Very Respectfully, &c,

W. G. Brownlow

SKETCHES

OF THE

RISE, PROGRESS, AND DECLINE

OF

SECESSION;

WITH A

Narrative of Personal Adventures among the Rebels.

By W. G. BROWNLOW,
EDITOR OF THE KNOXVILLE WHIG.

PHILADELPHIA:
GEORGE W. CHILDS,
628 & 630 CHESTNUT ST.
APPLEGATE & CO., 43 MAIN ST., CINCINNATI.
1862.

STEREOTYPED BY L. JOHNSON & CO.
PHILADELPHIA.

TO

Every honest Patriot citizen,
and unconditional Union man, who
loves Loyalty and despises Rebellion, whether
perpetrated North or South, under one pretence or
another, for the sake of office, power, fame, money, or
malicious resentment; To every intelligent reading
man, who, to whatever party he may belong, is unwilling
to see his Government overthrown by wicked and designing
men, and who has resolved to live and die beneath the folds of the
Star-Spangled Banner; To my companions in the Knoxville Jail, who,
with me, swore upon the altar of our country that, despite the gallows
and the prison, they would adhere to the Flag of the Federal Union, and who
look to the mild umpirage of the Union as the only shield of nationality, is this work

Dedicated by its Author,

Who, during the progress of this revolution, has opposed it at every step, regardless
of consequences personal to himself, and of what designing men might say or
think, or of what a corrupt and pensioned Southern Press might charge,
as to motives; who still bears in mind that it was WASHINGTON
who told us, "THE CONSTITUTION IS SACREDLY OBLIGATORY
UPON ALL;" and that it was JACKSON who said,
"THE UNION, IT MUST BE PRESERVED!"
This is a truth now revealed to us,
"Which kings and prophets waited for,
And sought, but never found."

PREFACE.

I HAVE prepared this work from the single stand-point of uncompromising devotion to the American Union as established by our fathers, and unmitigated hostility to the armed rebels who are seeking its destruction. My ancestors fought in its defence; and while their blood flows in my veins I shall instinctively recoil from bartering away the glory of its past and the prophecy of its future for the stained record of that vile thing, begotten by fraud, crime, and bad ambition, christened a Southern Confederacy. I cannot exchange historic renown for disgrace, national honor for infamy, how splendid soever may be the bribe or how violent soever may be the compulsion. This is my faith as an American citizen; and this book will show how sorely it has been put to the test. I claim, however, no merit, further than that arising from the discharge of a simple duty both of religion and patriotism. Thousands of my fellow-citizens have been equally faithful among the faithless. Their sufferings may be conceived from this narrative of my own.

Indeed, it is not from the slightest desire of self-glorification that I have spoken so freely of myself. It would have been sheer affectation of modesty to attempt by circumlocution of speech to do otherwise. For I have, in this matter, rather regarded myself as a type of the large body of loyal people in the border States, and have, accordingly, been the more unreserved, inasmuch as I felt that I might assume to some extent to speak in their behalf. It is important that our countrymen of the North should clearly understand the embarrassing position of this class, and the peculiar privations they have been compelled to undergo. It is chiefly due to them that the battle-field of the Rebellion has not been transferred to Northern homes. Their geographical location and political elements are such that, upon the soil which they inhabit, loyalty and treason have overlapped, and, being thus confronted face to face, they have been plunged into all the horrors of discord and anarchy, of divided communities and sundered households. In many respects, however, we of that region do not wholly sympathize with the North any more than with the extreme South. We deprecate alike the fanatical agitators of one section and the Disunion demagogues of the other. I believe I represent the views of multitudes of ever-true and now suffering patriots when I declare that, Southern man and slave-holder as I am, if the South in her madness and folly will force the issue upon the country, of Slavery and no Union, or a Union and no Slavery, I am for the Union, though every other institution in the country perish. I am for sustaining this Union if it shall require "coercion" or "subjugation," or, what is worse, the annihilation of the rebel population of the land. These peculiarities in my position, as an East-Tennesseean, it will be seen, have contributed to mould the views which I have expressed.

I am, therefore, prepared to expect that many readers will not concur in all that I have said. But I do verily believe that, as a National man,—having had an opportunity, as from an intermediate eminence, to view this question on both sides,—and having observed the bearings of the whole subject for thirty years past, I am enabled to suggest something worthy the consideration of my countrymen. Hence I have not consulted the opinions of others, nor reflected whether what I say would be acceptable or unacceptable, would render the writer popular or unpopular. I seek only to utter the profound convictions of my own mind, in order that, God willing, I may be of some benefit in my day and generation, and, without fear or favor, come weal or woe, may have the sad privilege of warning my fellow-citizens, even if I may not enjoy the cheerful satisfaction of convincing them.

I have suffered deeply in person and estate, have avoided no responsibility, have endured evil treatment and imprisonment, and been compelled day by day to contemplate the near prospect of a brutal death upon the gallows,—all in behalf of the sacred cause I have espoused. I avouch these things as evidence of sincerity. Not only so, but they have left me in no mood for the use of softened forms of speech in narrating such acts or depicting the actors. Hence I have spoken plainly. Extreme fastidiousness of taste may, perhaps, shrink with over-sensitiveness from some of the language I have employed. But it was no time for dalliance with polished sentences or enticing words; for an imminent necessity—like the "burden" of the old Hebrew prophets—was upon us, and the cause of our LORD and LAND could be best served by the sturdy rhetoric of defiance and the unanswerable logic of facts. The traitors merited a sword-thrust style, and deserved the strongest epithet I have applied. My persecution by them was such that I had a fair right to handle them roughly: they were not worth any other mode of treatment; and I have written what I have written.

I cannot close this preface without expressing my thanks for the generous reception I have met with at the North. In Cincinnati, Columbus, Chicago, Philadelphia, New York,—indeed, wherever I have gone,—I have been welcomed by individuals and by public bodies with demonstrations of honor and kindness which seem like a providential recompense for all I have endured. I shall preserve a life-long recollection of such universal and spontaneous sympathy, and leave its precious memory and memorials as an heir-loom to the latest generation of my descendants. I bear this testimony all the more willingly, because these courtesies vindicate me from aspersions, and are occasioned by no modification or concealment of my opinions. I have, everywhere, condemned the disorganizing propagandists of the North, and have publicly proclaimed that I was a Southerner by birth, education, and habits; yet, when I also announced that I was a National man and uncompromisingly for the Union, I found that other things were forgotten, and that I had touched a chord which made us all of kin.

God grant that we may, as Sections, Churches, and Individuals, realize how great a share each of us has had in bringing about our present calamities, and, consequently, how much of the responsibility falls upon *self* as well as upon others! When this shall be felt, and when a proper spirit shall accompany the conviction, the horrors of this wicked war will be appreciated, the hand of vengeance will be stayed, and

"Returning Justice lift aloft her scale."

W. G. B.

PHILADELPHIA, May, 1862.

CONTENTS.

BROWNLOW'S

EXPERIENCES AMONG THE REBELS.

CHAPTER I.

AUTOBIOGRAPHICAL SKETCH—NORTHERN AND SOUTHERN AGITATORS ALIKE TO BE DREADED—MUTINEERS ON BOARD THE SHIP OF STATE—SOUTH CAROLINA METHODISTS—THE RIGHT OF SECESSION ARGUED—JEFFERSON, MADISON, AND JACKSON ALL DENY THE RIGHT OF SECESSION.

It is a delicate task for a modest man to perform, when he undertakes to write out a memorial of himself, and especially when he shall undertake to give both his *private* and *public* life. But as I have never arisen to any thing like eminence, and as it is the custom of such only as have, to write out a full history of themselves, and to give their *bad* as well as *good* deeds to the world, I will be spared the labor and mortification of any unfavorable disclosures.

It will, perhaps, be urged that *both sides* of a man's picture of life should be given, and then the reader, having the *whole man* before him, will be the better prepared to award to him a righteous verdict. Others will insist that a man should so conduct himself as to

2

be wholly free from improprieties, especially if he be a member of the Church, or wear clerical robes. To this I reply, that if the memoirs of only such as have lived and died without fault, and without incurring the displeasure of designing and bad men, were written, we should seldom, if ever, see a production of the kind.

I lay no claim whatever to *inimitable excellencies;* but I do claim that my good and evil deeds, if placed in a scale, would not be so perfectly poised that neither end would preponderate! An anecdote of my life will illustrate my views of this subject.

Whilst in attendance at an Annual Conference of the Methodist Church, in Abingdon, Virginia, some twelve years ago, I suffered from an attack of fever; and, either from the influence of medicine, or of fever on the brain, I became a little flighty. The opinion prevailed that I would die, and the venerable BISHOP CAPERS, and other ministers, became anxious to know how the "eccentric Parson" felt in view of an exchange of worlds. Accordingly, they visited my room, and the Bishop read the Scriptures, and sang and prayed with and for me. On taking his leave of me,—holding me by the hand and looking me full in the face,—he inquired what my prospects were beyond the grave. It is said—and I have no doubt of the truth of the statement—that I returned for an answer, "Well, Bishop, if I had my life to live over again, I could improve it in many respects, and would try to do so. However, if the books have been properly kept in the other world, *there is a small balance in my favor!*"

I have lived long enough in this present evil world to have enlisted the sympathies of many friends, and at the same time to have excited the bitter resentments of many foes. This affords me proof that I have not been a *negative* character. That a man engaged in the work of propagating Christianity, in opposing error and defending the cause of truth, and, finally, in going about endeavoring to do good, should find himself exposed to enemies, or should meet with violent and protracted opposition, may seem strange. But history and observation inform us that such has been the lot of all *decided* public men, in a greater or less degree. While some emblazon a man's virtues, others will amplify his faults. A majority, however, labor

> "The struggling pangs of conscious truth to hide,
> To quench the blushes of ingenuous shame,"

rather than pursue the opposite course; and it is more than likely that on this account religious sectarians and political partisans have denied me justice. For it has certainly been my lot in life to have the shafts of unmerited censure hurled at me; and since this GREAT REBELLION has been inaugurated, I have been doomed to bear the base insinuations of invidious tongues and pens in Rebeldom!

Perhaps it will be asked, Who is the person that offers this volume to the world? In this the inquisitive reader shall be gratified; for short and simple are the domestic annals of the writer, though in his fifty-seventh year. I am the eldest son of JOSEPH A. BROWNLOW, who was born and raised in Rockbridge county, Virginia, and died in Sullivan county, in East Tennessee, in 1816. My father died when I was so young that I could not have been a judge of his character; but it has been a source of consolation to me to hear him spoken of by his old associates and schoolmates (General SAM HOUSTON among them) as a man of good sense, brave independence, and of sterling integrity. He was a private in a Tennessee company in the War of 1812. Two of his brothers were at the battle of the *Horseshoe*, under General JACKSON, two others of them died naval officers, and their remains sleep in Norfolk and New Orleans.

The death of my father was a grievous affliction to my mother, as she was left with five helpless children,—three sons and two daughters,—four of whom are now dead, having heard of the death of the last of the four since my banishment from home! My mother's maiden name was CATHARINE GANNAWAY,—a Virginian likewise, of respectable parentage, *and slave-owners.*

She departed this transitory life in less than three months after the death of her husband. Being naturally mild and agreeable in her temperament, she was warmly endeared to a large circle of friends and acquaintance. But their consolation was in this, that, while sinking into the cold embrace of death, she was happy in the religion of Christ.

I was born in Wythe county, Virginia, on the 29th of August, 1805. After the death of my parents, I lived with my mother's relations, who raised me up to hard labor, until I was eighteen years old, when I removed to Abingdon, in that State, and served as a regular apprentice to the trade of a house-carpenter. I have been a laboring-man all my life long, and have acted upon the Scriptural maxim of eating my bread in the sweat of my brow. Though a Southern man in feeling and principle, I do not think it *degrading* to a man to labor, as do most of the Southern Disunionists. Whether East or West, North or South, I recognize the *dignity of labor*, and look forward to a day, not very distant, when *educated labor* will be the salvation of this vast country!

My education was imperfect and irregular, even in those branches taught in the common-schools of the country. I labored, after obtaining a trade, until I acquired the means of again going to school. I afterwards entered the Methodist Travelling Ministry, and travelled ten years without intermission. I availed myself of this position to study and improve my limited education, which I did in all the English branches.

I am about six feet high, and have weighed as heavy as one hundred and seventy-five pounds,—have had as fine a constitution as any man need desire. I have very few gray hairs in my head, and, although rather *hard-favored* than otherwise, I will pass for a man of forty years. I have had as strong a voice as any man in East Tennessee, where I have resided for the last thirty years, and have a family of seven children. I have been speaking all that time; and for the last twenty-five years I have edited and published a WHIG newspaper having a larger circulation than any political paper in the State, and even larger than all the papers in East Tennessee put together. I have taken a part in all the religious and political controversies of my day and time.

I have written several books; but the one which has had the largest run is the one entitled, "The Iron Wheel Examined, and its False Spokes Extracted,"—being a vindication of the Methodist Church against the attacks of Rev. J. R. GRAVES, of Nashville. My reply was published by the Southern Methodist Publishing House, and at the earnest solicitation of the book-agents and other leading members of the Church. It is a work of great severity, but was written in reply to one of still greater severity.

In September, 1858, I was engaged in a debate upon the Slavery question, in Philadelphia, with Rev. ABRAM PRYNE, of New York, in which I defended the institution of Slavery as it exists in the South. The debate was published in Philadelphia, and exhibits my sentiments upon that great question, which have undergone no change since then.

I am known throughout the length and breadth of the land as the "Fighting Parson;" while I may say, without incurring the charge of egotism, that no man is more peaceable, as my neighbors will testify. Always poor, and always oppressed with *security* debts, few men in my section and of my limited means have given away more in the course of each year to charitable objects. I have never been arraigned in the Church for any immorality. I never played a card. I never was a profane swearer. I never drank a dram of liquor, until within a few years,—when it was taken as a medicine. I never had a cigar or chew of tobacco in my mouth. I never was in attendance at a theatre. I never attended a horse-race, and never witnessed their running, save on the fair-grounds of my own county. I never courted but one woman; and her I married.

I may be allowed to say that I have ever been, as I still am, quite a politician, though I have never been an office-seeker nor an office-holder. I began my political career in Tennessee in 1828, by espousing the cause of JOHN QUINCY ADAMS as against ANDREW JACKSON. The latter I regard as having been a true patriot and a sincere lover of his country. The former I admired because he was a learned statesman, of pure moral and private character, and because I regarded him as a FEDERALIST, representing my political opinions. I have all my life long been a FEDERAL

WHIG of the WASHINGTON AND ALEXANDER HAMILTON school. I am the advocate of a *concentrated* Federal Government, or of a strong *central* Government, able to maintain its dignity, to assert its authority, and to crush out any rebellion that may be inaugurated. I have never been a *Sectional*, but at all times a *National* man, supporting men for the Presidency and Vice-Presidency without any regard on which side of Mason & Dixon's Line they were born, or resided at the time of their nomination. In a word, I am, as I ever have been, an ardent WHIG, and CLAY and WEBSTER have ever been my standards of political orthodoxy. With the breaking up of old parties, I have merged every thing into the great question of the "Union, the Constitution, and the Enforcement of the Laws." Hence, I am an *unconditional* Union man, and advocate the preservation of the Union at the expense of all other considerations.

In 1832, I was chosen by the Holston Annual Conference as a member of the General Conference of the Methodist Church, which was held in Philadelphia. That year I travelled a circuit in South Carolina, having appointments in the districts or counties of Pickens and Anderson, and also in Franklin county, Georgia, south of the Tugaloo River. Nullification raged in South Carolina to a fearful extent, and men of all professions took sides, either in favor of the General Government or of the South Carolina

Ordinance of Disunion. Mr. CALHOUN, who was an able statesman and a man of most excellent private character, resided in Anderson, and was almost an object of worship among the Nullifiers. At least, when he took snuff, they all sneezed! The Union sentiment was very strong, but Union men were in the minority. I took a firm stand in favor of the Federal Government, and whatever influence I had was thrown into the scale against this wicked attempt of South Carolina to destroy the Government. So fierce was the opposition to me in consequence of the stand I took, that in the fall of that year I published a pamphlet vindicating myself. This was *thirty years ago;* and it will be refreshing to my Union friends to reproduce a few paragraphs from that defence:—

"It is urged against me that I have meddled in the politics of South Carolina and acted with the Union party. Nay, it has been said that I was the tool of Colonel SLOANE and Major PERRY. I plead guilty to the charge of having opposed the heresy of Nullification, but I deny having been the tool of any man, or set of men. Deeply as I have regretted the state of things existing here, and of the breaking up of the Churches, as well as the social intercourse of families and neighbors, I do not regret having taken sides in favor of the Tariff Acts complained of, of General JACKSON'S proclamation against Nullifiers, and in favor of enforcing the laws of Congress. If the Tariff Acts complained of were unconstitutional,—which I do not allow,—they afford no plea for dissolving this Union. South Carolina's remedy is at the ballot-box of the country, or in the Supreme Court of the United States, whose judges are able and, as I believe, impartial.

"South Carolina is looking to the formation of an independent *Province*, but will not be allowed any such privilege, as her leading men will infer from the proclamation of Old Hickory. I am threatened with proscription and starvation, because I have dared to assert that no law has been passed by Congress, touching the Tariff, at variance with the guarantees of the Constitution and the rights and liberties of the slave-holding States. So far as I am concerned, I ask no favors of the enemies of my Government, either in South Carolina or elsewhere. I can live without you, and live among a people who are loyal, and, having the fear of God before their eyes, they will be more likely to receive and appreciate the teachings of the gospel. That there are thousands of patriotic people in South Carolina, is true; but it is likewise true that there were more *Tories* here during the Revolutionary War than in all the other States put together. And that the descendants of these old Tories are now in the lead of this *Nullification Rebellion*, needs no proof whatever to make the charge good. I talk plainly, for one who is in your midst and liable to be mobbed every day; but this is the way to talk in times like these. I am not to be taught my duty by a set of gassy Union-destroyers such as constitute the staple of the South Carolina chivalry. This attempt by mob-law to nullify the laws of the General Government is but the development of a well-planned scheme for the ulterior but wicked purpose of destroying our Government. It is a wild, visionary, and supremely ridiculous scheme, and will be put down, at all hazards, by General JACKSON. In fact, he has now crushed it out, and I rejoice in its overthrow, though it may starve me out and drive me from your limits. I shall fall back into Tennessee, where the people appreciate the blessings of the best Government in the world, and where the gospel is likely to produce some other effect than that of arraying the people against the legal and constituted authorities of the land.

Thus did I write and publish *thirty years ago,* in the teeth of the Rebellion of South Carolina! The principles I then avowed I have cherished and acted upon ever since, and will continue so to do to the end of life. I am a Southern man by birth, raising, and education, and all my interests are there; but I am not of the number of those who believe that the South can any better preserve its rights *out* of the Union than *in it.* If those rights have been invaded,—which I deny,—I hold it to be the bounden duty of every man in the South, as well as his highest obligation, to protect them under the forms of law and the guarantees of the Constitution. These rights can never be maintained by Secession, but by a faithful observance of the Constitution and of the duties it imposes.

In October of the same year, being *thirty years ago*, I had a controversy with a Mr. POSEY, a Calvinistic preacher, a man of talents; and in a pamphlet printed by HIRAM BARRY, of Knoxville, on page 9, there appears the first paragraph I ever published upon the Slavery question. I herewith give it entire, and ask the reader to examine it, and compare the principles I then advocated with those I now avow:—

"When I drove Mr. POSEY to the wall, in our controversy, and convicted him of retailing all his slanders of me upon the authority of a negro slave of bad character, *Bacchus*, the property of his co-laborer in his dirty work, Dr. CARDES, he came out and taunted me with the false charges that Methodist preachers were the friends of negroes and opposed to slavery, and that WESLEY, their great idol, wrote and preached against slavery! Both of these specifications are false. Many of the Methodist preachers are opposed to slavery; but as many more of them own slaves and advocate the institution. I own none; but it is because of my poverty, and not because I am opposed to owning them. I am but a young man, and I notice the controversy going on between the advocates of slavery and its opponents. The Methodists in New England, and other denominations, take the ground that slave-holding is a sin, an injustice, a barbarism. I do not believe them: I believe with the Constitution of my country, that slaves are a lawful species of property, and that those who feed and clothe them well, and instruct them in religion, are better friends to them than those who set them at liberty.

"So far as Mr. WESLEY is involved, he wrote and preached against the *African kidnapping-business.* I denounce that, and so do all honest men, whether they live in New England or these Middle and Western States. The American Congress has condemned it as a piracy, and slave-holding members voted to do it. I have paid some attention to this subject, young as I am, because it is one day or other to shake this Government to its very foundation. I expect to live to see that day, and not be an old man at that. The *Tariff question* now threatens the overthrow of the Government, but the *Slavery question* is one to be dreaded. While I shall advocate the owning of 'men, women, and children,' as you say our Discipline styles slaves, I shall, if I am living, when the battle comes, stand by my Government and the Union formed by our fathers, as Mr. WESLEY stood by the British Government, of which he was a loyal subject. Where will you stand,

Mr. POSEY? Will you take sides against your own country? I shall expect you to advocate the *freedom of negroes*, as they seem to be the only class of beings who carry news to you!"

More recently, I held a debate in Philadelphia with Rev. Mr. PRYNE, of New York, upon the Slavery question, and the five discourses are bound in one volume, in the order in which they were delivered. In my fifth and last speech, I took up the subject of a dissolution of this Union, and I concluded as follows:—

"In saying this, I am not for separating from the North, or dissolving the Union. I am willing to live and die for America as she is and has been; but America without the South, and blight, ruin, and decay come upon us, and we bid a long farewell to the last remnant of earth's beauty, and the light of heaven!

"Who can estimate the value of the American Union? Proud, happy, thrice-happy America! The home of the oppressed, the asylum of the emigrant! where the citizen of every clime, and the child of every creed, roam free and untrammelled as the wild winds of heaven! Baptized at the fount of Liberty in fire and blood, cold must be the heart that thrills not at the name of the American Union!

"When the Old World, with 'all its pomp, and pride,

and circumstance,' shall be covered with oblivion,—when thrones shall have crumbled and dynasties shall have been forgotten,—may this glorious Union, *despite the mad schemes of Southern fire-eaters and Northern Abolitionists*, stand amid regal ruin and national desolation, towering sublime, like the last mountain in the Deluge,—majestic, immutable, and magnificent!

"In pursuance of this, let every conservative Northern man, who loves his country and her institutions, shake off the trammels of Northern fanaticism, and swear upon the altar of his country that he will stand by her Constitution and laws. Let every Southern man shake off the trammels of *disunion* and *nullification*, and *pledge his life and his sacred honor to stand by the* Constitution of his country *as it is*, the laws as enacted by Congress and interpreted by the Supreme Court. Then we shall see every heart a shield, and a drawn sword in every hand, to preserve the ark of our political safety! Then we shall see reared a fabric upon our national Constitution, which time cannot crumble, persecution shake, fanaticism disturb, nor revolution change, but which shall stand among us like some lofty and stupendous Apennine, while the earth rocks at its feet, and the thunder peals above its head!

"Contemplating our country and her Northern and Southern foes, a specimen of whom is here before us, may I not exclaim, with the poet?—

"'Country! on thy sons depending,
Strong in manhood, bright in bloom,
Hast thou seen thy pride descending
Shrouded to the unbounded tomb?
Rise! on eagle pinions soaring,
Rise! like one of godlike birth,
And, Jehovah's aid imploring,
Sweep the *spoiler* from the earth.'"

With a view still further to illustrate my views and demonstrate my *consistency*, I herewith submit a series of documents which appeared in the *Knoxville Whig* at the times indicated by the dates, bringing me down to the present year:—

Prayer During this Winter.

Seeing that the Episcopal Bishops of the Carolinas have composed prayers to be used by their clergy during the sessions of their Legislatures, we have deemed it proper, sustaining the relation to the Methodist Church we do in East Tennessee, to compose the following prayer, and order that it shall be used this winter by all *local* preachers in all their public ministrations:—

ALMIGHTY GOD, our heavenly Father, in whose hands are the hearts of men, and the issues of events, not mixed up with Locofocoism, nor rendered offensive in Thy sight by being identified with men of corrupt minds, evil designs, and damnable purposes, such as are seeking to up-turn the best form of government on earth, Thou hast graciously promised to hear the prayers of those who in an humble spirit, and with true faith,—such as no *Secessionist* can bring into exercise, —call upon Thee. Be pleased, we beseech Thee, favorably to look upon and bless the Union men of this Commonwealth, and sustain them in their praiseworthy efforts to perpetuate this Government, and, under it, the institutions of our holy religion. Possess their minds with the spirit of true patriotism, enlightened wisdom, and of persevering hostility towards those traitors, political gamblers, and selfish demagogues who are seeking to build up a miserable Southern Confederacy, and under it to inaugurate a new reading of the Ten Commandments, so as to teach that the *chief end of Man is Nigger!* In these days of trouble and perplexity, give the common people grace to perceive the right path, which, Thou knowest, leads from the camps of Southern mad-caps and Northern fanatics, and enable them steadfastly to walk therein!

So strengthen the common masses, O Lord, and so direct them, that they being hindered neither by the fear of fire-eaters, nor by the love of the corrupt men in power, nor by bribery, nor by an overcharge of mean whiskey, nor by any other *Democratic* passion, but being mindful of Thy constant superintendence, of the awful majesty of Thy righteousness, of Thy hatred of a corrupt Democracy and its profligate leaders, and of the strict account they must hereafter give to Thee, they may, in counsel, word, and deed, aim supremely at the fulfilment of their duty, which is to talk, vote, and pray against the wicked leaders of Abolitionism and the equally ungodly advocates of Secessionism. Grant that those of Thy professed ministers who are mixed up with *modern Democracy*, and have become so hardened in sin as openly to advocate the vile delusion, may speedily abandon their *un*ministerial habits, or go over to the cause of the devil, that their positions may at least be unequivocal, and that they may thereby advance the welfare of the country! And grant that these fire-eaters may soon run their race, that the course of this world may be so peaceably ordered, by Thy superintendence, that Thy Church, and Thy whole people, irrespective of sects, may joyfully serve Thee, in all godly quietness, through Jesus Christ our Lord. *Amen!*

Knoxville Whig, January, 1860.

To Reasonable Men in the South.

It is ascertained, beyond controversy, that Mr. Lincoln is President of the United States. And at a moment when a fierce struggle is going on between passion and reason, we propose, in a spirit of patriotism and compromise, to submit a few leading facts for the consideration of conservative men in the South. We are not so vain as to suppose that what we can say will stay the tide of passion in certain quarters in the South, and bring back the impetuous wanderers to consider great facts and principles. Yet the task of *trying* even those of our countrymen ought not to be shrunk from by conservative and patriotic men of the South, whose Southern birth and raising, and long services in behalf of the Union and the maintenance of the laws, may be urged as a reason why they are at least entitled to a patient and respectful hearing. It is an ungracious and thankless task to exhort the LEADERS of the Breckinridge party in South Carolina, Georgia, Florida, Virginia, Alabama, and Mississippi, to calmness, or to a patriotic reconsideration of the perilous position to which, under the apprehensions engendered by the election of a Northern Sectional President, they are plunging under the impulses of passion.

The fact which stares us in the face, and which all parties have to meet, whether they support Bell, Douglas, or Breckinridge, is Mr. Lincoln's election. Mr. Lincoln himself is no doubt a patriotic man, and a sincere lover of his country. He is to-day, what he has always been, an OLD CLAY WHIG, differing in no respect—not even upon the subject of *Slavery*—from the Sage of Ashland. The great objection with us to his election is the *sectional idea* upon which he was run, the *character of the partisans* who supported him and will, it is to be feared, to some extent control his administration. But Lincoln is chosen President, and, whether with or without the consent and participation of the South, will be, and *ought* to be, inaugurated on the 4th of March, 1861. True, as the lights before us indicate, we should say that Lincoln has not received more than one-third to two-fifths of the aggregate vote of the nation. Neither did Buchanan; and yet he, like Lincoln, has been elected by divisions among his opponents. Lincoln, then, has been chosen legally and constitutionally, without either fraud or violence, simply by the suffrages of an enormous majority of the people of the North, who have actually given him more Electoral votes than Buchanan received, who was permitted quietly to take his seat. Against the *manner* of his election nothing can be urged. It is true, as we have before stated, he was a *sectional* candidate; and it is equally true that, with trifling exceptions in Maryland, Virginia, Kentucky, and Missouri, he received no Southern votes. But do the Constitution or the laws of our country require a man to receive Southern votes before he can be inaugurated President? Do they compel a candidate to receive votes in *every State* before he shall be declared our Chief Magistrate? Certainly not. Then there is no just ground for resistance or revolutionary movement on that score.

But the argument of Secessionists is, that the administration of a Black Republican President must necessarily be of an aggressive character towards the South, and that the Slave States should forestall such iniquitous policy by withdrawing from the Union. Nay, the election of a man to the Presidency by a party known to be opposed to slavery, and who heretofore have never been successful in such a contest, is alleged to be a just cause for secession. This view of the subject is so fallacious, and so extremely shallow, that it ought not to mislead any one. The argument is, that the South is exposed to all the wiles and infamy of an Abolition Government,—an argument that we cannot accept as legitimate in fact or in reason. Did Lincoln receive the suffrages of the North under a pledge that, if elected, he would disregard his oath of office, violate the Constitution, and subvert the Union? Certainly not; for had he given that pledge, the day his election was announced, the entire South would have been united in carrying out a most thorough and determined revolution, and thousands of true men at the North would have joined us. But, now that Lincoln is elected, will he execute the purposes of Abolitionism? This he cannot do under the solemn oath to be administered at his inauguration. And who will say that he intends taking that oath with treason in his heart and perjury on his tongue? We have no right to judge of Lincoln by any thing but his *acts*, and these can only be appreciated *after* his inauguration. He knows very well that he cannot violate the Constitution in any serious particular, without rendering the dissolution of the Union necessary on the part of the South, and thereby involving the North in alarming troubles and certain ruin. The Constitution was planned by its sagacious and patriotic authors to protect the South in just such an emergency as this. If, then, Lincoln is not a patriot at *heart*,—and we assume no such thing,—the Constitution and his oath will make him administer the Government *patriotically*.

But the attempt to break up the Union, before awaiting a single overt act, or even the manifestation of the purpose of the President elect, would be wicked, treacherous, unjustifiable, unprecedented, and without the shadow of an excuse. And then, again, disunion is not a remedy for any evil in the Government, real or imaginary; and it is an uncertain and a perilous remedy, to be resorted to only in the last extremity, and as a refuge from wrongs more intolerable than the desperate remedy by which they are sought to be relieved. What the people of the Southern States should do may be summed up in a single word: PAUSE! It will be time enough to fight Lincoln with powder and sword—to resist him with regiments of "minute-men"—when we find that constitutional resistance fails, or that he and his party are bent on our humiliation and destruction. Let every man in every Southern State stand up for the Union as long as it is possible to prevent it. *Individually*, we are willing to go with the South, *even unto death*, but we feel bound to aid in making the South herself *go right!* Let all patriots, irrespective of parties, choose their position; let them resolve to stand by the Union as long as the Federal Government respects the rights of the people of the South. The Constitutional Union men of the South are largely in the majority, and they are pledged to the support of the rights and honor of the South as well as of the Union, and the maintenance of the spirit and form of our Government. They cannot do less; and they ask their *extreme* brethren to meet them upon a common basis and labor for the accomplishment of a common end.

They ask it in a spirit of mutual toleration, and they concede to thousands of others, who are shaping a different course, the same integrity of purpose, patriotism, and honor which they claim for themselves. Let the entire South unite with the thousands of conservative men North, bury their feuds, make common cause, and in 1864 the National Constitutional men of the country, North, South, East, and West, will overthrow the Sectionalists, and restore the Government to a better condition than it has been in for a quarter of a century. The night is dark, we confess, and troubled, but there are gleams of light along the line of the horizon. Lincoln is President; but he is nothing more. We trust that he contemplates no mischief, but, if he does, he can do none. The Senate, the House of Representatives, and the Supreme Court will hold him in check, and stand by the Constitution and the rights of all sections. Here, then, is our hope, and here is the platform that all conservative men should occupy, and time and reflection will, anon, inspire a sober second thought in quarters where at this moment the blind impulses of passion bear sway. The wise, the safe, and the only honorable course to pursue is pointed out in the following advice by the immortal author of the Declaration of American Independence. Here are his memorable words:—

"We must have patience and long endurance, then, with our brethren while under delusion. Give them time for reflection and experience of consequences; keep ourselves in a situation to profit by the chapter of accidents, and separate from our companions only when the sole alternatives left are the dissolution of our Union with them, or submission to a Government without limitation of powers."

There is one other consideration we wish to lay before the calm and considerate men of the South, and that is the division of power between the North and South since the organization of the Government. The South has held the Presidency as follows:—

Under			
George Washington, a Virginian	....	8	years.
Thomas Jefferson, "	....	8	"
James Madison, "	....	8	"
James Monroe, "	....	8	"
John Tyler, "	....	4	"
Andrew Jackson, a Tennesseean	....	8	"
James K. Polk, "	....	4	"
Total by the South	....	48	years.

The North has held the Presidency as follows, to wit:

Under

JOHN ADAMS, of Massachusetts............	4 years.
JOHN Q. ADAMS, "	4 "
MARTIN VAN BUREN, New York............	4 "
MILLARD FILLMORE, " "	4 "
FRANKLIN PIERCE, New Hampshire......	4 "
JAMES BUCHANAN, Pennsylvania...........	4 "
Total by the North....	24 years.

It will be seen that the South, though always in the minority, from the origin of the Government down to the 4th of March, 1861, has held the Presidency forty-eight years out of seventy-two. The North, on the other hand, has held it twenty-four years,—only one-third of the time! Let us do as we would be done by. True, it will be said that the South never furnished a *sectional*, but always a *national*, President. Those now complaining and threatening to go out of the Union have presented a *sectional* man, as much so as Lincoln is; and this cannot be denied!

Knoxville Whig, Nov. 17, 1860.

The Right of Secession.

The following correspondence will explain itself:—

GREENWOOD, S. C., NOV. 23, 1860.

W. G. BROWNLOW:—

SIR:—You will do me a favor by sending my account for the Knoxville Whig, and stop my paper. Secession now and forever! So say the Methodists of South Carolina. Yours, &c.,

R. H. APPLETON.

KNOXVILLE, NOV. 29, 1880.

MR. APPLETON:—

Your note, calling for account and ordering a discontinuance, is before me. You are not indebted to me for subscription, but, on the contrary, there are fifteen weeks of subscription due you. I take no offence whatever at your discontinuance, as *that* is every man's right in this free country. But, before parting with you, you must allow me to give you my views upon your favorite doctrine of "Secession." I am equally opposed to the wicked spirit of *Sectionalism* at the North and of *Secession* at the South. Your motto is, "Secession now and forever!" I offset this with the following patriotic sentiments from General JACKSON's Message of 1833:—

"THE CONSTITUTION AND THE LAW IS SUPREME, AND THE UNION IS INDISSOLUBLE."

Sir, the political journals, North and South, are discussing the right of a State to secede from the Union. For my part, I deny the right of secession altogether, though I admit the right of *revolution* when circumstances justify it. It must be an *extreme* case of oppression on the part of Government, and of *continued* oppression, that will justify revolution. Such a case was presented when the American Colonies revolted; and in that case revolution was called for and was successful.

But the idea of one of these States at its pleasure

claiming and exercising the right to secede from this Union, is a more monstrous and absurd doctrine than has ever been put forth in any republic. If the doctrine be true that the right exists, our Government is a mere rope of sand. Concede the truth of this dogma, and Cuba, after we may have paid *two hundred millions* for her purchase to Old Spain, may take offence, and, as a State, may at once secede, and leave the United States Treasury to whistle! We now have a case in point. Texas speaks of going out of the Union with Carolina, and I presume will do so. Less than twenty years ago, she was admitted into the Union upon her own solicitation, our Government paying millions to discharge her debts, and other millions to go into her coffers. Is she now at liberty to secede with all this booty, and array herself against this Government in all time to come? Certainly not. For, if she is, Louisiana, and all the States carved out of that purchase, for which we paid FIFTEEN MILLIONS, may do likewise, and carry with them the mouth of the Mississippi River, transferring it to any European Power.

So, too, States in which large amounts of Government property may be situated may at any time secede with that property,—just as South Carolina, Georgia, Florida, and Alabama, with their Government fortifications, arsenals, custom-houses, navy-yards, and other property, strung along the coasts from Charleston to Mobile, may at any time do. Construct a Pacific Railroad at an expense of millions paid from the common treasure, and the two or three States through which it passes, and which it so enriches, may take offence at something Maine and New Hampshire are doing, and decamp with the whole road, its stationary, running stock, and guarantees, taking all the property with them, and forming an alliance with some Government hostile to the very nation which built the road. Now, are Maryland, Virginia, Tennessee, Kentucky, and other States remaining loyal to the Union, to look quietly on, and even approve the exodus of those which have been thus enriched at their expense, and recognize the right of each of them to secede and take the common property of all the remaining States with them? I say most emphatically not!

This question of the right of secession is upon us, and we have to look it in the face, and meet it as it becomes men. Therefore let us reason together upon the subject, divesting ourselves of passion and prejudice. The right of secession, if it exist at all, is an *absolute* one, and a State has as much right to exercise it at one time as another. The Secessionists will concede the correctness of this position. If she may secede at will, she may do so in anticipation of a bloody and protracted war with a foreign Power, so as to avoid any draft upon her for men or money. If she can secede when she chooses, she owes no allegiance to the Government one hour after she decides to secede, but will then be just as independent of the Government as she is of France or England. In the midst of a violent and protracted foreign war, then, it will be the right of any one of the States of this Union, not only to desert our own Government, but at the same time to ally herself to the enemy the remaining States are fighting! Our Government, under such principles, if recognized, could not exist twenty-four hours. Other nations, and our own citizens, could have no faith in the permanence of such a Government. It would lack the vital principle of existence, because it would lack every thing like credit. No capitalist with a thimble-ful of sense would lend it a dollar; for no man could feel assured that such a Government would last long enough to pay a six months' loan, to say nothing of loans for a term of years. All who deal with Governments repose upon their *public faith;* and where this is destroyed they feel that all is lacking. Business must be destroyed; for men of sense and means would not embark either their industry or capital, unless it were under the shelter of laws and institutions not liable to change. In support of this, I need only call attention to the great fall in the price of State bonds, negroes, and all other property in the South, in *anticipation* of the rupture with which we are threatened. Things are bad enough with us in the South, and they are even worse at the North, because of what seems to be inevitable. And yet they are to grow worse each day we live in this state of uncertainty. And your good State of South Carolina, Mr. Appleton, is more to blame for these evils which affect the country than any one State in the Union.

I have, myself, no sympathy or respect for the anti-slavery men of the North, who are agitating this question, and enacting their "Personal Liberty Laws," with a view to defeat the operations of the "Fugitive Slave Law." I am a native of Virginia, as also were my parents before me, but for thirty years I have been a citizen of Tennessee, and I expect to end my days within her borders. My wife and children are natives of Tennessee, and all I have is here. I am a Union man in the fullest acceptation of that term, and I shall stand by the ship of state, as long as the storm is howling overhead, and the breakers are roaring on the lee-shore, though we have neither sun, moon, nor stars to light the way! And pardon me, sir, when I ask you, who but cowards would seek to desert the ship? Who but madmen would seek for safety out of it? Who but crazy mutineers would refuse to come to the rescue of the ship, passengers, and crew? South Carolina, at this trying moment, refuses to do duty. The storm affrights her. Her Senators and Representatives in Congress resign their seats, instead of remaining at their posts, and fighting the battle on the floor of Congress, where it ought to be fought and must be lost or won. Their hearts fail before the Northern Abolition

Simoon, and seeing only death, as they apprehend, staring them in the face, if they abide on board, they take to the boats, abandon the vessel in which we have all sailed together, through many a gale, these eighty years past, and intend, with *poles* and *paddles*, to *scuttle* through their cypress-swamps!

I admit the danger that menaces you all on board; but do you not multiply the peril tenfold by desertion? An overwhelming majority of the people of the Southern States have decided at the ballot-box in favor of the Union, voting for BELL and DOUGLAS. I regard the Abolitionists as the "mutineers;" and I ask you, I ask all South Carolina, is it manly, is it magnanimous, is it just, to throw yourselves into the sea, and leave these border States to destruction? No, Mr. Appleton, it is not magnanimous, it is not just! I tell you, and your Methodist brethren, in the language of the good Book they so much revere, that "Except ye abide in the ship, ye cannot be saved."

I am sorry to hear you say that the Methodists of South Carolina are now and forever the advocates of Secession! To appeal to them in behalf of the Union, is but beating the air, and wasting one's breath; but I say to them, through you, that I will stand to the Stars and Stripes—I shall cling to the Union! I say to them, however, as a heroic Christian apostle said to an equally panic-stricken generation of bolters, "Except ye abide in the ship, ye cannot be saved." You may leave the vessel,—you may go out in the rickety boats of your little State, and hoist your miserable *cabbage-leaf* of a Palmetto flag; but, depend upon it, men and brethren, you will be dashed to pieces on the rocks!

But the clergy,—the ministers of God, the followers on earth of the Prince of Peace,—at this threatening crisis, are going likewise! I know there are among that class of citizens, in South Carolina, some of the best men, as well as the most fearless and self-sacrificing men, of which the American people can boast. Why, oh, why are these men on the side of civil war, bloodshed, and revolution? They have offered up prayers and supplication, and made appeals to Heaven, but, alas! they have been—not for the preservation but for the destruction of the Union. I hear of no Paul among them, seeking to calm the minds of his companions, and to declare to them, "Except ye abide in the ship, ye cannot be saved." The venerable Dr. PIERCE, of Georgia, is an exception to this rule, and has spoken out like an American citizen and a Christian philosopher. To my mind it is clear that the clergy of South Carolina are wanting in *courage* to do what their "consciences dictate to be done." If they possessed the courage of their Master, they would from a Christian stand-point speak out in thunder tones! Jesus of Nazareth walked the earth thirty odd years, in the midst of millions of Roman Empire slaves, and dared to counsel them against rebellion and insurrection, and to exhort them to be *obedient to their masters.* Here was a courage worthy of God! Would that my South Carolina Methodist brethren would endeavor, humbly and courageously, to follow His example!

I believe the Union is in danger, and in regard to the consequences of its dissolution I shall not lengthen out this epistle in an attempt to portray the consequences. What I have to say to your ministers and church-going people is, that the importance of the times demands the grave and serious reflection and prayerful deliberation of every individual and State, before they proceed to take any action. One false step, such as contemplated by South Carolina, may plunge the people of the United States into unutterable woe! We now need the cool deliberation, the conservatism, and the wisdom of the nation, to "pour oil upon the troubled waters,"—to calm the storm now raging in the political elements, and to save this Union. And to no class of men living have we greater cause to look for help in this good work, than to the ministers and members of the Methodist Church, whose Discipline and Constitution, as well as their Bible, require loyalty to the civil Government, obedience to rulers, and a devotion to a country that forbids their assenting to its overthrow, directly or indirectly! The South should resist unlawful aggressions, but she should do it *in* the Union, *under* the Constitution, and with a scrupulous regard to the *forms* of law. Secession is no remedy for any evils in our Government, real or imaginary, past, present, or to come.

I will go further, if you please, and affirm that the Constitution has, in the clearest terms, recognized the right of property in slaves. That sacred instrument prohibits any State into which a slave may have fled, from passing any law to discharge him from bondage, and declares that he shall be surrendered to his lawful owner by the authorities of any State within whose limits he may be found. More than this, sir, the Constitution makes the existence of slavery our foundation of political power, by giving to the Slave States representatives in Congress not only in proportion to the whole number of free negroes, but also in proportion to the *three-fifths of the number of slaves.* The Northern States, by their "Personal Liberty Laws," have placed themselves in a state of revolution, and unless they repeal these laws, the revolution—a thing that never goes backward—must go on, until these rebellious States are declared out of the Union, and the truly conservative States take the Union in charge!

I have, my dear sir, defined my position, and in such terms as not to be misunderstood. I have already extended my remarks beyond what I intended in the outset. I will therefore close with brief extracts from the pens of three distinguished men, and I ask your attention to what they have said. The two first assisted in framing the Constitution. Mr. JEFFERSON remarked, in a letter to John Taylor, dated June 1, 1798,

"If on the temporary superiority of the one party the other is to resort to a scission of the Union, no Federal Government can ever exist.

"Who can say what would be the evils of a scission, and when and where they would end? Better keep together as we are; haul off from Europe as soon as we can, and from attachments to all portions; and, if they show their power just sufficiently to hoop us together, it will be the happiest situation in which we can exist. If the game were sometimes against us at home, we must have patience till luck turns, and then we shall have opportunity to win back the principles we have lost."

Mr. MADISON, in a paper he drew up a short time before his death, gives us this advice:—

"The advice nearest my heart and deepest in my conviction is, that the Union of the States be cherished and perpetuated. Let the open enemy to it be regarded as a Pandora with her box opened, and the disguised one as the serpent creeping with his deadly wiles into Paradise."

Gen. JACKSON, in his message to Congress, January 7, 1833, thus disposes of the question of Secession:—

"The right of the people of a single State to absolve themselves at will, and without the consent of the other States, from their most solemn obligations, and hazard the liberties and happiness of the millions composing this Union, cannot be acknowledged. Such authority is believed utterly repugnant both to the principles upon which the General Government is constituted, and to the objects which it was expressly formed to attain."

To these sentiments I subscribe as heartily and as unswervingly as I do to those I have preceded them with. Very respectfully, &c.,

W. G. BROWNLOW.

Knoxville Whig, December 8, 1860.

To the People of East Tennessee.

The Governor has issued a call for the meeting of the Legislature on Monday, the 7th of January, and that body will call a Convention of the State, to act upon the great and only issue of the day,—the breaking up of this Union by the secession of certain States from the Confederacy. We shall then be called upon to elect men from all of our Legislative districts, Representative and Senatorial, to represent us in that Convention; and this election will be upon us in a very short time, say two or three months. The single issue will then be, *secession or no secession;* or, in other words, *Shall Tennessee follow the Cotton States out of the Union, or remain in the Union, true to the Constitution and the laws?* Let those who dare to favor disunion become candidates, and show their hands. They will not be allowed to dodge the issue: they must declare either *for* or *against* secession. The people will force every man to define his position. We desire to see a candidate in every county on each side of the question, so as fully to test it; and we hope to see the ablest men in the State in the field, on both tickets. It will not be Whig and Democrat, Bell and Breckinridge, or Douglas, but *Union or Disunion.*

The Cotton States have spurned the offer of certain border States to meet them in a friendly conference,—declare they are going rashly and headlong out of the Union, and that these border States may either follow them or remain where they are. They allege our unity of *interests,* but refuse us harmony of *action.* Five refractory States claim the right to dictate to TEN conservative States, and to involve them in all the horrors of civil war, extending along a border of fifteen hundred miles; but they indignantly refuse to confer with these TEN States. If these border States were their *enemies,* then there would be some propriety in refusing their *counsels.* The border States have been their *friends,* through evil and good report; they have been their companions in arms, and side by side they have fought many a battle and triumphed over the British and Indians. But *now,* in matters in which we are as deeply interested as they are, they give us the cold shoulder, and refuse to meet us in counsel, to see if some course of procedure cannot be agreed upon by which *all* who are identified in interest should unite forces against our enemies.

We are, in fact, "in the midst of a revolution,"—a phrase whose dreadful meaning, as interpreted in the history of nations, none of us now realize the force of. The honest yeomanry of these border States, whose families live by their hard licks, four-fifths of whom own no negroes and never expect to own any, are to be drafted,—forced to leave their wives and children to toil and suffer, while they fight for the purse-proud aristocrats of the Cotton States, whose pecuniary abilities will enable them to hire substitutes! Revolution, or civil war, is no *holiday affair;* and those who expect to carry it on by the bright and shining light of pleasure and prosperity are to experience the saddest of disappointments.

Let us be calm, fellow-countrymen of the border States, and weigh well every step we take towards meeting these avowed enemies of the Union in counsel. That great teacher—history—shows a multitude of cases in which whole communities, and sometimes nations, have been led into disastrous and wholesale calamities, under excitements not so terrific as that which now agitates these States. In proof of this, we could refer to the South-Carolina-like insanity which seized upon whole nations of Europe, and led them to inhospitable graves on the bloody fields of battle. The most impressive and notable of these is furnished by the terrific French Revolution, which *began with a Convention,* culminated in the decapitation of a king, and ended in the worst form of a military despotism. Tennesseeans! let us not disregard these stern teachings of history. Human nature and man are essentially the same in all ages. The demagogues who denied to us before the late Presidential election that they were at all favorable to Secession, now make light of, and affect to despise, the dangers which are only a few brief months ahead of us. We are urged to go into a Southern Confederacy at once; and in a few months thereafter we shall be drafted as soldiers, and forced to abandon our peaceful homes, never to see them more, to perish by exposure, or hunger, or disease, on long and dreary marches, or to fall by the hands of our countrymen, in a war that never ought to have been waged. This dreadful state of things is just before us in the portentous future, and we are rushing into the jaws of death, led on by the *ignis-fatuus* of the wild and visionary theorists of the South, who believe that the chief end of man is *nigger!*

But it is said that five or six Cotton States will go out of the Union, and we of the border States will be forced to follow. We say, Let them go, if they are bent upon self-destruction, but let us, Tennesseeans, remain in the Union, whose Constitution and laws *provide adequate protection to the rights of all the States of the Confederacy;* and let us look to that instrument for defence *within* the Union, warned by the experience of the past, the dangers of the present, and the hopes of the future. It is worse than idle—it is fool-hardy—to discuss the question of the relative merits of the two Governments, the new and the old. The *spirit* manifested by the Disunionists of the South shows most clearly that they are not the men to make laws for our Government, or to frame a Government for conservative Union men to live under. We may as well live under the government of the *William L. Garrisons* of the North, as the *William L. Yanceys* of the South. In case of disruption, the formation of a Southern Confederacy, by direct taxation, by means of military encampments, and by calling off the yeomanry of the country from agricultural pursuits, will involve us all in one common ruin, in financial embarrassments, and in the overthrow of the best Government the world ever knew. One can but involuntarily turn even from the contemplation of this state of things. Shall we be precipitated into this dreadful state of things by a set of men who denied to us, but three months ago, that they favored Disunion, because they then wanted our votes? If time were given to the North, she would do the South justice: therefore let these border States be guided by moderation. Let us, Tennesseeans, stand by the Union; let us hope on, and when hope is gone—so far as we are concerned—life will have lost its value for us!

Knoxville Whig, Dec. 22, 1860.

Disunion Party Revived.

The old Nullifiers of the days of JACKSON have revived under the lead of BRECKINRIDGE, and in the name of National Democracy. They were for Disunion, Secession, and Nullification, during the reign of JACKSON; but his devotion to the Union, his iron will and towering popularity, enabled him to crush them out.

JOHN C. CALHOUN was a man of iron will, scarcely behind the hero of New Orleans. He was honest, bold, frank, and fearless,—above all taint of corruption, all suspicion of his integrity, virtue, and courage. To the majesty of this man's towering intellect, and his high moral, social, and political worth, the Senate, in the palmiest days of Clay, Webster, Berrien, Leigh, Wright, Benton, Tazewell, White, Poindexter, and other Senators of the truest antique Roman mould, bowed in admiration. But, representing the Disunion sentiment of the times, he was crushed beneath the heel of ANDREW JACKSON, and he was sustained in crushing him out by the real people, irrespective of parties; for then, outside of the *Province* of South Carolina, all were intensely Union men. Then, too, the Democratic party were all Union men. Not so now: the pernicious heresy of Disunion, which strikes its accursed roots so broadly and deeply into Southern soil, is confined to the Democratic ranks.

This fiercely aggressive spirit of Disunion, South, next showed itself in the *Hartford* Convention held at Nashville, and then, as now, was confined to the Democratic organization. Their pretext for holding that treasonable convocation was *slavery*, but their craven object was *Disunion*. They broke up the Whig party in the South, and merged all opposition into the Democratic party; what opposition remained they denounced as *Abolition*. The next thing, and the last thing, was to break up the Democratic party as a national party, so as to bring the slave-holding and non-slave-holding States into conflict, divided upon a geographical line. They well knew the Union could not long survive such a division of parties, and for that reason alone brought it about.

Now, the men who seceded from the Charleston Convention in April last are the men who have been engineering for years to break up the union of these States and to establish a Southern Confederacy. They are the followers of that Calhoun school which ANDREW JACKSON broke up in 1831. BRECKINRIDGE has loaned himself to these bad men to be used as a tool, in the sacred name of Democracy, to do a deed that entitles all concerned to an ignominious death under the gallows. Ay, we have the strange spectacle presented, of men whose principles JACKSON denounced as those of traitors, setting themselves up for leaders of Democracy, while true and consistent Democrats are thrust aside for devotion to the Jackson creed!

BRECKINRIDGE now stands upon the narrow sectional ground that CALHOUN occupied in his day; and the issue between BRECKINRIDGE and the other tickets in the field, disguise it as they may, is the issue of Union or Disunion; it is an issue between the *United States* and a *Southern Confederacy*. The Disunion men of the South have chosen their candidate; and that man is JOHN C. BRECKINRIDGE. Those who act with them favor the cause of Disunion, whether they intend to do so or not.

Knoxville Whig, August 11, 1860.

"Brownlow's Flag."

It is known to this community and to the people of this county that I have had the Stars and Stripes, in the character of a small flag, floating over my dwelling, in East Knoxville, since February. This flag has become very offensive to certain leaders of the Secession party in this town, and to certain would-be leaders, and the more so as it is about the only one of the kind floating in the city. Squads of troops, from three to twenty, have come over to my house, within the last several days, cursing the flag in front of my house, and threatening to take it down, greatly to the annoyance of my wife and children. No attack has been made upon it, and consequently we have had no difficulty. It is due to the Tennessee troops to say that they have never made any such demonstrations. Other troops from the Southern States, passing on to Virginia, have been induced to do so, by certain cowardly, sneaking, white-livered scoundrels, residing here, who have not the *melt* to undertake what they urge strangers to do.

One of the Louisiana squads proclaimed in front of my house, on Thursday, that they were told to take it down by citizens of Knoxville.

Now, I wish to say a few things to the public in connection with this subject. This flag is private property, upon a private dwelling, in a State that has *never voted herself out of the Union* or into the Southern Confederacy, and is therefore lawfully and constitutionally under these same Stars and Stripes I have floating over my house. Until the State, by her citizens, through the ballot-box, changes her Federal relations, her citizens have a right to fling this banner to the breeze. Those who are in rebellion against the Government represented by the Stars and Stripes have up the Rebel flag, and it is a high piece of work to deny loyal citizens of the Union the privilege of displaying their colors!

But there is one other feature of this tyranny and of these mobocratic assaults I wish to lay before the people, irrespective of parties. There are but a few of the leaders of this Secession movement in Knoxville—less than half a dozen—for whom I entertain any sort of respect, or whose good opinions I esteem. With one of these I had a free and full conversation, more than two weeks ago, in regard to this whole question. I told him that we Union men would make the best fight we could at the ballot-box, on the 8th of June, to keep the State in the Union; but that if we were overpowered, and a majority of the people of the State should say in this constitutional way that she must secede, we should have to come down, and bring our flags with us, bowing to the will of the majority with the best grace we could. I made the same statement to the colonel who got up a regiment here, and to one of his subordinate officers. I made the same statement to the president of the railroad, and I have repeatedly made the same statement through my paper. The whole Secession party here know this to be the position and purpose of the Union party; but a portion of them seek to bring about personal conflicts, and to engage strangers, under the influence of whiskey, to do a dirty and villainous work they have the meanness to do, without the courage.

If these God-forsaken scoundrels and hell-deserving assassins want satisfaction out of me for what I have said about them,—and it has been no little,—they can find me on these streets every day of my life but Sunday. I am at all times prepared to give them satisfaction. I take back nothing I have ever said against the corrupt and unprincipled villains, but reiterate all, cast it in their dastardly faces, and hurl down their lying throats their own infamous calumnies.

Finally, the destroying of my small flag or of my town-property is a small matter. The carrying out of the State upon the mad wave of Secession is also a small matter, compared with the great PRINCIPLE involved. Sink or swim, live or die, survive or perish, I am a Union man, and owe my allegiance to the Stars and

Stripes of my country. Nor can I, in any possible contingency, have any respect for the Government of the Confederated States, originating as it did with, and being controlled by, the worst men in the South. And any man saying—whether of high or low degree—that I am an Abolitionist or a Black Republican, is a LIAR and a SCOUNDREL.

W. G. BROWNLOW,
Editor of the Knoxville Whig.

Knoxville Whig, May 25, 1861.

Twelve Months Ago.

On Saturday morning, July 28, 1860, or a year ago, the following leading editorial appeared in our Tri-Weekly Whig, and again, on the following Saturday, in the Weekly Whig. We copy it by way of vindicating our claims to *consistency*, and invite attention to it, as an article having more interest about it than it had when it was first published. It was then *prophetic;* it is now prophecy *fulfilled:—*

"THIS UNION AND ITS FUTURE."

We had occasion, while at the White Sulphur Springs, to answer a long letter addressed to us by a gentleman in New York, who was raised in the South, on the subject of national politics. In reply to that letter he says:—

"I have perused your letter with as much interest as I read your paper. In most of your positions I agree with you; in some I do not. Give us in your next issue your honest views as to *this Union and its future.* I ask this because I hear it said you are a Disunionist, and by others that you are opposed to the Secessionists. Your editorials satisfy me that you are holding on to the Union."

We are now, as we have always been, a Union man. We say, let the Union stand; let the principles and compromises of the Constitution be observed; let the spirit of our forefathers, who framed out of discordant materials this noble fabric of government, prevail; let the work of the clear heads of Adams, Hancock, Jefferson, Carroll, Harrison, and a host of others, equally true and patriotic, be perpetual; let sectionalism, as held by the Republicans of the North and the Democrats of the South, and the evil passions of vile demagogues, who seek *their own,* not *their country's* good, sink to the lowest hell; and let unity of opinion, tolerance of differences, and patriotic sentiments alone be heard in our national councils.

The foregoing are briefly our sentiments, and they have never been otherwise during the twenty-one years of our active editorial and political life. But will these opinions prevail in this country? We think not. There is at the North a powerful party, called the Republican party, whose leading principle is opposition to the spread of slavery over territory now free: into this party, purely *sectional*, are going all the shades of opinion opposed to the institution of negro slavery. There is also at the North a party calling itself Democratic, by no means consistent, and having no fixed principles, willing to stand on any sort of platform which will secure to it the vote of the South for the Presidency and the spoils of office. In the South, there is in every State an equally sectional organization, calling itself Democratic, which is dominant in all the fifteen States but Maryland. Southern Democracy is by no means consistent with itself. A portion of them hold on to save the Government from disunion; another portion cling to the organization expressly to overthrow the Union!

The large demands of the leaders of Southern Democracy, their violence and ultraism, are thinning the ranks of the Northern Democracy, and driving them over to the Northern anti-slavery party. Some go directly, others indirectly by supporting Douglas, whose principles end in Republicanism. It is clear to our mind that the Democratic party has become *sectional*, and that the contest before the Charleston Convention is to turn alone on the Slavery question. All interests, State and National, are discarded; all feelings are absorbed in the one question, and that a sectional issue that never ought to have been agitated in Congress. This state of things cannot last many years longer. It has but one issue,—that of *disunion*. The waters of the Mississippi lead not more certainly to the Gulf of Mexico than do these sectional issues, in the hands of these parties, carry our Government to certain destruction. In other words, we think the Union will be dissolved. We are sorry to say it, and sorry that we have been brought to believe it; but we are unable to resist the evidence driving us to this melancholy conclusion!

Knoxville Whig, July, 1861.

The North and the South.

With all our progressive developments in the South,—and we hail them all with pleasure,—still we are, *ex necessitate rei*, largely dependent upon the mind and labor of the North. If this dependence be a sin, as Southern fire-eaters contend it is, how deeply we are all involved in transgression! The very knives and combs in our pockets, the hats upon our heads, the shoes upon our feet, the clothes upon our backs, the razors with which we shave, the cologne with which we perfume our hair, to say nothing of the furniture of our parlors, the ware upon our tables, the implements of husbandry in our fields, the coffins in which we are buried, the spades with which our graves are dug,—all come from the North, and will rise up and condemn us. When we have erected manufacturing establishments, and applauded them as Southern enterprises, the truth still stares us all in the face that they have nevertheless been inaugurated by Northern genius, supplied by Northern machinery, and worked by Northern men. The very *types* on which the South is dependent for the issue of her scores of newspapers and periodicals, as well as our printing-presses and ink, to black these types, come from the North! While, therefore, we consent to share the *shame* of this our humiliating dependency, let us be a little more slow to censure harshly the noble enterprise of our neighbors beyond the Potomac, and equally so to anathematize our Southern neighbors who deal with them, until we provide at home the *necessaries* of both life and death.

When South Carolina goes out of the Union, and a few other "Cotton States" follow her iniquitous example, where will they get shoes and coarse clothes for their negroes? Where will they get types and presses to print their fire-eating journals and doctrines? The truth is, we are acting the fool at the South, and the Abolitionists are playing the same game at the North. We can't do without their productions, and they can't do without our rice, sugar, and cotton. Had we not, then, better "live and let live"?

Knoxville Whig, Nov. 10, 1861.

Multum in Parvo.

"CAMDEN, ARK., June 30, 1860.

"W. G. BROWNLOW:—I have learned with pleasure, upon what I consider reliable authority, that you have made up your mind to join the Democratic party, and in future to act with us for the benefit of the country.

When will you come out and announce it? It will have a good effect in the present election, if you will make it known over your own signature. Hoping to hear from you, I am, very truly,

"JORDAN CLARK."

KNOXVILLE, August 6, 1860.

MR. JORDAN CLARK:—I have your letter of the 30th ult., and hasten to let you know the *precise time* when I expect to come out and formally announce that I have joined the Democratic party. When the sun shines at midnight and the moon at mid-day; when man forgets to be selfish, or Democrats lose their inclination to steal; when nature stops her onward march to rest, or all the water-courses in America flow up stream; when flowers lose their odor, and trees shed no leaves; when birds talk, and beasts of burden laugh; when damned spirits swap hell for heaven with the angels of light, and pay them the boot in mean whiskey; when impossibilities are in fashion, and no proposition is too absurd to be believed,—you may credit the report that I have joined the Democrats!

I join the Democrats! Never, so long as there are sects in churches, weeds in gardens, fleas in hog-pens, dirt in victuals, disputes in families, wars with nations, water in the ocean, bad men in America, or base women in France! No, Jordan Clark, you may hope, you may congratulate, you may reason, you may sneer, but that cannot be. The thrones of the Old World, the courts of the universe, the governments of the world, may all fall and crumble into ruin,—the New World may commit the national suicide of dissolving this Union,—but all this, and more, must occur before I join the Democracy!

I join the Democracy! Jordan Clark, you know not what you say. When I join Democracy, the Pope of Rome will join the Methodist Church. When Jordan Clark, of Arkansas, is President of the Republic of Great Britain by the universal suffrage of a contented people; when Queen Victoria consents to be divorced from Prince Albert by a county court in Kansas; when Congress obliges, by law, James Buchanan to marry a European princess; when the Pope leases the Capitol at Washington for his city residence; when Alexander of Russia and Napoleon of France are elected Senators in Congress from New Mexico; when good men cease to go to heaven, or bad men to hell; when this world is turned upside down; when proof is afforded, both clear and unquestionable, that there is no God; when men turn to ants, and ants to elephants,—I will change my political faith and come out on the side of Democracy!

Supposing that this full and frank letter will enable you to fix upon *the period* when I will come out a full-grown Democrat, and to communicate the same to all whom it may concern in Arkansas,

I have the honor to be, &c.,

W. G. BROWNLOW.

CHAPTER II.

THIRTY-NINE LASHES AND A COAT OF TAR AND FEATHERS PROMISED ME—REPLY TO W. L. YANCEY ON THE PLATFORM IN KNOXVILLE—DENYING THE RIGHT OF SECESSION—PRONOUNCING THE AFRICAN SLAVE-TRADE PIRACY—MY ANCESTORS FIGHTING FOR THIS COUNTRY—SOUTH CAROLINA THE RESORT OF TORIES—NULLIFICATION IN 1832—NULLIFICATION AMONG THE ANCIENTS.

A South Carolina Correspondent.

WE have received the following epistle from a *dignitary* in South Carolina, which we think is worth laying before the public, and with it we give our reply:—

"UNIONVILLE, S.C., Oct. 4, 1860.

"W. G. BROWNLOW:—

"SIR:—I have been taking your paper some time, believing you to be honest in your views. But your remarks to Yancey convince me fully you are a traitor to the South and to your country. As to what you say of the Secessionists, that is true. I expect to find you and your followers in the ranks of the Abolitionists, and if so, so help me God, I will kill you the first man. If it should be that we ever meet on the soil of South Carolina, I expect to be one of the number that will give you thirty-nine lashes on your bare back, and a coat of tar and feathers afterwards to heal up the stripes.

"If my time is not out, stop my paper, anyhow. I make you a present of all you owe me, believing you would steal it if I did not.

"Nothing more at present.

"JOHN W. PALMER."

KNOXVILLE, Oct. 12, 1860.

MR. JOHN W. PALMER:—

I have your *polite* favor of the 4th inst., requesting a discontinuance of the Whig to your address, and *kindly* making me a present of "*all*" I am owing you. I respectfully decline your *liberal* offer, and enclose you twenty-four cents in postage-stamps, the amount due you for the six remaining weeks required to complete your year.

Your proposal to be "one of a number" who will first thrash and then tar and feather me, illustrates the *spirit* of the party with which you act, as well as its *courage*. If a *number* of Secessionists will join you, you will undertake to mob me. This is the *argument* of your party, and especially in South Carolina. If you will undertake the task "solitary and alone," furnishing me with reliable proof of your respectability, I will give you an opportunity of carrying out your threats at such time and place as you may designate

I can, I think, survive the shock of your withdrawal

from my subscription-list. I have a paying list of twelve thousand subscribers,—more than any other political paper in this State can boast of,—and I can afford to part with every Disunionist on my list, and really desire to be rid of them. And if the world were rid of them, it would be better for the country.

My remarks to Yancey, upon the stand, when he spoke here, are the immediate cause of your withdrawal, and proof to you that you will find me and my followers in the ranks of the Abolitionists. Now, sir, what were my remarks, and what is their true import? The question was, would the election of Lincoln be a sufficient cause for dissolving this Union? I stood forth upon the stand, by the side of Mr. YANCEY, and answered in the following terms:—

> "Yes, I endorse all Bell has said, and I go further than he has gone. I am one of a numerous party at the South, who will, if even Lincoln shall be elected under the forms of our Constitution, and by the authority of law, *without committing any other offence than being elected*, force the vile Disunionists and Secessionists of the South TO PASS OVER OUR DEAD BODIES ON THEIR MARCH TO WASHINGTON TO BREAK UP THIS GOVERNMENT!"

However offensive the foregoing sentiment may be to Southern Disunionists, I am proud of it, and take nothing back. Our Government is the greatest and the best the world has ever seen. I am, therefore, opposed to dissolving it because a man not acceptable to me is elected President, and elected upon a sectional issue. The object aimed at by the Disunionists is, that *they may re-open the slave-trade.* They prefer Disunion with the slave-trade, to the Union without it; although the Congress of the United States, and the Supreme Court, have declared it to be PIRACY.

The man who calculates upon a *peaceable* dissolution of the Union is either a madman or a fool. I am among those who believe that the Union is not going to be dissolved, because the Disunionists have no right to do that thing; they have no power, if the right existed; and there is no *cause* for a dissolution,—not even after Lincoln shall have been elected. I even deny the right of secession, and I could here quote from JEFFERSON, MADISON, RITCHIE, JACKSON, and others, to show that the right of secession does not exist; but this would extend my letter beyond the limits I have prescribed. The American Constitution, adopted in Convention, and ratified by the States, is higher authority than even these great statesmen; and that declares:—

"This Constitution, and the laws of the United States which shall be made in pursuance thereof, and all treaties made, or which shall be made under the authority of the United States, shall be the *supreme* law of the land, and the judges in every State shall be bound thereby, *any thing* in the Constitution or laws of any State to the contrary notwithstanding."—*Art.* VI. *Sec.* 2.

For argument's sake, I will concede what the Disunionists claim,—to wit, that the right of secession is a "reserved right." Let us illustrate that point. One State has as much right to secede as another. Our Government acquired Louisiana by purchase from Spain, and paid a round sum of money: suppose Louisiana should take offence at some Federal law, or at the election of Lincoln, and *secede.* What would become of all we paid in the purchase? We paid millions for Texas; and if she were to *secede,* what becomes of all that money?

But I am not yet done with this *supposable case* of the election of Lincoln. I will say more than I have said, and I will go on to state my position in the event of his election; and I am free to confess that his chances are now better than those of any other candidate in the field. Should Lincoln be elected, and should he, for instance, recommend the abolition of the slave-trade between the States, I shall advocate waiting to see if Congress will sustain him. If Congress will sustain him in the outrage and violation of the Constitution, I shall advocate an appeal to the Supreme Court; and if that tribunal sustain Lincoln, I would take the ground that *the time for Revolution has come,*—that all the Southern States should go into it; AND I WOULD GO WITH THEM! Here is where I stand, and where all Union-loving and law-abiding men are bound to stand, whether they were born North or South.

But, Mr. Palmer, you say I am a traitor to the South and to my country. I am willing to compare notes with you, or any man in the Disunion party South. Your idol, Yancey, characterized the Bell men, in his speech here, as the *descendants of Tories.* This charge is too base and contemptible to attempt a refutation of it, and no man but a malicious slanderer would urge it in the indiscriminate terms Yancey did. But how stands the case as between you and myself? I am, as were my parents before me, a native of Virginia. A portion of my relatives on my mother's side were in the War of 1812,—the second War of Independence,—and lost their lives at Norfolk. My father was a "high private" in Captain Landon's company from Sullivan county, Tennessee, when peace was made and terminated that war. My uncle, WM. L. BROWNLOW, was a captain in the United States Navy, died in the service, and his bones repose in the navy-yard at Norfolk. Another, ALEXANDER BROWNLOW, was first lieutenant in the Navy in that same war, and his bones rest in the graveyard at New Orleans, having died in the service. A third uncle, SAMUEL L. BROWNLOW, was a wagon-master under General JACKSON, and was in the battle of the Horseshoe. A fourth uncle, ISAAC BROWNLOW, was an inferior officer under General JACKSON, and bore his dispatches from the Creek War to Huntsville, swimming the Tennessee River on horseback. A fifth uncle, JOHN BROWNLOW, was an inferior officer in the Navy, and died at sea.

Now, sir, what is your pedigree? You hail from a State which mustered more Tories in the War of the Revolution than all the other States in the Confederacy put together. There are, I am free to allow, many Union-loving, law-abiding, patriotic, and gallant citizens in South Carolina, and there were during the War of the Revolution; but still, I repeat, it was the resort of Tories, and the home of traitors, during that dark and trying period of our history. And I have no doubt that your ancestors, on both sides, were operating in the cypress-swamps, and figured with that illustrious class of robbers who were hunted down by General MARION, the "Swamp Fox," for giving "aid and comfort" to the British army.

I have no doubt there are Tories enough still in South Carolina, and the descendants of Tories, to influence an attempt to go out of the Union in the event of Lincoln's election. And I think it a great misfortune that the Constitution does not provide some means of letting that State out peaceably. As matters stand, she will have to be *thrashed into line.* It will not, however, become necessary to send an army to South Carolina, if she should attempt to *secede.* Let the Government blockade her ports; and then let all mail-communications with the State be closed, and she will herself propose liberal terms of compromise.

I resided in South Carolina in 1832, when *Nullification* raged, and when the *Ordinance* of the Nullifiers was put forth, which called for the proclamation of General Jackson. I took sides in favor of the General Government then, as I do now; while the Churches were enveloped in the smoke of faction, and many of the ministers—Presbyterians, Baptists, and Methodists—volunteered to support the "Ordinance," and preached expressly on Nullification, declaring that it was both *scriptural* and *right*. They received new commissions to "Go into all the world and preach *Nullification* to every creature;" and, like the deluded followers of Mohammed, they carried the *Alkoran* of Nullification in one hand, and the sword of vengeance in the other.

The Nullifiers throughout the country, in that memorable day, distinguished themselves by wearing a cockade on their hats, made of *blue ribbon*. The *boys*, not free from the apron-strings of their mothers, had these badges displayed in bold relief and in the true style of chivalry. A vast number of the common people left the country, as they will do again, not feeling exactly willing to fight the battles of demagogues and designing leaders.

It is plain to be seen that the same spirit of disloyalty to the Union which prevailed there in 1832 is now working in the hearts of the Breckinridge unbelievers; and a similar fate awaits them. Nullification has been attended with the worst of consequences in all ages. In the garden of Eden, our first parents were induced by the devil, in the form of a serpent, to *nullify* the laws of God; and, believing it to be a "peaceful remedy," they made the dreadful "experiment." Cain, in the case of Abel, *nullified* the law of God; and he was branded in the forehead as a traitorous murderer. The nation of Jews who perished in the siege of Jerusalem were all *nullifiers*. So were the rebellious inhabitants of Sodom and Gomorrah. And the antediluvians, for their *South-Carolina politics*, encountered the very devil, in the days of the Flood. And the King of Egypt, in trying to carry his "Ordinance" into effect, lost his life in the Red Sea. And had the South Carolina Nullifiers gone a little further with their scheme of secession, Old Hickory Jackson would have drowned them in the harbor of Charleston. Indeed, General Scott was ordered to the port of Charleston with the regular army, and the writ of old Jackson was in the hands of the United States Marshal for the arrest of the leaders of the rebellion, with a view to hanging them. Knowing this, they came to terms, and a compromise was effected.

And, by way of admonition to all Disunionists, I conclude this epistle in the language of Holy Writ:— "Let every soul be subject unto the higher powers.

For there is no power but of God: the powers that be are ordained of God. Whosoever therefore resisteth the power, resisteth the *ordinance* of God: and they that resist shall receive to themselves DAMNATION."

W. G. BROWNLOW,
Editor of the Knoxville Whig.

Knoxville Whig, Oct. 13, 1860.

CHAPTER III.

CASE OF REV. DR. NEELY, THE ALABAMA SECESSIONIST—PRAYING THE SOUTH NOT TO SUBMIT TO THE INAUGURATION OF LINCOLN—EXHORTATION TO MODERATION.

Another Withdrawal from our List.

THE following correspondence will explain itself; and we therefore leave it to our readers to pass upon:—

"JEFFERSON, ALA., Oct. 4, 1860.

"REV. W. G. BROWNLOW:

"DEAR SIR:—I subscribed for your paper a month or so ago, in the belief that you would *honorably* advocate the principles of the party to which I belong, and use all *proper* means to secure the election of Bell and Everett. But, a short time since, to my utter astonishment, you published a short editorial about Dr. Neely, of the Alabama Conference, which I think is very far from honorable, and shows your unscrupulousness, and the little regard you have for the reputation of others, and is also a reflection upon the Church to which Dr. Neely belongs, and a slander upon the Alabama Conference, before which he was tried and *fully acquitted of improper motives*, and has gone forth for the last ten years with the endorsement of this body. I am a strong party man, but love my Church and the reputation of her ministry more than party; and I have no confidence in the political honesty of a man who will defame the name of a minister and slander such a body of men as I know the Alabama Conference to be, for party purposes. I am no satellite of Dr. Neely's: I am barely acquainted with him,—only regard him with that friendship I have in common for the ministers of the Church to which I belong. You will please discontinue your *slanderous sheet* to my address, and I will bestow my patronage upon those who will promote my political principles in an honorable and gentlemanly way.

"Yours, &c.,
"A. W. Cooper."

Knoxville, Oct. 15, 1860.

Mr. A. W. Cooper:—I have before me your insulting and dictatorial epistle, ordering a discontinuance of your paper with something of a flourish,—all characteristic of its author, who is known to be a self-willed and self-conceited man, suffering greatly from a disease, common among men of your calibre, known as the *big-head*. You have only *thirteen* weeks of the paper due you, after receiving the issue containing this correspondence; and, when you speak of ordering a discontinuance, confine yourself to the truth in this respect.

It seems that I have offended you by my well-timed, but moderate, castigation of Rev. P. P. Neely, a Methodist travelling preacher in the Alabama Conference, for making *stump-speeches* favorable to the cause of Breckinridge and of an organized band of traitors and hell-hounds in the South, who seek to overthrow this Government and to erect upon its ruins a Southern Confederacy, where a few corrupt and ambitious demagogues may get offices and spoils they can never enjoy while the Union is preserved. You say that you will bestow your patronage elsewhere. Do so, and carry with you as many bigoted Neely men and as many blind partisan Methodists as you can influence. I can live without your patronage or theirs; and, to be candid with you and them, I want the names of no such partisan fools upon my list. Nay, I invite you and Neely, and all such men as can be enlisted, to take the field and the *stump* against me and my paper; and the only effect of your opposition will be to increase my list of paying subscribers!

Now, Mr. Cooper, you write as "one having authority, and not as these little scribes;" and, if you do not represent the "Alabama Conference," you at least represent Neely and his clique. Let me review you and your esteemed pastor Neely for a brief spell.

It was in the Sumpter (Ala.) *Democrat* of September 1, I first learned that Mr. Neely had made a stump-speech in the court-house in Livingston in favor of the

Breckinridge-Yancey ticket. After this, I found an account of this Livingston speech by Neely in the Montgomery *Advertiser*, from which I take this brief extract, premising that the *Advertiser* characterized it as a "patriotic and Christian sentiment:"—

> "Whilst he was not a disunionist *per se*, yet '*he would get down on his knees to every man in the South, and beseech him not to submit to the inauguration of a Black Republican or his administration.*'"

Now, I, in commenting on this passage from Neely's speech, declared that in counselling resistance to the inauguration and administration of a man elected by a majority of the voters of the country, under our Constitution and forms of law, Mr. Neely was neither representing the sentiments of the Southern Methodist Church nor the teachings of Christ and his apostles. I also stated that, as the *salaried* agent of the Methodist Publishing House at Nashville, he was not required to *fall upon his knees before any man in the South, and beseech him to resist, "with force and arms," the inauguration and administration of a Black Republican!* I also stated that the neighbors and friends of Mr. Bell were doing, and had done, more for the "Southern Book Concern" than the neighbors and friends of Breckinridge had ever done or ever would do. I stated—and now repeat—that there are more Bell-and-Everett men in the South connected with the Methodist Church South, than there are advocating Breckinridge and Lane, and that

Bell-and-Everett Methodists did not care to see the Church pay any man a large salary to do the dirty work of *falling upon his knees and beseeching Southern men to resist the Constitution and laws of the country* and "precipitate the Cotton States into a revolution." Our gospel is one of *peace*, and not supported for the purpose of plunging the country into all the horrors of civil war!

For this, you say I have resorted to *dishonorable means* to secure the election of Bell and Everett, and that I am unscrupulous and have but little regard for the reputation of others. Nay, you say that I am a slanderer, and have reflected upon the Alabama Conference. In what respect have I slandered Neely or the Alabama Conference? I said nothing about the Alabama Conference in any publication I made; and you have only *evaded the truth* in shielding Neely behind that Conference. I seek no controversy with the Alabama Conference; but, at the same time, I ask no favors of that body. I know what my rights are, and I know *where* my remedy is in a matter of church controversy.

* * * * * *

In conclusion, sir, if you can have any control over the deluded friends and admirers of Mr. Neely, prevail on them to cease their clamors in his behalf, and especially their letter-writing and their newspaper eulogies of him at the expense of better men; and let the low murmurings of the autumnal night-winds, sighing among the tree-tops, waft his faults and imperfections to the distant shores of oblivion! Prevail on him to humble himself before God, and pray much, repudiating all agitation of the questions now dividing the political parties of the day. And then shall the pale moonbeams of forgetfulness sleep around the tomb of his follies, in deathlike stillness, no more making the air hideous with the mournful cadences of his past indiscretions.

W. G. BROWNLOW,
Editor of the Knoxville Whig.

Knoxville Whig, Oct. 13, 1860.

CHAPTER IV.

SOUTH CAROLINA IN 1780—HER CITIZENS TORIES AND ON THE SIDE OF THE BRITISH CROWN—TWO HUNDRED AND TWENTY-SIX TORIES IN CHARLESTON ADDRESSING SIR HENRY CLINTON—R. BARNWELL RHETT CHANGES HIS NAME—THE DESCENDANTS OF THESE TORIES SPREAD OVER THE SOUTH—SOUTH CAROLINA ROYALTY.

South Carolina in 1780.

IN the spring of 1780, Sir Henry Clinton and Vice-Admiral Arbuthnot appeared before Charleston and demanded a surrender to His British Majesty's forces. The gallant General LINCOLN, in command of the American forces, repulsed this arrogant demand with the scorn and contempt of a brave officer. They have hated the name of Lincoln ever since! The people of Charleston, and of nearly all South Carolina, being Tories of the basest character, took the matter into their own hands, and threatened the gallant Lincoln with betraying him into the hands of the British forces if he did not come to such terms as pleased *them*. And Sir Henry Clinton, writing to Lord George Germaine, one of His Majesty's principal Secretaries of State, from "Head Quarters, Charles-Town, South Carolina, June 4th, 1780," by way of boast, says,—

"With the greatest pleasure I further report to your lordship that the inhabitants from every quarter repair to the detachments of the army, and to this garrison, to declare their allegiance to the King, and *to offer their services in arms in support of his government. In many instances they have brought prisoners their former oppressors or leaders; and I may venture to assert that there are few men in South Carolina who are not either our prisoners or in arms with us.*"

The very day after Sir Henry Clinton wrote that letter disclosing the Toryism of South Carolina, two hundred and twenty-six of their leading citizens, representing almost every family connection in the State, addressed the following begging, supplicating petition to Sir Henry, furnishing the proof of their own infamy:—

"*To their Excellencies* SIR HENRY CLINTON, *Knight of the Bath, General of His Majesty's Forces, and* MARIOT ARBUTHNOT, *Esq., Vice-Admiral of the Blue, His Majesty's Commissioners to restore peace and good government in the several colonies in rebellion in North America:*

"THE HUMBLE ADDRESS OF DIVERS INHABITANTS OF CHARLES-TOWN:

"The inhabitants of Charles-Town, by the articles of capitulation, are declared prisoners on parole; but we the underwriters, having every inducement to return to our allegiance, and ardently hoping speedily to be readmitted to the character and condition of British subjects, take this opportunity of tendering to your Excellencies our warmest congratulations on the restoration of this capital and Province to their political connection with the Crown and Government of Great

Britain; an event which will add lustre to your Excellencies' characters, and, we trust, entitle you to the most distinguished mark of the Royal favor. Although the right of taxing America in Parliament excited considerable ferments in the minds of the people of the Province, yet it may, with a religious adherence to truth, be affirmed, that they did not entertain the most distant thought of dissolving the union which so happily subsisted between them and their parent country; and when, in the progress of that fatal controversy, THE DOCTRINE OF INDEPENDENCY, WHICH ORIGINATED IN THE MORE NORTHERN COLONIES, made its appearance among us, OUR NATURE REVOLTED AT THE IDEA, and we look back with the most painful regret on those convulsions that gave existence to a power of subverting a Constitution, for which we always had, and ever shall retain, the most profound veneration, and substituting in its stead a RANK DEMOCRACY, which, however carefully digested in theory, on being reduced into practice, has exhibited a system of tyrannic domination only to be found among the uncivilized part of mankind, or in the history of the dark and barbarous ages of antiquity.

"We sincerely lament, that after the repeal of those statutes which gave rise to the troubles in America, the overtures made by His Majesty's Commissioners, from time to time, were not regarded by our late rulers. To this fatal inattention are to be attributed those calamities which have involved our country in a state of misery and ruin, from which, however, we trust, it will soon emerge, by the wisdom and clemency of His Majesty's auspicious Government, and the influence of prudential laws, adapted to the nature of the evils we labor under; and that the people will be restored to those privileges, in the enjoyment whereof their former felicity consisted.

"Animated with these hopes, we entreat your Excellencies' interposition, in assuring His Majesty that we shall glory in every occasion of manifesting that zeal and affection for his person and Government, with which gratitude can inspire a free and joyful people.

"CHARLES-TOWN, June 5, 1780.

John Wragg,
Wm. Glinn,
John Stopton,
John Rose,
Wm. Greenwood,
Jacob Vulk,
Robert Wilson,
Leonard Askew,
And. McKenzie,
Rob. Lithgow,
Wm. Wayne,
Jas. G. Williams,
James Ross,
John Moncrief,
John Wells, jr.,
Allard Bellin,
John Wogner,
John Ward Taylor,
Jock Holmes,
James Mesgown
Wm. Davie,
James Dunning,
John Sprisd,
Wm. Nervcob,
John Daniel,
John Collum,
John Smith,
Lewis Dutarque,
James McKlown,
Wm. Burt,
John Watson,
Anthony Montell,
James Lynch,
And. Mitchell,
Parq. McCollum,
George Adamson,
Wm. Vallentine,
Christo. Williman,
D. Pendergass,
Daniel Bell,
Edw. Cure,
Thomas Timms,
Thomas Buckle, sr.,
Hopkins Price,
George Denholm,
Roger Brown,
James Strictland,
Wm. McKinney,
John Abercrombie,
David Bruce,
John Gray,
Thos. Dawson,
Tho. Winstanley,
Cha. Ramadge,
Wm. Bower,
Alex. Walker,
John Lyon,
Robert Philip,
Robert Johnson,
David Tayler,
John Latuff,
John Gillsnocz,
John Barson,
Jo. Donaven, jr.,
Nicholas Boden,
Ja. McKenzie,

George Grant,
Abraham Pearce,
John Miot,
Fred. Augustine,
John Webb,
Robert Williams,
Alex. Macbeth,
John Robertson,
John Liber,
Hugh Rose,
Patrick Bower,
Thomas Todd,
Brian Foskie,
Thomas Eustace,
Emanuel Marshall,
Thomas Clary,
Thomas Hooper,
Ch. Sutter,
Robert Lindsey,
Tho. Richardson,
James Rach,
Peter Dumont,
Tho. Saunders,
Ed. Legge,
Henry Hardroff,
Aaron Locoock,
Arch. Brown,
Wm. Russell,
Thomas Coram,
James Hartley,
Andrew Thompson,
William Layton,
Nich. Smith,
Andrew Stewart,
John Hartley,
James Cook,
Ch. Fitz Simmons,
John Davis,
Henry Walsh,
Isaac Clarke,
John Durst,
William Cameron,
John Russell,
John Bell,
John Hayes,
James McKie,
James Gillandeau,
Hugh Truir,
Lewis Coffere,
Hugh Kirkham,
Wm. Farrow,
Wm. Arisam,
Tho. Deighton,
Robert Paterson,
John Parkinson,
John Love,
Alex. Ingles,
William Mills,
James Duncan,
Ja. Blackburn,
John Johnston,
Samuel Perry,
Geo. R. Williams,
Matthias Hunkin,
Edm. Petrie,
Wm. Nisbett,
Geo. Cook,
Tho. Stewart,
Gideon Dupont, jr.,
Jer. Savage,
Andrew Reid,
Jeph Kingsby,
Alex. Oliphant,
Paul Hamilton,
Ch. Bouchomeau,
John Bury,

Benj. Baker, sen.,
John Fisher,
Charles Atkins,
Wm. Edwards,
Thos. Buckle, jr.,
Henry Ephram,
John Hartley,
James Carmichael,
Samuel Adams,
Chr. Shutts,
Alex. Smith,
John McCall,
Michael Hubert,
Joseph Jones,
Henry Branton,
John Callagan,
John Ralph,
Samuel Bower,
George Young,
Jas. Milligan,
Anthony Geaubeau,
William Smith,
Jas. Robertson,
Michael Quin,
John Gornley,
Walter Rosewell,
Richard Dennis,
John W. Gibbs,
Benj. Sinker,
John Rartels,
Wm. Miller,
John Burges,
Daniel Boyne,
Peter Lambert,
Hen. Bookless,
Thomas Hutchinson,
Thomas Mise,
Alex. Harvey,
John Pafford,
Tho. Phepoe,
Samuel Knight,
Archibald Carson,
Tho. Elliott,
Gilbert Chaliner,
Arch. Downs,
Alex. Johnstone,
James Fagan,
Ja. Bryant,
James Courtonque,
Joseph Wyatt,
John Cuple,
James McLinachus,
Wm. Jennings,
Patrick McKam,
Robert Beard,
Stephen Townshend,
Ja. Snead,
Ch. Burnham,
Charles H. Simonds,
Rob. McIntosh,
G. Thompson,
Isaac Lessenes,
Isaac Manyeh,
Peter Procue."

We print the names of these infamous Tories, because their descendants are spread all over the South, and a portion of them are now figuring in this Secession movement, and some of them ever in their late Convention. They have a hereditary title to the contempt of all honest and patriotic men. ☞ Did not a man by the name of *R. Barnwell Smith*, some twenty-five or thirty years ago, have his name changed to that of *Rhett*, by the Legislature? and, if so, what was the motive? Was he not prominent in the late Convention, in declaring South Carolina out of this Union? We ask for information; because there have been more names changed in South Carolina, by Act of General Assembly, than in any State in the Union!

In thus showing up the original Toryism of South Carolina, we have desired to retort upon Mr. Yancey, who stood upon the platform in Knoxville last summer, and gave it as his opinion that the Bell-and-Everett men of the South were the descendants of the Tories of the Revolution. Mr. Yancey is a native of South Carolina; and who among this list of names were his "illustrious predecessors"? He may perhaps be able to say, when he inspects the list!

All who have noticed with care the proceedings in the South Carolina Convention must have been struck with the *royalty* displayed, when their President was marched in, dressed in *mazarine blue*, and attended by *Lords* and *Commoners*, equalling the coronation services in the installation of a king. There is a great deal of this *monarchical* and *despotic* feeling in South Carolina. To this very day, they clothe their circuit judges in *black silk gowns*, and attend them to and from the court-room every time court aajourns, with a sheriff and his deputy on either side, wearing cocked hats, and carrying drawn swords in their hands! We have witnessed this mock-royalty time and again, and laughed in our sleeves, as these dignitaries approached!

These are not the people to head a Confederacy for Tennesseeans to fall into. Their notions of royalty, and their contempt for the common people, will never suit Tennesseeans. In Tennessee, free white men vote who are twenty-one years of age, and they are not required to own land and negroes before they are qualified to vote. In a late speech made by *R. Barnwell Rhett*—who, by the way, was the leading spirit in this Convention—he distinctly enunciated that *capital* and *property* must hereafter be represented at the ballot-box. It is not strange that Andy Johnson, a tailor by trade, should denounce this whole movement in a speech in the Senate! And nine-tenths of our people will veto this Southern Confederacy at the ballot-box, and vote to stay in the Confederacy founded by GEORGE WASHINGTON and others, who thought a poor but honest man should be entitled to vote for or against those who were to rule over him! Let Tennessee once go into this *Empire of Cotton States*, and all poor men will at once become the *free negroes of the Empire!* We are down upon the whole scheme.

Knoxville Whig, Jan. 12, 1861.

CHAPTER V.

THREATENING TO HANG US FOR OUR PRINCIPLES—CHARGES US WITH BEING A YANKEE—THE WICKEDNESS OF SECESSION—ORIGIN OF SECESSION—SOUTH CAROLINA FIRES THE FIRST GUN—FREEDOM OF SPEECH TO BE DENIED—STANDING OUT FOR THE UNION.

Threatening to Hang us!

WE call attention to the two following letters, as they are from men responsible in the ranks of the Secessionists, and reflect the sentiments and feelings of the great Southern mob known by this name. The Georgia letter regards us as *seceding from the South*, and threatens violence. This letter we give entire. The one from Mississippi comes out in the proscriptive and mobocratic spirit of this whole party in the South. We give an extract:—

"COVINGTON, Jan. 8, 1861.

"BROTHER BROWNLOW:—

Having been a subscriber to your *once readable* paper for a goodly number of years, and having through the agency of its columns formed an opinion of your character which I must in candor own was favorable, I take the privilege which my age, experience, and position in society afford me, to *advise*, *entreat*, and *warn* you of your approaching danger. Among the most important things in which we have noticed your deviation from the path of rectitude is, that in this present political commotion you have *dabbled* more than becomes you. From all appearances, you have turned from a *private* and *respected citizen* to a *contentious, quarrelsome* politician,—from a Southern-Rights man to a friend of the North,—from a *Union* man to a *Secessionist*. Can these charges be true? Am I not deceived? I hope so. Yet these reports come from every quarter, and are strengthened by the *tone* of your paper. With you alone, my dear brother, it remains to refute them by your future conduct. These remarks are prompted by a generous heart, and the feeling that causes a friend to inform another of his errors, hoping thereby to correct them. We will close, as 'a word to the wise is sufficient.' That a speedy reformation may take place, is the wish of

"Your affectionate friend,

"GEORGE P. NICKOLS."

"CORINTH, MISS., Jan. 10, 1861.

"MR. BROWNLOW, OF THE UNITED STATES OF AMERICA:—I see, in a late issue of your dirty sheet, that you are full of braggadocio, and that you declare positively that if Tennessee, and the South generally, secede, you will still cling to that most abominable of all abominations, the Union. Now, Parson, if you adopt this policy, what do you think will be the consequence? You will certainly be hung, as all dogs should be, until you are 'dead, dead.' Your crime will be treason of the deepest dye.

"I have never believed you to be a Southern man, but a shrewd, money-making Yankee; and, if you will give me time, I will look into your nativity. When Tennessee secedes, I will head a company of Tennesseeans and Mississippians and proceed to hang you by law, or by force if need be. The South can look upon you in no other light than as a traitor and a Tory, and the twin brother of *Andrew Johnson.* Remember, and beware, you shall be hung in the year 1861, unless you conclude to live the life of an exile.

"Yours, &c.,

"W. M. YANCEY."

KNOXVILLE, Jan. 15, 1861.

MATCHLESS SIRS:—

In a brief reply to your letters, I will first correct the error into which one of you has fallen as it regards my nativity, &c. I am not "a shrewd, money-making Yankee," nor am I a money-making man at all,—never was. My town-property and printing-office I estimate to be worth about *ten thousand dollars.* This is all I have, and is fully as much as I ever did own at any one time. I am, therefore, a poor man, and never expect to be any thing else. It would have been otherwise with me, if I had not *given away* half of all I ever did make, and if I had *sought* to make money.

As it regards my nativity, I was born and raised in Wythe county, Virginia, and my parents were both natives of the same State. I have lived in East Tennessee for thirty years; and, although I am now fifty-five years of age, I walk erect, have but few gray hairs, and *look* to be younger than any whiskey-drinking, tobacco-chewing, profane-swearing Secessionist in any of the Cotton States, of forty years.

As it regards your threats, (and both of your letters are of a threatening character,) they have no terrors for me. I have no doubt but there are thousands of Secessionists in the South who would be willing to see me hung, and would assist in swinging me up, could they have the slightest pretext for so doing, and meet with an opportunity. When you come to East Tennessee, with a company of Tennesseeans, Mississippians, and Georgians, to hang me, please give me ten days' notice, and I will muster men enough in the county where I reside, to hang the last rascal among you, and then use your carcasses for wolf-bait!

This whole scheme of Secession is the most wicked, diabolical, and infernal scheme ever set on foot for the ruin of any country. It has long been contemplated by the Tory leaders of the Cotton States, and the details of it, I see, have just come to light through the *National Intelligencer*, one of the most reliable journals in

America. The scheme to avoid a collision about the revenue, is to declare Southern ports free to the commerce of the world, raise their revenues by direct taxation and forced loans, and leave the United States and foreign Governments to fight out the question of the collection of the revenue. Another one of their schemes was to seize upon all the forts and Southern fortifications along the entire coast from Maryland to Texas; and this, like lawless rebels, they have been doing, even before they have seceded. This was all agreed upon before the Charleston Convention, and a part of the programme was to break it up in a row, and prevent the nomination of Douglas, for if nominated they knew he could be elected, and this would prolong the existence of "that most abominable of all abominations, the Union," at least four years longer.

South Carolina, Alabama, Mississippi, and Florida have actually gone out of the Union, and Georgia, Louisiana, Arkansas, and Texas will soon follow. The first four States named have passed their Ordinances of Secession, and published them to the world. They call them *ordinances;* I call them so many covenants with death and agreements with hell! They are so many decrees to carry out the behests of *madmen* and *traitors*. Each ordinance is the twin sister of treason,—"treason *de facto*." O Secessionism! "hell is moved at thy coming;" for hell and its infinitely infernal Government are thy offspring. The fallen angels were the first seceders from Paradise, and declared their "*independence*" by promulgating an ordinance in "a lake that burns with fire and brimstone," and "where there is weeping, wailing, and gnashing of teeth; and where the smoke of their torment ascends up for ever and ever,"—the reward of their treason being "eternal damnation."

But war has commenced. The first guns have been fired,—and fired by South Carolina rebels upon unoffending American soldiers sailing into port under the Stars and Stripes of their country. In four of the States of this Confederacy rebellion bids defiance to law, and "bloody treason flourishes over us." Throughout these four States, judgment and truth seem to have "fled to brutish beasts, and men have lost their reason." Even in the halls of our national Capitol traitors stalk unblushingly, and openly proclaim their treason, denouncing the Government and declaring their purpose to destroy it. Traitors stand on the floor of the American Senate and receive nine dollars per day for proclaiming treason, rank and damning,—for which they ought to be hung, and would be if the laws of the land were enforced.

Every man who is worthy of the name of an American citizen will denounce this treason, and rally to the defence of our Constitution and laws. They are the bonds of our Union, and around that Union cluster the hallowed memories of the past and the brightest hopes and dearest interests of the future. Blood, it is plain to be seen, will be shed in its defence; but upon these Secession aggressors be the consequences and responsibilities.

I am for my country, and on the side of the General Government; and in every contest, either at sea or on land, I shall rejoice in the triumph of the Government troops fighting under the Stars and Stripes. Should Tennessee go out of the Union, I shall continue to denounce Secessionism, and war against the storms of fanaticism at the North and the assaults of demagogues and traitors at the South, though their number be legion. In all candor, I believe that in a Southern Confederacy the freedom of speech and of the press will be denied; and for the exercise of them I will be hung. But, come what may, through weal or woe, in peace or war, no earthly power shall keep me from denouncing the enemies of my country until my tongue and pen are paralyzed in death! Once destroyed, this Union can never be reconstructed. And, with others, I have resolved that no earthly power shall prevail against it; that it shall be "perpetual," as our fathers intended it,—"one and indivisible, now and forever."

W. G. BROWNLOW,
Editor of Knoxville Whig.

Knoxville Whig, Jan. 19, 1861.

CHAPTER VI.

PATRONAGE WITHDRAWN FROM MY PAPER—PREDICTING THE SUCCESS OF SECESSION—THE AUTHOR ALWAYS AFTER OFFICE—INDEBTEDNESS TO STORES—OUR OWN PARTISANS REFUSING TO ENDORSE US—MEMBERS OF THE CHURCH SPURNING US.

A South Carolina Correspondent.

We are receiving quite a number of letters from South Carolina, and it is only at intervals that we *condescend* to notice one, and then only when the name of the writer is given. The following *polite* note we publish on account of *its information derived from Knoxville*:—

"Abbeville C. H., S.C., Jan. 27, 1861.

"W. G. Brownlow:—

"Sir:—I wrote to you a few days ago under the signature of 'T. J. C.,' and informed you that you were the greatest liar out of hell, and one of the most infamous scoundrels living between heaven and earth; and I then told you, and now repeat, that nothing would afford us as much pleasure as to see you in Abbeville, where we could treat you to a coat of tar and feathers. I told you in that brief letter that my understanding was that the people of Knoxville were a respectable and intelligent people, and that it was a matter of surprise that they would allow you to remain in their midst,—a vile scamp, as you have shown yourself to be.

"Since writing that note to you, I have seen a long and interesting letter from Knoxville to a citizen of this Republic, giving some facts in regard to you that I am resolved the world shall know, at least to the extent of the circulation of Southern papers. I was permitted to take down the *points* made against you in the Knoxville letter, and they are as follows:—

"1. The Southern States having withdrawn their patronage from your Abolition sheet, you no longer have subscribers enough to defray the expenses of publication, and you are about to starve out.

"2. The town and county in which you publish your slanderous sheet will shortly cast a majority of their votes for Secession, and so will your State.

"3. You have repeatedly thrust yourself forward as a candidate for office, but never have been elected.

"4. You are indebted to every store in your town,—and nothing can be made out of you at law,—until you cannot get credit in any store for a suit of clothes!

"5. Your own partisans refuse, upon the stump, to endorse any thing you say, and will not be held to an account for your doctrines; while the common people send off to other sections of your State for newspapers.

"6. The members of your Church have no respect

for you, and the better class refuse to speak to you, either publicly or privately.

"This, you lying old hypocrite, is your character furnished by a South Carolinian from your own town, where you are best known.

"T. J. CINCLAIR."

KNOXVILLE, Feb. 14, 1861.

T. J. CINCLAIR:—Your insulting letter is before me, and I take the opportunity to reply, though I have no idea that I am replying to a *gentleman*, or a man who pays his just debts, or tells the truth in common conversation. I am not ignorant of the deadly opposition to me in South Carolina, and more especially from the blackguard portion of her citizens, of whom *you* are a fit representative. I expect that the vials of contumely, reproach, and defamation will be poured upon me by a hireling press of a corrupt and plundering Southern Confederacy, by the insolvent bullies, hardened liars, and vulgar cut-throats whose only ambition is to serve as tools under an arrogant and hateful pack of aristocratic leaders. But while I have strength to wield a pen, my nerve shall be exerted in defence of that *Union* which was purchased with blood. Under the mantle of freedom, dark assassins of our National Constitution are endeavoring to insinuate themselves into the temple of those privileges, our rights to which were secured by the toil of our fathers and sealed with their blood. But these border States will teach you that our Constitution is not built upon such a sandy foundation as to be shaken and demolished without the rotten pillar of reputed South Carolina orthodoxy to support it.

As it regards your Knoxville letter-writer, he is a *liar* and a *coward*, and *dare* not give his name to the public. My neighbors, without distinction of parties, will testify that he is a liar. Even my *enemies*—and I have some—will testify from their own personal knowledge that he is a liar. I do not believe, for one moment, that any citizen of Knoxville ever wrote any such letter to South Carolina. You have been duped for once, or else some straggling subject of your contemptible Southern Confederacy has passed through here and sent to your would-be Republic the infinitely infernal production from which you quote your six propositions.

I would as soon be engaged in importing the plague from the East, as in helping to build up a Southern Confederacy upon the ruins of the American Constitution. I expect to be abused for my defence of the Union. "Tray, Blanche, and Sweetheart" will all bark at me. The kennel is now unloosed: all the pack—from the deep-mouthed bloodhound of South Carolina and Florida to the growling cur of Georgia—are baying at me. If I were to stop to throw stones at all the snarling puppies that yelp at my heels in South

Carolina and elsewhere, I should have little time to do any thing else.

Your first falsehood, as gathered from a Knoxville writer, is that my subscription has so diminished of late that my office does not pay expenses. There are twelve newspapers in East Tennessee besides mine, and I have more paying subscribers than all of them put together. I have the largest list of any political paper in the State; and my list of yearly subscribers is now larger than it ever was before,—increasing now at the rate of two hundred per week, and the rise of that. So much for my prospects of starving out.

2. But my town and county have cast a majority of their votes for Secession, and my State was to have done so! Well, sir, on Saturday last our election was held, and a full vote was had all over the State,—the issue being Union or Disunion. In my town, out of a vote of 960 the Secession ticket received 113, and in the remainder of the county the Secession ticket received about 100 votes, leaving the Union majority in the county and town *upwards of three thousand!* In the State at large the Secession ticket is so badly beaten as to be absolutely disgraced. It has been "routed, horse, foot, and dragoon," the Secessionists having elected only about *half a dozen* members to the State Convention!

3. As to my thirst for office, I simply have to say that I never declared myself for office in my life. I

have been frequently urged to run, but declined. There is but one office within the gift of my State that I would accept, and that is the office of *Governor;* and I am not sure that I will not run for this. I would like to fill that office for two years, in order to meet the issues that will be raised by the seceding States and traitors of the South; and, further, to take the State Bank and its numerous branches out of the hands of the Secessionists, who now have them in charge.

4. I am indebted to no stores in this or any other town, and I would not give the Republic of South Carolina twenty-five dollars to pay all my store-debts in this world. I have never been refused credit in any store here, and I am of the opinion that there is not a store in this city but would be willing to credit me for more than they can induce me to purchase.

5. The assertion that my partisan friends refuse to endorse any thing I say is simply an unmitigated falsehood. The Secession candidates have never made such an issue, and, if they were to, they would be promptly met by my "partisan friends." As it regards the sending to other sections of the State for papers by the common people of my county, it is simply a lie. I have, to-day, a larger list of subscribers in this county than any paper ever had, published in or out of the county. The "common people" are with me in sentiment, and the recent election shows that in this large county, voting something under four thousand votes,

9*

only two hundred and thirty-eight of them refused to endorse my "doctrines" at the ballot-box.

6. The last of your six propositions is the only one that contains a *squinting* towards the truth, and it, as a whole, is basely false. There are a few of the members of the Methodist Church in this city, Democrats and Secessionists, who do not interchange civilities with me, and have, for aught I know to the contrary, no sort of respect for me. If these entertain more profound contempt for me than I do for them, they are truly objects of pity. And if the great body of the "common people," in the town and county, have no more respect for me and my "doctrines" than they have for these Methodist brethren of mine, I would leave the country, and settle where I could find persons agreeing with me in "doctrines." Upon these persons, wanting in respect for me as they are, I have no disposition to make war. The alarming and wasteful disease of *Disunion* is now raging among them and *prostrating* its victims. If their symptoms grow worse, and the disease continue to spread, I may, through compassion, convert the basement of my office into a *hospital* for the afflicted! Already their elongated faces evince to the passers-by that they have passed the Rubicon!

In conclusion, allow me to inform you, Mr. Cinclair, that in Tennessee the heresy of Secession, sick with contradiction and crazed with a superabundance of inconsistency, is flying to falsehood as a remedy, and expiring from the venom of its own fangs. The night of TREASON has passed away in Tennessee; the purple morn of PATRIOTISM has dawned. Already do the tints of truth appear, while the gloomy mists rising from the swamps of a polluted Southern Confederacy fade in the distance, and sink below the horizon to rise no more! A cloudless day is breaking around us in Tennessee; emerging from the ocean of the UNION, the sun of American liberty is rising along the whole line of the border States, refulgent in light, brilliant with patriotism, and resplendent in glory! The hallowed name of the AMERICAN UNION, more fragrant than the spicy gales of Arabia, more balmy than Gilead's air, thrills the bosom of the patriot, where despair once revelled, and whispers *good tidings for all lovers of the Union!* Trophies of victory, in smiles and peace, deck the brows of those who were once saddened with doubt and uncertainty and sunk with sorrows to the depth of hell.

Parent of good, these are thy works! Thou art the great mover in the minds of deluded and distracted men, and wilt turn them "as the rivers are turned," until they shall see thy glory, bask in the sunshine of our national prosperity, and drink living waters at the wells of American salvation!

Finally, sir, when you put forth your batch of villainous falsehoods, through the *brawling Jacobin jour-*

nals of a demoralized Southern Confederacy, have the *candor* and *charity* to accompany them with this reply, and I will remain the defiant opponent of a wilful and despicable South Carolina rascal!

W. G. Brownlow,
Editor of the Knoxville Whig.

Knoxville Whig, Feb. 16, 1861.

CHAPTER VII.

POSITION OF BORDER-STATE UNION MEN—THE AUTHOR'S VIEWS OF SLAVERY GIVEN BY REQUEST—BLOW UPON FORT SUMTER STRUCK WITH A VIEW TO FORCE VIRGINIA TO SECEDE—NORTHERN AND SOUTHERN CLERGY—REIGN OF TERROR IN THE SOUTH—VIRGINIA STATESMEN ALL DEAD—FOR THE UNION UNDER ALL CIRCUMSTANCES.

Position of Union Men.

THE following correspondence will explain itself. We will only say that the writer of the letter from Albany resides in the city of New York, is a Marylander by birth, and was a Breckinridge Democrat in the late Presidential election:—

"ALBANY, N.Y., May 8, 1861.

"W. G. BROWNLOW, Esq.:—

"I send you by mail the Albany *Evening Journal*, containing Hon. Benj. Nott's speech on the crisis. Judge Nott is a life-long Democrat, of the Hard-Shell school, and an avowed advocate of the Dred Scott decision.

"I read your paper with great interest, and your course is the subject of conversation in every circle North, meeting the approval of all parties, for all parties here are for the Union. We understand you to be a pro-

Slavery man, but for the Union, opposed to Secession, —not even regarding the election of Lincoln as any just cause for dissolving the Union. Can't you give us a leading editorial on these points, and at the same time state the position of the Union men in the border Slave States in the event the Administration were to interfere in any way with the institution of slavery?

"The masses of the Northern people have no feelings but the most friendly towards their brethren of the South, and are ready to concede to them all their rights. They are even for returning to them their slaves who have escaped, as the law requires. This Administration would protect Southern rights, and if it would not of choice, the public would require it to be done. And, in saying this, I assure you I am no Lincoln man. But this you very well know.

"Hoping that you may be sustained, and live to see the Stars and Stripes float on every hill-top, and in every valley, from the St. Lawrence to the Rio Grande, I remain, very truly, L. M. E."

KNOXVILLE, May 14, 1861.

To L. M. E.:—

I have your letter of the 8th, and also the *Evening Journal*. I have perused the speech of Judge Nott: it is able, conservative, and eminently patriotic. Had you more Notts in the North, and fewer Slavery agitators, and had we fewer Rhetts, Yanceys, and Davises, in the South, none of these troubles would now be upon the country.

You correctly interpret the Union men of the border Slave States when you pronounce them "pro-Slavery men." I think I correctly represent them in my paper, as I shall do in this brief epistle, except, perhaps, that I am more *ultra* than most of them. I am a native of Virginia, and so were my parents before me, and, together with a numerous train of relatives, they were and are slave-holders. For thirty years I have lived in Tennessee, and my wife and children are native Tennesseeans. My native State did more to form the old Confederacy and to form the Constitution of the United States than any other State; her soil is now the resting-place of the honored dead, the most ultra old Unionists dead or alive,—Washington, Jefferson, Madison, Monroe, Marshall, Henry, and a host of others. I am sorry to have to record that it has, in the mysterious providence of God, been reserved to Virginia to do more towards overthrowing the Confederacy and the Constitution than any other State, South Carolina not even excepted. It took the Virginia Convention of 1861 to overthrow her State Government,—changing her organic political *status* contrary to the expressed direction of her people at the ballot-box when they elected the men who perpetrated the deed! Virginia, I am sorry to say, if I may be allowed to use an humble illustration, is like a *hill of potatoes*,—the best part under ground: the part above ground reminds me but of *vines.* When citizens of other States are called upon to name their great statesmen, they point to *living men.* Make the call upon Virginians, and they ask you out into *a graveyard,* when they will point you to the tomb of Washington, the monument erected over Madison, or the grave of Jefferson!

I am a pro-Slavery man, and so are the Union men generally of the border Slave States. I have long since made up my mind upon the Slavery question, but not without studying it thoroughly. The result of my investigation is, that there is not a single passage in the New Testament, nor a single act in the records of the Church, during her early history even for centuries, containing any direct, professed, or *intended* censure of slavery. Christ and the apostles found the institution existing under the authority and sanction of law; and in their labors among the people, unlike *ultra* Abolitionists, *masters* and *slaves* bowed at the same altars, and were taken into the same Church, communing together around the same table,—the Saviour and his apostles exhorting *owners* to treat *slaves* as became the gospel, and slaves to obedience and honesty, that their religious profession might not be evil spoken of.

The original Church of Christ not only admitted the lawfulness of slavery, but in various ways, by her teachings and discipline, expressed her *approbation* of it, enforcing the observance of "Fugitive Slave Laws" which had been enacted by the State. God intended the relation of master and slave to exist, both *in* and *out* of his Church. Hence, when Christ and his apostles found slavery *incorporated with every department of society*, they went to work and adopted rules for the government of the Church providing alike for the *rights* of slave-holders and the *wants* of slaves. Slavery in the days of the apostles had so penetrated society, and was so intimately interwoven with it, that a religion *preaching freedom to the slaves* would have arrayed against it the civil authorities, armed against it the whole power of the State, and destroyed the usefulness of its preachers.

Finally, I hold—and thirty years of observation and experience among slave-holders in the South have convinced me that I am not mistaken—that all the finer feelings of humanity may be cherished in the bosoms of slave-owners; that there are thousands of devout slave-owners and slaves in the South who are acceptable to God, through Christ. And, however much the bonds of the slaves of the South may provoke the wrath of the ultra Abolitionists of the North, the Redeemer of the world smiles alike upon the devout master and the pious slave!

Now, sir, allow me further to say that the Union men of the border Slave States are loyal to their Government, and do not regard the election of Lincoln as any just cause for dissolving this Union. We believe that slavery had very little to do with inaugurating armed secession, which commenced at Charleston, to overthrow the United States Government: it was the loss of the offices, power, and patronage of the Government by corrupt politicians and bad men in the South, who had long controlled the Government. Believing this, as we honestly do, we can never, like Mexico, inaugurate political conflicts and anarchy by armed secession. We can never agree to assist in the inauguration of a Government of conventions by armed secession,—which Government, in the case of England and her Rump Parliament, resulted in the Protectorate of Cromwell, and in France, in the military despotism of Bonaparte, and in both cases resulted in anarchy, as it is bound to do in this country if not put down by the power of the Government.

Whilst I say this, let me say, in all candor, that if we were once convinced in the border Slave States that the Administration at Washington, and the people of the North who are backing up the Administration with men and money, contemplated the *subjugation* of the South or the *abolishing* of slavery, there would not be a Union man among us in twenty-four hours. Come what might, sink or swim, survive or perish, we would fight you to the death, and we would unite our fortunes and destinies with even these demoralized seceded States, for whose leaders and laws we have no sort of respect. But we have not believed, nor do we yet believe, that the Administration has such purposes in view. Demagogues and designing men charge it here, and by this means enlist thousands under their banner who, otherwise, would never support their wicked schemes of Secession. We Union men believe that the blow was struck upon Fort Sumter to induce Virginia to go out, and to create sympathy elsewhere, and that the Administration at Washington is seeking to repossess its forts and property and to preserve its existence; and, as long as we believe this, we are for the Union and the Administration. I, of course, speak for Union men in the general. We are sustained in this by the Mobile *Advertiser*, which glories in the fact that the seven Confederated States "*struck the first blow in the conflict*," and "*threw down the glove of mortal combat to their powerful foe.*" The Mobile organ of Secession adds, "It was plucky in the seven Confederates: it was more,—it was sublimely courageous and patriotic."

Allow me to say that the curse of the country has been that, for years, north of Mason & Dixon's line, you have kept pulpits open to the abuse of Southern slavery and of the Southern people.

In like manner, the clergy of the South,—without distinction of sects,—men of talents, learning, and influence,—have raised the howl of Secession, and it falls like an Indian war-cry upon our citizens from their prostituted pulpits every Sabbath. Many of them go so far as to petition their God, in their public prayers, to *blast* the people of the North! I have no idea that a God of peace will answer any such blasphemous supplications; but it shows the spirit of these minions of anarchy, who have sworn allegiance to the kingdom of Davis, and have been released from any further obligations to the kingdom of Jesus,—at least during the war! Some of our clergy are officers in volunteer companies, with swords hung to their sides, and stripes on their pants. Others, having an eye to the loaves and fishes, are anxious to serve as chaplains.

We are in the midst of a reign of terror in Tennessee, and where it will end, and in what, I am not able to conjecture. We vote for or against the Ordinance of Secession on the 8th of June; and, although there is a majority of the voters of the State utterly and irreconcilably opposed to Secession, I can't promise you that it will not carry. Fraud and force, and all the other appliances of Secessionism, will be brought to bear in carrying the State out of the Union. When overpowered and voted down, we shall be forced to submit. When I surrender, it will be because I can no longer help myself; but it shall be under protest, claiming the right, as a Union man, to curse this whole movement in my heart of hearts! And, whether in or out of the Union, as long as I remember it was Washington who told us, "*The Constitution is sacredly obligatory upon all;*" and that it was Jackson who told us, "*The Union, it must be preserved,*"—I shall offer this prayer upon the altar of my country: Mania to the brain of him who would conceive, and palsy to the arm of him who would perpetrate, the dissolution of the Union!

And, whether my humble voice is hushed in death, or my press is muzzled by foul legislation, I beg you, and all into whose hands this letter may fall, to credit no Secession falsehood which may represent me as having changed.

W. G. Brownlow,
Editor of the Knoxville Whig.

Knoxville Whig, May 18, 1861.

CHAPTER VIII.

THE GREAT ENEMY OF THE COTTON STATES—NOT AN ABOLITIONIST—OUR SYMPATHIES WITH THE GOVERNMENT—THE REBELLION ORIGINATED WITH THE SOUTH—CHARGE OF SEEKING TO SUBJUGATE THE SOUTH A FALSE ISSUE—THE KNOXVILLE WHIG REFUSING TO LIE AND BOAST FOR THE TRAITORS—NOT LOOKING TO REWARD IN DOLLARS AND CENTS—STANDING OR FALLING UPON A PLATFORM OF PRINCIPLES!

Doctors will Differ.

THE following correspondence will explain itself. We take the writer of the letter to us to be a clever man carried astray upon the Secession wave that has swept over the land, blinding the eyes of honest men to all sense of duty, and burying beneath it the last remnant of the privileges of the Constitution:—

"CEDAR GROVE, FLA., June 15, 1861.

"DR. BROWNLOW:—

"As a freeman, you have a right to your opinions, in common with other men, but, sir, you have no right to defame those who are laboring to throw off the yoke of Northern oppression. I have ever been an admirer of yours, and of your principles; but permit me to tell you this morning that you are doing more injury to the Cotton States than any of the Greeleys or

Webbs of Yankeedom. I do not believe you to be an Abolitionist, as some do in this quarter. These being my honest opinions, I do not wish to read your paper longer. If there be any thing due me on my subscription, I wish it applied to the family of Jackson the martyr. Very truly, &c.,

"R. M. SCARBOROUGH."

KNOXVILLE, June 25, 1861.

MR. SCARBOROUGH:—

I received your letter of the 15th only on yesterday, and I hasten to reply very briefly. Upon examination, I find thirty cents due you on my book, and I enclose you the amount in United States stamps, which you can transmit to "the family of Jackson the martyr," who can use them in their locality.

You are correct in supposing me free from the taint of Abolitionism. I have fought the agitators of the Slavery question at the North for the last two-and-twenty years, during which time I have edited a Whig paper in Tennessee. With my *Government*, and its *Constitution* and *laws*, I intend to stand or fall, having no regard to who may be President for the time being. This rebellion is utterly without cause. Nothing but force will put it down; and hence there never was a more necessary, just, and lawful war than this, to preserve a necessary, just, and noble Government against inexcusable, unnatural, and villainous rebellion. This rebellion, on the part of the South, originated in falsehood, fraud, and perjury, and the men who inaugurated it, and are now at its head, are as bad men as ever agitated the Slavery question in New England, or any who suffer the vengeance of eternal fire for having flagrantly violated God's law through a long and eventful life of wickedness! Knowing this, or rather believing it, as I honestly do, I can have no sympathy with the men in the South who have brought about this war and are urging it on. No mad-dog cry of the invasion of the sacred soil of the South by the Vandals of the North can blind my eyes to the *facts* in the case, or shift the responsibilities of its origin upon those who are fighting to preserve the Government. Men need not talk to me about the unnatural, fratricidal, and horrible war Lincoln is waging! Why is it unnatural? I think it the most natural thing in the world for a nation to fight for its Government against a vile rebellion which has never yet been able to allege an excuse. That any portion of the people should stand aloof from such a cause, is indeed unnatural, but that does not make the war unnatural.

That any people should rebel against so benign a Government, and make war upon it, is most unnatural. It is the greatest crime that could be committed against humanity, for it and its consequences include all other crimes. It was not the falsely-alleged Slavery question that excited the Cotton States to the *fatal* point, and brought about their acts of secession. It was because they lost the race for the Presidency, and with it the spoils and power of a Government they had been plundering and living off of for years. Hence, it was only when the Government changed hands, and, in the legitimate exercise of its lawful powers, resorted to the only means that would preserve it and a vestige of liberty to the American people, that the war became unnatural, fratricidal, and horrible to the advocates of a Southern Confederacy. Southern-Rights politicians and hypocritical clergymen may ejaculate that their heads may be made water, and their eyes fountains of tears, that they may weep day and night over the unnatural war of the best Government that has ever existed, against the most villainous rebellion that history gives any account of, and they can never excite my sympathies but in favor of the Government.

The Secessionists, for the purpose of hiding their traitorous course, create a false issue before the people. They assert that the effort to preserve the Government is an attempt on the part of the North to crush the South, and that a sectional fight is the real issue before the people. This attempt to create a false issue is an acknowledgment on their part that they dare not meet the true one. The effort to enforce the law is not a fight against the South, but it is a fight against the traitors to the General Government; and, whether they appear North or South, it is the duty of the Government to crush the treason. When Southern traitors resist the laws of the land, they call all attempts on the part of the Administration to enforce those laws, outrageous acts of oppression,—attempts to invade and subjugate the free and independent people of fifteen sovereign States. Rebellion with this class of men is liberty, whilst they denounce all attempts to execute the laws of the land as the essence of despotism. To such subterfuges are Secessionists driven to sustain the rebellious course they have entered upon under a Southern Confederacy.

For daring to oppose Secession, the chivalry of my own section have denounced me in unmeasured terms, and declared me less sane than the inmates of Bedlam. And because I have refused to lavish volumes of whimsical abuse upon the North for their defence of the National Government, I have been pelted with a most horrible bombardment of uncleanly epithets by the veracious chroniclers who control the pensioned press of the South. The complaint against me is, that my paper has not teemed with bragging and fantastical lies about the origin of this war, and the ability of one Southern soldier to whip five Yankees. I have been even required by my Southern subscribers to declare, upon the receipt of the news of every engagement by scouting-parties, that the Yankees took to their heels, and that soon the Southern troops would have the Yankees harnessed tandem-fashion, and with their own hands conveying them back to their Southern plantations in a Broadway omnibus! I have been expected to state in every issue of my paper, that the mantle of Washington sits well on Jeff Davis! This would be a funny publication. The bow of Ulysses in the hands of a pigmy! The robes of the giant adorning Tom Thumb! The curls of a Hyperion on the brow of a Satyr! The Aurora Borealis of a cotton farm melting down the icy North! This would be to metamorphose a *minnow* into a WHALE!

I never look through telescopes made of cotton-stalks, and hence I never make these ridiculous discoveries. And I tell the misguided men of the South, who have been laboring to make a demi-god of Davis, to undeceive themselves, and look at men "as trees walking." Look at battles as they occur, and at chances as they are. The deception they are imposing upon the honest masses is only temporary. It will become more and more apparent, as their humbugged victims draw near to the sober realities of a war which must terminate fatally for the interests of the South.

I assure you, my dear sir, that I am honest in my convictions of right, and that in advocating my Government I am not looking to a reward in dollars and cents. Indeed, I am a loser by my course, as I knew I would be; but I feel tranquil under losses incurred in the manly defence of PRINCIPLES. I shall look on the progress of affairs with as much interest as any one man in the country. If the Federal Government prevails, it will prove that the Union was a nationality; if the Cotton States make good their independence, it will prove that the Union was a partnership during pleasure. In other words, if we have a Government, I want to know it; and this war will determine the issue.

I am, sir, very truly,

W. G. BROWNLOW.

Knoxville Whig, June 29, 1861.

CHAPTER IX.

SECESSION FORGERIES AT KNOXVILLE—ATTEMPT TO DESTROY SENATOR JOHNSON, AND TO EMBEZZLE MONEY FROM AMOS A. LAWRENCE—THE GUILTY PARTIES DETECTED—A WARNING TO ALL FUTURE CONSPIRATORS.

SENATOR JOHNSON has at length captured the hell-hounds, letter-forgers, and thieves, at Knoxville, who have been seeking his ruin by means as foul as the parties are corrupt, and as wicked as the deeds of the infernal regions. Let the people of Tennessee ponder over this worse than "Gunpowder Plot," this dark and damning attempt to have a Senator assassinated, and ask themselves if the guilty perpetrators of the forgery and attempt at theft do not merit the vengeance of eternal fire. Ought such traitors, slanderers, thieves, and assassins be allowed to live longer in any community? Never before have we been brought to witness such perfidy, malice, and corruption on the part of any clique as is now proven upon the Secession clique in Knoxville, *who are concerned* in this disgraceful, hell-born, and hell-bound expedition against the reputation and life of Andrew Johnson.

We here insert the letters forged, and remarks of

Governor Johnson just as he has published them, and to the whole we annex a few paragraphs which will throw some further light upon this most infamous transaction.

"BOSTON, May 18.

"DEAR SIR:—If your note to me were printed in our newspapers, it would be good for ten thousand dollars in three days' time. But, of course, I must only use it as a private letter.

"In order that you may be sure of something at once, I write below this a draft, which some of your Union bankers or merchants may be willing to cash at the usual premium for East exchange. Probably Gardner & Co., Evans & Co., Douglas & Co., of Nashville, will know it.

"The Government will soon exhibit a power which will astonish even you. The Nullifiers have been playing into Scott's hand for three weeks, and now they have lost the game.

"Yours, with regard,

"AMOS A. LAWRENCE.

"If you cannot use the draft, return it, and tell me what to send.

"BOSTON, May 18, 1861.

"At sight, without grace, pay to Andrew Johnson, or order, one thousand dollars, for value received, and charge to my account.

"AMOS A. LAWRENCE.

"To MASON, LAWRENCE & Co., Boston.

"Across the face of the draft is the acceptance of Mason, Lawrence & Co.

"No one, I am sure, could have been more surprised than I at the appearance of the above article. As I had *never* written to Amos A. Lawrence, Esq., upon the subject of East Tennessee affairs with the view of obtaining either money or other material aid, I saw at a glance that forgery, fraud, and robbery of the mails formed the basis of this mendacious article, and I therefore wrote to Mr. Lawrence, (*the first and only letter ever written by me to Mr. L. upon any subject whatever*,) requesting him to forward to me the original letter or letters upon which his draft had been predicated.

"I have just received his reply thereto, in which he expresses his regret at the deception practised, and encloses two letters purporting to have been written by me, as follows:—

"[Private.] KNOXVILLE, TENN., May 15, 1861.

"AMOS A. LAWRENCE, ESQ., NEAR BOSTON, MASS.

"DEAR SIR:—I received your kind favor on yesterday, and hasten to reply.

"Thank you for the high regard you seem to have for my patriotism and my devotion to my country.

"What assurances can I have from you and your people of *material aid* in the way of money, men, and arms, if I can succeed in arousing my people to resistance to this damnable treason in the South? This is very important. We have a formidable Union element in East Tennessee, which can be judiciously managed if we can obtain the aid alluded to. Harris, Governor of this State, will not let us have arms nor money: therefore we *must appeal* to you. Let me hear from you forthwith.

"Very respectfully, your obedient servant,

"ANDREW JOHNSON.

"KNOXVILLE, TENN., June 6, 1861.

"AMOS A. LAWRENCE, ESQ., NEAR BOSTON, MASS.

"MY DEAR SIR:—I have received your two letters to-day. Thank you most sincerely for your proffered aid. We need it,—need it badly. As yet I have not been able to use your draft; I am afraid to do so. Send me, if you can, $5000 or $10,000 in New England currency, in large bills, by mail, via Cincinnati. Be sure to do it promptly. Don't delay. I can now purchase a lot of arms if I had the means.

"How do you propose to introduce aid or arms into East Tennessee? By what route, and by what method? Answer soon.

"Respectfully, your obedient servant,

"ANDREW JOHNSON.

"I pronounce both of the above letters deliberate, wilful, and unmitigated forgeries, perpetrated, no doubt, with the view not only of injuring me, but of damaging the Union party of Tennessee, by connecting me with Northern men and Northern means in a manner supposed to be obnoxious to the noble patriots of my own State.

"The letter of the 15th ultimo, it seems, is the private letter to which Mr. Lawrence refers in his letter as published in the *Enquirer*, and upon which the draft was drawn. This is the first forgery.

"The letter of the 6th instant clearly shows that the draft—which could not be made available, so palpable was the fraud—was to be retained and used in the work of injuring me just as circumstances might favor; while the call for '$5000 or $10,000 in New England currency, in *large bills*,' if responded to, would have served individual purposes, and, I doubt not, would have been unhesitatingly used therefor. To make this fraud and bold attempt at robbery still more conclusive, I will state the fact that, on the 15th of May, the date of the first letter, I was present at and addressed a large Union meeting in Elizabethton, one hundred and eighteen miles from Knoxville, where the above letters were written and mailed; and on the 6th of June, the date of the second letter, I was filling one of a series of appointments at Montgomery, about forty miles west of Knoxville. This town of Knoxville, let it be remembered, is about seventy-five miles distant from Greeneville, my post-office address. I will add, further, that there is not, either in the body of the letters or the signature thereto, the slightest similarity to my handwriting or signature.

"It would have been impossible for such a fraudulent and mail-robbing transaction to have been carried out in the post-office at Knoxville without the knowledge or consent of the postmaster, and he and his confederates must be held responsible for it by an enlightened public judgment. Time may develop all the facts connected with this and other transactions of a similar character perpetrated at this same post-office.

"I have not made this statement of facts for the purpose of exonerating myself from the charge of treachery, treason, and corruption based upon the publication of the Richmond *Enquirer*, for I feel that I stand beyond the reach of the shafts of calumny and defamation; but my object is to expose the dishonorable and wicked means resorted to by 'Secession' to carry out its nefarious and corrupt designs in attempting to overthrow and break up the best Government the world ever saw.

"ANDREW JOHNSON.

"WASHINGTON CITY, June 30, 1861."

REMARKS.—Upon the subject of this most *infamous* transaction on the part of the vile *author* or *authors* we shall make but few remarks; but they shall be pointed, and such as the facts call for.

1. The letters purporting to be from Johnson to Lawrence are base forgeries, not in Johnson's handwriting,—forged here by Secessionists, and at two several times when Johnson was speaking in Elizabethton, one hundred and eighteen miles east, and at Montgomery, forty-five miles northwest, of Knoxville. When we published the Lawrence letter and the copy of the one-thousand-dollar draft, we charged the corruption of intercepting and the infamy of the forgery upon Nashville and Knoxville; but, from our knowledge of some of the Secession materials here, we give the preference to *Knoxville!*

2. The scoundrel, cut-throat, and midnight assassin who forged the letters was first aiming to *steal money* through this medium. He could not use the draft without forging the name of Johnson, and in this he would have been detected by the banker or broker to whom he might have passed it off. But for this, Governor Harris would not have been furnished with the original letter and draft with which to expose Johnson. Now, as Governor Harris is mixed up with this matter, and has furnished copies of the letter and draft for publication, he owes it to himself to tell the world *who sent him the original from Knoxville!* Will he tell? or will he seek to shield the guilty, and make himself a party to the nefarious transaction?

3. Had the "$5000 or $10,000 in New England currency, in large bills," been furnished by Lawrence, the

thief would have used them for his own purposes, and for the purposes of such as may have been connected with him in thus getting money under false pretences. The scoundrel ought at once to be sent to the penitentiary. Whoever he may be, he can, no doubt, throw some light upon the history and mystery of the SEVENTEEN HUNDRED DOLLARS lost in this office and belonging to the branch of the Bank of Tennessee at Athens! That dark transaction was traced to this place by Mr. Francis and others, Government officials, and mysteriously and suddenly hushed into profound silence! We speak of it, because it is alluded to by Governor Johnson, and known to this whole community. We have no information as to who is even *suspected*. A poor devil of a dancing-master was sent to the penitentiary for taking out of this office and opening a letter not his own; but these Secession forgers and stealers of large sums of money are allowed to go scot-free!

4. Certain Secessionists in Knoxville know these letters to have been forged, and they know *who* perpetrated the forgery, though we are not informed who the parties are. Nay, when the corrupt liar, low-down drunkard, irresponsible vagabond, and infamous coward of the *Register* paraded these documents before the world as evidence of Johnson's corruption, *he then knew them to have been forged*. A man capable of such scoundrelism, corruption, fraud, and duplicity is a dangerous man in any community,—not too good to burn

a house down in the dead hour of the night, and capable of bribing a runaway negro or convict to assassinate an enemy!

5. Governor Johnson has implicated the Knoxville postmaster and his confederates. This they can't complain of, upon a moment's reflection, for the facts in the case deeply involve the postmaster and all who were acting as deputies and clerks at the time. The public will hold them responsible, and they owe it to themselves to explain. They are welcome to our columns to do so, free of charge. They ought to tell the public *who* mailed letters there under the forged frank of Andrew Johnson, addressed to Amos Lawrence! If they are not able to do this, let them tell to *whom they handed out letters addressed to Andrew Johnson*, postmarked Boston, one of which contained a check for one thousand dollars! These things need explanation. Johnson's signature is as peculiar as that of Andrew Jackson: it is coarse, heavy, and bold, and can't be mistaken. The post-office employés are familiar with it; and, what is more, they knew Johnson was not in or near Knoxville at the time these letters were deposited under this forged frank!

6. This desperate effort to destroy Johnson will multiply his friends in every direction, and cause thousands to come out in his favor who have heretofore felt indifferent, and occupied neutral ground, so far as he is concerned. And, to-day, there is not an *honorable*

enemy to Johnson in this State who will hesitate to pronounce him a gentleman, a patriot, and a Christian, compared with any man concerned in this base, dark, and infinitely infernal transaction!

Knoxville Whig, July 20, 1861.

After learning as I did that the guilt of this transaction attached to a prominent Secessionist, a citizen of Knoxville, I *stereotyped* the following article, and kept it in my paper until it was suppressed the last of October:—

Keep it before the People.

Keep it before the people, That the Secessionists of Knoxville actually forged the name of Governor Johnson, and carried on a correspondence with Amos Lawrence, of Boston, with a view, first, to destroy Johnson's character, and to have him assassinated, and, next, to steal money, upon the credit of Johnson's name and political position, from a Northern capitalist.

Keep it before the people, That the forgery is traced to this town, and is known to have been perpetrated here, and the fact, as well as the author of the forgery, are alike known, and can be proven by Secession authority of respectability.

Keep it before the people, That the letter containing one thousand dollars, enclosed to Johnson here, in answer to this vile forgery of his name, was handed out of the post-office here to the forger or his representative, and that the letters in reply were mailed here, upon which Johnson's frank was forged, and, although this has been charged time and again, in this paper, no one has dared to deny it!

Keep it before the people, That Governor Harris was furnished with this forger's letters drawn from Lawrence, and with the check for one thousand dollars, and he gave out copies of them to the prejudice of Johnson; and, while he knows them to have been obtained by forgery and theft, he refuses to tell who his villainous Knoxville correspondent is, or to say or publish one word that will go to do an act of justice to Johnson.

Keep it before the people, That all concerned in this dark, damning, and most infamous transaction should be held up to public gaze, as objects for the scorn, contempt, and hatred of all honest men of all parties in all time to come!

Keep it before the people, That Johnson has procured from Lawrence the original forged letters, written and mailed in Knoxville,—that he recognizes the handwriting, and will in due time expose the forger.

Keep it before the people, That as many as a half-dozen respectable East Tennesseeans have been to Washington, inspected these base forgeries, in Johnson's possession,—that they report them clear and palpable cases of forgery, and that they readily recognized the handwriting *as the production of Knoxville.*

Keep it before the people, That the Knoxville *Register*, edited and published in the buildings where the post-office was kept during this *diplomatic and financial correspondence,* and familiar with the turpitude of the whole affair, nevertheless paraded the correspondence before its readers as a wonderful discovery, and as evidence of Johnson's corruption and Abolitionism.

Keep it before the people, That this whole case of forgery is before the leading men of the Confederate Government at Richmond, and that they know who the guilty parties are; and, however little they may think of Governor Johnson, they cannot think well of the *means* resorted to to destroy him.

P. S. I have since seen the original letters, and find them to be in the handwriting of W. G. Swan, a lawyer, and at present the Rebel Congressman from the Knoxville District. Other citizens of Knoxville have seen the letters, and they recognize the handwriting of the same man. But the question comes up, How came he to be elected to their Congress? First, such conduct is no draw-back upon a man in the Southern Confederacy; and, next, this man only received from seven to eight hundred votes. The people refused to vote, as they had previously given ten thousand votes to Horace Maynard, whom they elected to represent them in the Congress of the United States.

As further evidence of the turpitude of this affair, it is susceptible of proof at Knoxville that *Rev. Mr. Charlton* exhibited the forged letters written to Lawrence before they were mailed, in his office, to as many as two different men! Mr. Charlton is a Methodist preacher of intense Secession proclivities, and the postmaster at Knoxville. Besides, Senator Wigfall stated in Richmond that *Swan* had written there that such letters were passing between Johnson and Lawrence even before they came to light. What a commentary upon the morality and integrity of this bogus Confederacy!

CHAPTER X.

THE SPIRIT OF SECESSION—SAVAGE TREATMENT OF A PREACHER—ATTEMPTING TO GIVE THE AUTHOR THE SMALL-POX—PROPOSITION TO HAVE US MOBBED—TREATMENT OF AN OLD MAN—ARREST OF MR. DICKINSON—PERSONAL ASSAULTS IN PRAYER—RAISING LINCOLN'S BLOCKADE BY PRAYER—THE PRAYER-MEETING SIGN—FORMING A UNION CHURCH—SHEPHERDS FEEDING THIER FLOCKS—SECESSION AN EPIDEMIC—THE REAL TRAITORS—FALSE DISPATCHES—AT THEIR OLD TRICKS AGAIN.

UNDER the heading of this chapter I propose to give various brief editorials from my paper during the months of July, August, September, and October, 1861, as they go far to disclose the vile spirit that works in the hearts of the rebel children of disobedience in the so-called Confederacy.

The McMinn County Arrests.

Some twenty-five persons, citizens of McMinn county, were brought before Judge Humphreys on Monday, about twenty of whom were released on the ground that there was *nothing* against them. The truth is, they had voted the Union ticket, and they had voted for years against certain men; and this explains their arrest. They were taxed with small fees to pay costs, and required to take the oath, although they had committed no offence.

The other five were retained for further hearing, and sent into camps, under a military escort, for the night. Among these was Rev. Wm. H. H. Duggan, a member of the Holston Annual Conference, and the preacher in charge of the Athens circuit. He was arrested at a quarterly meeting, on Friday night, and marched on foot on Saturday *nine miles*, being refused the privilege of riding his own horse, and on Sabbath he was landed at Knoxville. He is a large, fleshy man, weighs two hundred and eighty-one pounds, and was recovering from a long spell of fever. He gave out at a spring some seven miles from where he started. The day was warm, and his feet were sorely blistered. He begged permission to ride: he was refused, cursed, and denounced, and threatened with *bayonets!* His horse was led after him, as if to aggravate him. They even refused him water to drink, or any thing to eat, until Sunday.

On Thursday evening he was discharged without entering into bonds or taking any oath. The indictment was read to him by Attorney Ramsey, and charged that he had *prayed for the Government of the United States;* but this praying was the previous winter and spring. Duggan is a very poor man, with a wife and six helpless children. He is a man of truth and of strict integrity, and has the confidence of men of other denominations. He has been most shamefully treated.

This was in October, and he would have suffered with cold at night, but for the fact that my wife sent him several blankets.

The Spirit of Secession.

One day last week, the Southern mail brought us a small package, done up precisely like a newspaper, and about equal in size to one of our exchanges, with the usual endorsement, "Brownlow's Whig, Knoxville, Tennessee," and postpaid. Upon opening it, we found it to contain about half a yard of brown domestic, with an appearance resembling that of a cloth taken from some one afflicted with small-pox. We had it burned in the front yard of our printing-office, after handling it with tongs! This is the *spirit* of Secession,—its mode of warfare, and its sense of honor. Clever men, heretofore high-minded, will not be long in their ranks until they will openly justify even this mode of warfare against Union men.

This attempt at our death, by the planting of a masked battery manned by the iniquitous spirit of Secession, entitles the cowardly villain who did it, to the honor of being picketed in the deepest gorge leading to hell! Not only so, but he should be required to make nightly advances upon the ambuscades of the devil; and every morning of his life, by way of healthful exercise, he should make a reconnoissance of the damned, having the entire control of the guerrilla rebels of the infernal regions.

A Band of Villains.

An officer accompanying some troops from Mississippi informed us that men, unknown to him, but looking like citizens, advised the troops, while changing cars at Chattanooga, to mob *us* on their arrival at Knoxville. Two young soldiers, associated with our sons in Emory & Henry College, said similar advice was given to some of the Louisiana troops by officials on the railroad between Chattanooga and Knoxville. And it is a well-ascertained fact that citizens of this town have repeatedly urged the same thing upon troops, and have sought to do so when they found them under the influence of ardent spirits.

These unmitigated cowards, God-forsaken scoundrels, hell-deserving villains, and black-hearted assassins and murderers, seek to induce strangers in the army to take up quarrels and fight battles which they themselves are too cowardly to fight. For years we have held up a portion of these unprincipled dastards, dishonest, lying, swindling scoundrels, and revolting hypocrites, to the scorn, contempt, and hatred of honest men, passing and re-passing them, day by day, and it never occurred to the loathsome villains that they ought to resent it, until an opportunity offered to hide behind some infuriated troops, made drunk for the occasion. Some of them are white-livered cowards, who live by lying and swindling; others are cloaking their deceit, adultery, and numerous acts of baseness in one or another of the Churches, under a pretence of being religious; and others of them are acting for pay, as the tools of men of position and property. The superiors of many of these men in honor are in the penitentiary; and the superiors of others of them in morals and piety are in hell!

July 6, 1861.

Treatment of an Old Man.

Bryant Breeden, an old man, some sixty years of age, and a very respectable citizen of Sevier county, recently had a daughter to die in Illinois, leaving several helpless and unprotected children. Mr. Breeden determined to go after his grandchildren, and took *Memphis* on his way. There he fell into the hands of the Secessionists, whose great concern for the *safety* of the South and her *rights* led them to arrest him. Upon learning that he hailed from East Tennessee, and from the odious Union county of Sevier, they procured a *rope*, and led him around, threatening every moment to hang him. He had, therefore, to abandon his trip, and leave his poor little orphan grandchildren to the mercy of strangers in Illinois. He was a quiet man while in Memphis, as he is at home,—disturbed no one,—but, when interrogated, acknowledged himself to be a Union man from East Tennessee, and for this, and no other offence, was he thus treated. This is the *spirit* which everywhere actuates the self-constituted Secession Committees of Safety, and the leaders of those most intolerant and odious organizations. No wonder that freemen of East Tennessee, by thousands, have resolved not to go into this Southern Confederacy! No wonder that the Union men of the thirty counties of East Tennessee should desire to be cut loose from the rest of the State, and allowed to form a separate State. To live in such a Confederacy, under the control of such men, actuated by such a spirit, is literally to live in hell!

June 29, 1861.

Arrest of Mr. Dickinson.

On Saturday evening, Mr. Perez Dickinson, for the last thirty years a successful merchant of Knoxville, returned from the North, whither he had gone, with the written permit of Governor Harris, to attend to business connected with the two firms of which he is a member. On Monday morning he was arrested upon a warrant, based upon an affidavit filed by Attorney Ramsey, setting forth that said Dickinson was born in the State of Massachusetts, and that he had recently been to the North and held intercourse with the Northern people. This was the charge, and this affidavit was all the proof offered against him. His Honor Judge Humphreys bore testimony to the good character and high standing of Mr. Dickinson, and proposed to him that he should at once, and without any investigation, take an oath of allegiance and fidelity to the Confederate States. Mr. Dickinson rose, and responded in a brief address, spoke of his coming here when a boy, some thirty years ago,—of his being an orderly and law-abiding citizen,—of his all being here, and of the bones of his mother, sisters, and brother resting here,—denied that he had held any intercourse with the people of the North, in violation of his parole to Governor Harris,—and declined, under the circumstances of compulsion surrounding him, to take the oath. His Honor then instructed him that he would have to give a bond of *ten thousand dollars* for his good behaviour during the few days allowed him to remain in the State. He gave the required bond, and was discharged.

Thus, a man who has spent his life here,—acquired by industry and business talents a fortune,—a man whose relatives sleep in these graveyards,—a man who has committed no offence but the one committed by his parents in allowing him to be born in Massachusetts, —is forced to leave his property and abandon the home of his adoption and choice, and go into exile! He has less than one week allowed him to get out of the State; and he has made up his mind to go. From such oppression and tyranny may God deliver the people of this distracted and ruined country!

Personal Assaults in Prayer.

It is becoming the practice of our Secession clergymen, in part, to take the hides off Union men by holding them up before their congregations in prayer, and pretending to pray for them,—condemning their "reported" offences and deprecating their "reported" treachery to their country. We think that in all cases of *attack*, whether in public or private prayers, the parties assailed ought to be present, and allowed *a division of time*, in laying the other side before the Lord. We admit the fairness of telling the Lord that we formed our charges against individuals upon "reports," and thus *conditionally* pray for their destruction. We also allow that the Lord ought to be *posted* as to the numerous "reports" put in circulation by Secessionists, the enemies of the parties accused. It would be proper, too, in presenting the case of a "traitor" to God in prayer, to state to the Most High what we admit in private,—to wit, that we make the assault to gratify certain members of our congregations. This would enable the Lord to receive what we say with certain "grains of allowance." But, in all cases where the heads of families are to be attacked from our *praying batteries*, let the *females* of the family be previously notified by the deacons or elders, that they may not be mortified and insulted, have their feelings outraged, and be constrained to go home crying through the streets. These are only suggestions thrown out by us in kindness to preachers and people. Let them pass for what they are worth.

This attack was made upon Hon. Horace Maynard, who was at Washington, by *Rev. Mr. Martin,* pastor of the Second Presbyterian Church in Knoxville. He prayed that his traitorous feet might never again press the soil of Tennessee. Mr. Maynard was an elder in his church, and his estimable wife then in the congregation. Next day the parson called on her, and excused himself on the ground that he was urged by some of his members to make the attack!

Raising Lincoln's Blockade.

We are informed that one of the pastors of our city actually appointed a prayer-meeting last Sabbath night to especially pray for the raising of the blockade, and that he called on God, in fervent prayer, to strike Lincoln's ships with lightning and scatter them to the four winds of heaven! The idea of a Secession preacher heaving and setting at a throne of grace,—like a ram at a gate-post,—asking God to raise Lincoln's blockade, is a bright idea and a rich conception, in our judgment. That churches throughout the country have become demoralized, that preachers have prostituted themselves, for Secession, is as plain as the nose on a man's face; but it does not yet appear that the Almighty has mixed Himself up with any such scenes.

This parson was *Rev. Mr. Harrison,* pastor of the First Presbyterian Church in Knoxville. He held his prayer-meeting, and, assisted by several old *clericals,* made a desperate effort to raise the blockade! God, in answer to their prayer, gave them a lift on Roanoke Island, some weeks after the prayer-meeting, when the entire Rebel forces were either killed or taken prisoners by Burnside's blockading squadron.

This man *Harrison* is the same preacher who boasted in his pulpit that Jesus Christ was a *Southerner,* born on Southern soil, and so were His apostles, except Judas, whom he denominated a *Northern* man! Speaking of the Bible, he said he would sooner have a Bible printed and bound in hell, than one printed and bound north of Mason & Dixon's line!

The Prayer-Meeting Sign.

It is well known to our citizens that a Union Prayer-Meeting has been kept up for several years in this city by the several religious denominations, and that they occupy a room on the corner of Gay and Main Streets, where there is a modest sign out, with the inscription, in bronzed or gold-leaf letters, "Union Prayer-Meeting Room." Not long since, some troops from one of the Cotton States were passing through the streets, looking at the town, and, burning with indignation for the old defunct Union, could not bear to see a sign up with a word upon it that would call the

Union to mind. They halted, looked at it, and swore, by the God who made them, "That d—d thing must come down!" One of the Secession leaders of the town approached them, and assured them that the allusion on the sign was not to the Federal Union, but to a *union of denominations*. But the infuriated advocates of Southern rights brought it down, and destroyed it on the street.

Forming a Union Church.

A gentleman of character and influence suggests that portions of us, belonging to different denominations, and even to no sect, organize a new congregation for religious worship, and that we employ some man of talents and piety to preach to us, irrespective of creeds or confessions of faith. We like this idea, and bring it before our readers as a well-timed suggestion. We want some man to instruct us all in the *common gospel of God our Saviour*, who will not mix up the sacred truths of holy writ with the abominable heresy of Secession, who will refrain from denouncing one party in his congregation as traitors to their country and their God, and who will not attack private families in public prayer. We have—among us—brought disgrace upon the church, destroyed confidence in the ministry, disbanded our congregations, and broken up the social and religious ties that formerly bound us together. It is useless for us to meet in our churches on the Sabbath, put on long,

Brutal treatment of Rev. Wm. H. H. Duggan by the Rebels. (Page 135.)

pious faces, offer up long prayers, hand round the bread and wine, and then pass out in society and vilify each other as a set of pickpockets, liars, and traitors, and keep up this holy and patriotic warfare until we meet again the next Sabbath. The fool, the wayfaring man, and the untutored African can see that we are wicked, and on the high-road to the devil! Let us break up our hypocritical organizations called churches, and out of a half-dozen of them make up one new one, whose pastor and members shall neither preach, exhort, nor pray any thing connected with party politics.

August 10, 1861.

"Shepherd, Feed my Sheep."

This was the command of Christ to His apostles, and through them, in all time to come, to His ministers. The *nourishment* given in the earlier days of the gospel dispensation was any thing but what it is now, under the *improvements* of our age. "Repent and believe the gospel," was the first dish; "Give all diligence to make your calling and election sure," was the second *course*. The *dessert*, which was the closing out of the meal, was to the effect, that "if ye do these things ye shall never perish."

Then we were not prepared to see our Southern preachers, so early as 1861, following the bad example of these *false teachers*, by preaching *Secession*, profaning the Sabbath, and taking commissions in the army to aid in carrying on a most wicked and unholy war,—seeking the overthrow of the best Government the world has ever known. Ascending the sacred pulpit on the Lord's day, under a pretence of "feeding the sheep," these reverend traitors to God and their country deliver inflammatory stump-speeches, excite the worst passions of a people not extravagantly given to prayer, and thus more effectually serve the cause of the devil than all the ultra Abolition preachers of the North have been doing for a quarter of a century past. The South is now full of these reverend traitors, and every branch of the Christian Church is cursed with their labors. They can find nothing in the teachings or example of the meek and lowly Jesus to justify them in feeding their flocks on the treasonable doctrines of Secession and Southern Rights, or the still more damnable heresy of the right of a State of this Union to secede at pleasure from the Federal compact, merely because a few bad men and corrupt politicians have been turned out of the Federal offices by the vote of the people.

Preachers, all must admit, have a right to their opinions and to the exercise of the right of suffrage, but they have no right to disgrace their pulpits on Sunday by delivering inflammatory stump-speeches, under the pretence of preaching Christ to the people. They have no right to abandon the congregations to whom they say God has called them to preach, and sew stripes upon their pants, swing swords to their sides, and actually turn *rowdies* in the camps of Jeff Davis! And these reverend gentlemen should remember—as very few of them do—that preachers don't make any *better* traitors than the most abandoned sinners in the country. Counterfeiting money, or forging checks upon a bank, are not less wicked acts because perpetrated by a preacher than they would be if perpetrated by an infamous gambler.

July 6, 1861.

Secession an Epidemic.

Secession has assumed an *epidemic* form in most of the Southern States, and men become Secessionists with marvellous rapidity. It is nothing to know that a particular man was a Union man last night: how is he this morning? This is the question, and where *inducements* are held out to fall in with the heresy, it is well to inquire of men, morning, evening, and at noon, where they stand upon this great office-and-money question. Men change in a night. Men rise up and dress as Union men, and turn Secessionists before breakfast is over. The worst symptom is the morbid excitement of the organ of credulity. The cry of a loss of one's *rights* originates the disease, and it never abates till the patient "goes clear out." If a man is pressed for money, and some one in favor of "immediate separation" has some to lend *on time*, the man wanting to borrow sees that our only safety is in "a united South." If a man is a Union mechanic, and out of work, the furnishing him with a small job at once discloses the startling fact that Lincoln commenced this war, that it is a war of conquest, and that the sacred soil of the South is to be invaded and the negroes all set at liberty. The malady is short; the disease runs its course in twenty-four hours, and the patient heads a committee to order better men than himself to leave the State in a given time. He believes every lie he hears, and swears to the truth of every lie he tells. He drinks mean whiskey, and associates with men whom the day before he would have scorned. The disease is contagious, and a clever man will contract it by drinking mean whiskey out of the same tumbler with one afflicted with it.

July 6.

The Real Traitors.

Much is said of late about the traitors who have brought the existing troubles upon the country, and a good deal is said, by way of *dispute*, as to who they are. Portions of them live on both sides of Mason & Dixon's line. But the real traitors who are responsible for the disruption of the American Union, and the present civil war, threatening such fearful consequences, are Yancey, Rhett, Toombs, Pryor, Davis, Keitt, Iverson, Wise, Mason, Wigfall, and Breckinridge and Lane, who lent themselves to these miserable purposes. If there are any men in this country who deserve the doom of traitors, it is these authors of our national calamities. And if the war continue three to five years, the men we have named, and other smaller lights, will be fugitives in foreign countries. They have misled and deceived the Southern people to the ruin of the country. And when the reaction takes place,—as it surely will,—popular vengeance will seek them for punishment. When disaster and suffering pervade the South, as they surely will,—when the innocent people cry out under the burden of taxes and debt which this war will force upon them,—then will come the day of reckoning for the real traitors, the political demagogues, who are the authors of the nation's calamity. To avoid this doom, these men will make superhuman efforts to carry the day on the field of battle, and thus prevent the reaction which promises their ruin. But they cannot evade their accountability to God and to an outraged people.

July 6.

False Dispatches.

We find in Secession papers some of the most notoriously false dispatches ever published in the world. These appear frequently, under sensation heads, displayed in large capitals, and with exclamation-points. We never copy them; and the reason is that we are satisfied that they do not contain a word of truth. They have turned out to be false, and, as a natural result, they have destroyed public confidence in these Secession sensation dispatches. Usually, they carry the lie upon their faces, representing a few hundred Southern troops as whipping several thousand Yankees, killing and wounding so many, while nobody is hurt on the Confederate side. To listen to the "loud-swelling words" uttered by these men, one would suppose that a regiment of Yankees will take to flight upon seeing one Southern man in uniform. We never give these exciting dispatches to our readers, and for the reason, we repeat, that we do not believe one word they set forth, and do not wish to humbug our readers, many of whom take no journal but ours.

July 6.

At their Old Tricks again.

We see letters, and extracts from letters, in several Southern Secession papers, boasting of the vast numbers of Union men in East Tennessee who are coming out for Secession since the late election. Nay, one gifted writer in a Georgia paper speaks of whole counties having turned over to Secession. This is a revival of their system of wholesale lying carried on before the February election, and again before the late June election. In this late election their lying letters and dispatches, published in the Nashville and Memphis papers, claimed that they would carry East Tennessee. And yet when the votes were polled they lacked some twenty thousand votes of carrying East Tennessee, whilst out of thirty-one counties they carried five,—four of these by small majorities.

As soon as one defeat is over, they prepare for another, and tell, write, and publish the most extravagant falsehoods as to changes that are going on. We notify them that the ballot-box, on the first Thursday in August, will again convict them of lying. If they have the recruits they boast of, let them elect members to Congress and to the Legislature from East Tennessee. We give them notice that the Union men intend to elect, and that they will do it fairly by majorities, and through the ballot-box.

July 6.

CHAPTER XI.

THE DISTINCTION BETWEEN THE PARTIES—INFAMY OF THE LEADERS OF THIS REBELLION—REBEL STEALING IN TENNESSEE—REBEL STEALING IN RICHMOND—SWINDLING HORSE-CONTRACTS—THE SCRIPTURES AGAINST THESE EXTORTIONERS.

As a general thing, in speaking of the troops of the two contending armies we speak of them as "Union troops" and "Confederates." The European papers call the former the "Federal troops." The Government troops should be called the *National* troops, because ours is a NATION, and has been ever since we abandoned the old "Confederation" and established a National Government.

The Southern troops should not be designated as "Confederates," for we do not recognize their right to separate themselves from the National Government. They are legally nothing more nor less than *rebels*, or *insurgents*, and they should be so characterized when we have occasion to speak of them. There is much in a name. Let the two parties, then, in all time to come, be known as the Rebels and Nationals.

The day is coming when the originators of this rebellion will be *pilloried* in history, as history must name them, and can only name them with scorn. I do not allude to those in obscurity, persons of no mark, who have retired within the veil of the obscurity of mediocrity; but I allude to the leaders,—the men raised to high public positions, who led off in this infernal crusade, and now head their bogus Government and their retreating army. They are now being despised by thousands who have been their tools, and who had not nerve enough to resist their bad designs in the outset. These villains will stand conspicuous in all coming time, as a man upon the gallows stands; and, to increase their misery, they will have no sympathy from any quarter. No loyal man will welcome one of them to his house, or call a child by his name. Their careers will end before their lives, and after death—if not before—their names will become the synonyms of dishonor and contempt.

Rebel swindling has outstripped any other thieving heard of in the history of this war. I could give many instances, but will content myself with a few, authenticated by Rebel papers. The Clarksville (Tenn.) *Chronicle* thus rebukes certain unmitigated Shylocks in Middle Tennessee:—

"When we think of the self-sacrificing patriotism of our brave volunteers, and then look at the Shylocks at home who extort the last cent from their families for the necessaries of life, the contrast is painfully disgusting. The cause of the South must suffer severely under such a state of things; and should the war continue long, the country will learn, to its cost, that men will not volunteer to fight its battles, leaving their dependent wives and daughters to the tender charities of the sharpers who have no higher or holier ambition than to speculate upon the scanty pittance of daily bread that prolongs, without comforting, life. The soldier has no spirit to fight the common enemy when he knows that he leaves behind him a deadly foe to the comforts of his family, and is made to feel that every danger he encounters and every hardship he endures is for the defence of the mercenary and heartless speculators who make dire necessity the pretext for oppression. The press, in every section of the Confederacy, is loud in its complaints against such unnatural conduct, and in North Carolina the Government has found it necessary to interpose its authority for the protection of families against the monopolizing greed of those who seek to build up fortunes upon the necessities of the times. If common humanity, or a sense of shame, cannot reach these men, and the laws will not, the time is not distant when Judge Lynch will pass sentence upon them."

The Richmond *Examiner*—the organ of Jeff Davis—for January 17, thus notices the frauds in the Treasury Department at Richmond:—

"We are aware of the recent occurrence of some bold frauds on the Treasury, which have been conveniently hushed up in that department. We have avoided any particular statement of the facts, as Mr. Memminger, instead of bringing the matter to the examination of the civil courts, where it would have got to the public, adopted the expedient of turning out all the clerks in one of the rooms of the department, thereby confounding the innocent with the guilty, on account of the former of whom we were loath to make the subject one of publication in the newspapers.

"In the matter, however, of these frauds there has been an amount of official carelessness and negligence to which we not only feel free, but are constrained by public duty, to refer. It appears that the fraud consisted in the abstraction of whole sheets of signed Treasury notes. At one time one sheet was abstracted, and the fraud reported to Mr. Memminger. But a few days ago two sheets were abstracted. In *both instances*, occurring at different times, the fraud was accomplished *by the neglect in the department to count the sheets as they passed from hand to hand.* Each sheet probably represented several thousand dollars, and was as good as so much money; and the practice of shuffling them from hand to hand, and taking no account of them, affords not only an instance of the grossest carelessness ever heard of in a Government, but actually offered a premium for the fraud of clerks. What would be thought of not counting coin in a mint? And yet it would be less reckless than the omission to count sheets of paper representing thousands of dollars, any one of which might be abstracted as easily as a single gold eagle from a heap of coin."

The Richmond *Examiner* for January 15 thus exposes the swindling of its partisans in "horse-contracts:"—

The Horse-Contracts.

"We have reason to believe that, in some of the purchasing departments of the Government, monstrous and audacious frauds have been perpetrated; and we expect soon to be in possession of the facts to authorize a complete exposure of this matter. There is talk on the street that one single horse-contract of a well-known official here has realized him a fortune. We have more than once had our attention called to the curious management of a fraud in the purchase of horses for the Government. It is for the purchasing officer, in the first instance, to reject horses that are offered, as not coming up to the Government standard or as unsound; a pimp or accomplice is kept to buy the horse, after he is rejected, at a reduced price, and then the purchasing officer buys from the accomplice, and charges the horse, of course, at the full Government price.

"The subjoined statement of a correspondent hints at this acute trick of complicity by which the Government is defrauded:—

"'Some time since, I rode to one of the Government stables in the neighborhood of the Potomac, and offered to sell to the agent there a very fine pony, both for riding and working purposes; but the agent said he did not want said horse at any price. He was too small, &c. &c. I concluded that I would take a look at the horses there, expecting to see them all large and fine; but, to my great surprise, I found horses there not much more than half as heavy as my own, with sore backs, swollen legs, hip-caps gone, lame, big heads and little bodies, sharp behind and low before, legs scarred from kicking in gear, &c. &c. The mules were in similar condition. I asked the men who were attending to them if the agent there bought those horses for the Government. They said he had. I then remarked that said agent would not purchase mine at any price, and yet I would not give him for a stable full of such horses as I saw there. An old man, who stammered badly, replied, by saying, "M-m-aster, I-I-I r-r-reckon, s-s-sir, you do-don't be-be-long to-to dat par-party whar-whar dey fa-fa-favors, s-sir." Of course, I disclaimed all connection with that party. I had heard a report before this, that only a certain party or parties could sell horses there, and that a handsome profit was made out of the Government on every horse purchased. How true the report is, I can't say; but certainly an investigation ought to be had in the matter. Horse-dealers had told me that I could not sell any horse to the Government,—that he must get into certain other hands first. I wonder if such is true?'"

This stealing from their bogus Government and defrauding the common soldier, has been going on all over the so-called Confederacy. They have no faith in the ultimate triumph of their arms, and hence they seek to make out of the Rebellion all they can,—thieving and singing,—

> When we're here a few more days,
> A fobbing public money,
> We'll have less ways to make a raise
> Than when we begun-ah!

For the edification of those of them who vend goods, wares, and merchandise for all that they can get, and swindle their bogus Government, I advise their whiskey-drinking chaplains to preach to them from the following passages of holy writ:—

Ezekiel xxii. 12.—"In thee have they taken gifts to shed blood; thou hast taken usury and increase, and thou hast greedily gained of thy neighbors by extortion, and hast forgotten me, saith the Lord God."

Isa. xvi. 4.—"Let mine outcasts dwell with thee, Moab; be thou a covert to them from the face of the spoiler; for the extortioner is at an end, the spoiler ceaseth, the oppressors are consumed out of the land."

1 Cor. vi. 10.—"Nor thieves, nor covetous, nor drunkards, nor revilers, nor extortioners, shall inherit the kingdom of God."

CHAPTER XII.

THE CONSPIRACY TO BREAK UP THE GOVERNMENT—THE PLOT AND ITS DEVELOPMENTS—TESTIMONY OF SECESSION WITNESSES—DOCUMENTS WORTHY OF BEING PRESERVED, AND WORTHY OF BEING STUDIED BY THE FRIENDS OF THE UNION.

In one of the issues of our paper we published an article nearly two columns in length, with the proof carefully arranged, going to convict this Breckinridge-Yancey party of Seceders of the foul crime of seeking to disrupt this Government. They are guilty; it is what they are after,—what they had in view when they bolted at Baltimore and nominated Breckinridge. We can establish it beyond doubt; it is due to the public that we do so; and, for reference among the friends of the Union, we here insert the whole story.

The *conspiracy* against this Union by that wing of the Democratic party which has gone off in the Breckinridge crusade, is now established beyond controversy. But, with a view to open the eyes of honest and patriotic men in the Democratic ranks, of whom there are thousands, we will submit other proof, and still more convincing evidence, so that none need be in doubt who will read, and read the testimony of *Demo-*

crats. Their infernal plot was, *themselves* being witnesses, to break up the Union, to revolutionize the Government, and to establish upon its ruins a Southern Confederacy. They have gone with cold-blooded, deliberate malice into the plot, and Breckinridge has lent himself, as the tool of these conspirators, to head them, and really deserves to be hung. Their treason and fraud no longer burrow beneath the surface in the names of *Nashville Southern Convention* or *Southern Commercial Convention*. They have now thrown off the mask and raised their traitorous heads to the view of the world.

Old *Davy Hubbard*, an ex-Congressman from Alabama, and a delegate to Charleston and Baltimore, thus discoursed to his Disunion brethren on the great struggle between the factions:—

> "Let us proceed at once to examine the relation sustained by each section to the great issue, 'Negro or No Negro,' now before the country, and which has brought these dissensions,—the *main issue, before which all others should and will give way, until it is settled,—emancipation and equality of races on one side, protection by the Union Government in, or protection out of it, on the other.*"

Governor Wise, who was afterwards so anxious to give the vote of the Old Dominion to Breckinridge, addressed letters to all the Southern Democratic Governors, in 1856, with a view of concerting measures to prevent the inauguration of Fremont in the event of his election, which amounted to revolution and disunion. Here is the letter as it since appeared in the papers:—

"RICHMOND, VA., Sept. 15, 1856.

"DEAR SIR:—

"Events are approaching which address themselves to your responsibilities and to mine as chief Executives of slave-holding States. Contingencies may soon happen which would require preparation for the worst of evils to the people. Ought we not to admonish ourselves by joint counsel of the extraordinary duties which may devolve upon us from the dangers which so palpably threaten our common peace and safety? When, how, or to what extent may we act, separately or unitedly, to ward off dangers if we can, to meet them most effectually if we must?

"I propose that, as early as convenient, the Governors of Maryland, Virginia, North Carolina, South Carolina, Georgia, Florida, Alabama, Louisiana, Texas, Arkansas, Mississippi, and Tennessee, shall assemble at Raleigh, North Carolina, for the purpose generally of consultation upon the state of the country, upon the best means of preserving its peace, and especially of protecting the honor and interests of the slave-holding States. I have addressed the States only having *Democratic* Executives, for obvious reasons.

"This should be done as early as possible before the Presidential election, and I would suggest Monday,

13th of October next. Will you please give me an early answer, and oblige,

"Yours, most truly and respectfully,

"HENRY A. WISE.

"His Excellency THOMAS W. LIGON, Governor of Maryland."

The same to Thomas Bragg, Governor of North Carolina; James H. Adams, Governor of South Carolina; H. V. Johnson, Governor of Georgia; James C. Broome, Governor of Florida; John A. Winston, Governor of Alabama; John J. McRae, Governor of Mississippi; Robert Wickliffe, Jr., Governor of Louisiana; Edmund M. Pease, Governor of Texas; Elias N. Canway, Governor of Arkansas; and Andrew Johnson, Governor of Tennessee.

Mr. Spratt, of South Carolina, afterwards a supporter of Breckinridge, said, in the Southern Commercial Convention at Vicksburg,—

"It might be said that the slave-trade could not be legalized within the Union, and that to re-establish it the Union would have to be dissolved. *Let it be so.* The men of the South had higher trusts than to preserve the Union."

Judge Jones, of Georgia, afterwards for Breckinridge, said, in this same Vicksburg Convention,—

"He proclaimed himself a Disunionist since 1829, but he did not believe the Southern States would go out of the Union unless they were kicked out. He believed there was no chance of equality in the Union; and he would rather die a poor wolf in the woods than live a fat dog with any man's collar on his neck. *He owed no allegiance to any power but Georgia!* He urged the fallacy of the apprenticeship-theory. They would be brought here as apprentices, and as soon as their time was out they would be sold as slaves. That might not be slave-stealing, but to him it squinted a good deal like it. [Applause.] If he were on a jury, and a man were tried before him under the slave-trade acts, he would never find him guilty, because they were unconstitutional."

In 1858, this Southern Breckinridge party put forth a pamphlet, with which they flooded the Southern States, avowedly with a view to form a "*great Southern party*," and, after a Disunion preamble, the first of a series of resolutions is in these words:—

"*Resolved*,—1. That, with that purity of motive, consciousness of rectitude, and noble determination to do right, we recommend, and *will do* ALL WE CAN *to bring about*, an honorable and, if possible, a peaceable *separation of the Southern Slave States from the Northern free States*."

Senator Iverson, of Georgia, afterwards an ardent Breckinridge man, said in the United States Senate, 7th of January, 1859,—

"Sir, there is but one path of safety for the institution of slavery in the South when this mighty avalanche of fanaticism and folly shall press upon us, and that path lies through separation and a Southern Confederacy. This is the great ultimate security for the rights, honor, and prosperity of the South. Sir, there are even now thousands of her sons who believe that the Slave States, formed into a separate Confederacy and united under such a government as experience and wisdom would dictate, would combine elements of more political power, national prosperity, social security, and individual happiness, than any nation of ancient or modern times; and, sir, *I am among the number.*"

South Carolina was for Breckinridge, and her Legislature cast her Electoral vote for him. Here is a resolution adopted by that same Legislature, *in advance:*

"*Resolved,* That the election of a President of the United States by a sectional party, with views adverse to the institution of domestic slavery as it exists in the slave-holding States and Territories, or of one who is opposed to the grant of the protection claimed in the foregoing resolution, would so threaten a destruction of the ends for which the Constitution was formed, as to justify the slave-holding States in taking counsel together for their separate protection and safety."

Alabama was *furious* in her support of Breckinridge; and here is a resolution adopted by her Legislature with absolute unanimity:—

"2d. *Be it further resolved,* That in the absence of any preparation for a systematic co-operation of the Southern States in resisting the aggressions of their enemies, Alabama, acting for herself, has solemnly declared that under no circumstances will she submit to the foul domination of a sectional Northern party, has provided for the call of a convention in the event of the triumph of such a faction in the approaching Presidential election, and, *to maintain the position thus deliberately assumed, has appropriated the sum of*

$200,000 *for the military contingencies which such a course may involve.*"

Governor Mouton, of Louisiana, was a delegate in the Charleston Convention, and was for Breckinridge. He offered the following resolution in the State Convention on the 6th of March, 1860; and it was adopted by acclamation:—

"6. That in case of the election of a President on the avowed principles of the Black Republican party, we concur in the opinion that Louisiana should meet in council her sister slave-holding States to consult as to the means of future protection."

Texas, also for Breckinridge, adopted the following resolution in a State Convention at Galveston, in April, 1860:—

"*Resolved*, That we regard with great aversion the unnatural efforts of a sectional party at the North to carry on an 'irrepressible conflict' against the institution of slavery; and whenever that party shall succeed in electing a President upon their platform, we deem it to be the duty of the people of the State of Texas to hold themselves in readiness to co-operate with our sister States of the South in convention, to take into consideration such measures as may be necessary for our protection, or to secure out of the Confederacy that protection of their rights which they can no longer hope for in it."

The Mississippi State Convention in January, 1860, adopted this resolution, and the men who were most prominent in that Convention were for Breckinridge:—

"*Resolved*, That in the event of the election of a Black Republican candidate to the Presidency by the suffrages of one portion of the Union only, to rule over the whole United States, upon the avowed purpose of that organization, Mississippi will regard it as a declaration of hostility, and will hold herself in readiness to co-operate with her sister States of the South in whatever measure they may deem necessary for the maintenance of their rights as co-equal members of the Confederacy."

We could add any number of the treasonable sayings of the men and States who backed up Breckinridge, but the proof of their infamous conspiracy is now complete. Breckinridge himself was aware of the designs of the men who procured his nomination, and he went into it *understandingly*. He expected what was coming, and *sympathized with this infernal movement*. In a speech delivered at Frankfort, and written out by himself for publication, he said:—

"Perhaps the most imminent danger springs from the possible action of certain members of the Confederacy. The representatives from South Carolina, Georgia, Alabama, and Mississippi, not to mention other Southern States, say that they represent their constituents,—nay, that they scarcely go so far as their constituents; and most of them declare that they are ready at any moment for a separate organization. Some of the Southern Legislatures have passed resolves of this character; and we may safely assume that is the true feeling of the people."

In other portions of the speech, Mr. Breckinridge

tells the people of Kentucky that *resistance must be resorted to, sooner or later!* And General Martin, of South Carolina, in a late ratification speech of his, thus alludes to Breckinridge:—

"And having read carefully his speech, delivered at Frankfort, Kentucky, when he could not have expected a nomination, I am now better satisfied that he is a States Rights man of the strictest school, more satisfied than I was when I gave him my vote at Richmond. In that speech he lays down a broad ground,—a ground that I will close my remarks with, and save me a great deal of what I intended otherwise to say. He tells his people that the Democratic party was a very good thing in itself, but they were not to rely upon the Democratic party or any party. They were to rely upon themselves. The South must rely upon its own strong arm, and be prepared for any and every emergency."

We will only add that every prominent Disunion man in the South was for Breckinridge.

W. L. Yancey, of Alabama, is the *bell-wether* of the Disunion flock in the South, and the man who had an interview with Breckinridge at Washington and coaxed him into the lead of the traitorous gang who have conspired to subvert this Government. Here is said Yancey's celebrated Slaughter letter, which defines his principles, and which will *slaughter* Breckinridge, and all others engaged in the same infamous cause of Disunion, and their children after them in all time to come. We predicted that twelve months from that time, *Aaron*

Burr will be regarded as a patriot, compared with the movers, speakers, and active partisans in this Disunion scheme :—

"MONTGOMERY, June 15, 1858.

"DEAR SIR :—

"Your kind letter of the 15th is received. I hardly agree with you that a general movement can be made that will clean out the Augean stable. If the Democracy were overthrown, it would result in giving place to a greater and hungrier swarm of flies.

"The remedy of the South is not in such a process. It is in a diligent organization of her true men for the prompt resistance of her next aggression. It must come in the nature of things. *No national party can save us; no sectional party can ever do it. But if we should do as our fathers did,—organize committees of safety all over the Cotton States, (and it is only in them we can hope for any effective movement,)—we shall fire the Southern heart, instruct the Southern mind, give courage to each other, and at the proper moment, by one organized, concerted action,* WE CAN PRECIPITATE THE COTTON STATES INTO A REVOLUTION.

"The idea has been shadowed forth in the South by Mr. Ruffin,—has been taken up and recommended by the *Advertiser*, under the name of 'League of United Southerners,' who, keeping up the old party relations on all other questions, will hold the Southern issue paramount, and will influence parties, Legislatures, and statesmen. I have no time to enlarge, but to suggest merely.

"In haste, yours, &c.,

"W. L. YANCEY.

"To JAMES SLAUGHTER, Esq."

But why disguise the issue? This Breckinridge party made up the issue of Disunion, and throughout the South boasted of their purpose to convene a Congress at Richmond and go out of the Union. A Breckinridge meeting in Louisiana adopted a string of twenty-seven resolutions, and a friend at Homer, Louisiana, enclosed them to us in a printed slip. The following are two of these resolutions:—

"*Resolved*, That, while we place a high value on the Union, we place a still higher on the institution of slavery, and if unfortunately we must be compelled to part with one or the other, we cannot hesitate to part with the *Union*.

"*Resolved*, That we will use all possible means to keep the yellow fever from New Orleans and other seaport towns of the Slave States, by establishing and enforcing the quarantine law, and encourage emigration from the whole world to the great commercial city of the South, where health and prosperity is most abundantly found."

Hon. James O. Harrison, a Douglas Democrat, made an able speech at Lexington, Kentucky,—at the door

Rebels whipping a man for expressing Union sentiments. (P[illegible]

of Breckinridge, as it were,—and said he could sustain the following five propositions:—

1. That there was a Disunion party South *prior* to the Charleston and Baltimore Conventions.
2. That the party entered the convention with the design of dividing the Democracy on the slave line, as a preparatory step to Disunion.
3. That it aided in the formation of a Southern sectional platform, plausible, but dangerously delusive, on which said party knew *national* Democrats neither would nor could unite.
4. That this sectional platform has been adopted by the Secessionists, and that the Disunionists now stand on it.
5. (A natural sequence.) That the tendency of the platform is to Disunion, by bringing on an irrepressible conflict; and that this tendency is increased by the Disunionists who stand on it.

General John McQueen, a Representative in Congress from South Carolina, made a speech on the 4th of July, at Bennettsville, in that State, of which a sketch is given in the local paper,—*Son of Temperance.* It says,—

"He reviewed the Federal politics of the day, cordially endorsed the nomination of Breckinridge and Lane for the Presidency and Vice-Presidency,—said they were good and true men for the South to support, and would maintain the constitutional rights of the Confederacy, and should be supported by every Soutnern man.

* * * * * *

"If they submit, and permit Lincoln to be inaugurated President, without resisting and seceding from the Union, in such an event he, for one, believed that we were a degraded people, and a thousand times more than the colonies were under Great Britain. He counselled secession of the South from the Union if a Black Republican was elected President of the Government; for it would be an open declaration of an irrepressible conflict against our peculiar institutions, which are as dear to us as our lives."

Hon. Lawrence M. Keitt, another Representative in Congress from South Carolina, in a letter, said,—

"But, should the Black Republican party obtain power, and the South remain passive,—what then? While I invoke co-operation,—while I appeal to the States around us to be true to their honor,—yet, if these fail, I will counsel this State alone, if necessary, and at all hazards, to secede from the Union.

* * * * * *

"This Union is just as travellers tell us many Eastern habitations are,—a palace to look upon, all fair on its outside, and presenting the appearance of a house that should last for generations; but the master puts his walking-stick or his boot-heel through the rafters, and he finds that the white ants have eaten all the substance of the timbers, and that all that he sees about him is a coating of paint, which an intrusive blow may disperse in a cloud of dust. The skirting-boards have already perished; the rafters are now ready to tumble in."

A few extracts from some Breckinridge-Yancey papers in the South, in this connection, may throw further light on this plot against the Union:—

(From the Camden [Ala.] Democrat.)

"We run up our flag to-day for Breckinridge and Lane, the Democratic nominees for President and Vice-President of the United States. We have unwaveringly contended for the last ten years that it would be better for all concerned to make two or more distinct Governments of the territory constituting the United States of America,—and that such will ultimately be done with fairness and justice to every section of the Union; and, believing that the party to which we belong is the only reliable one to carry out this measure and secure to our own section all her rights, we intend to battle for its principles to the fullest extent of our ability."

(From the Montgomery [Ala.] Mail.)

"Run three Presidential tickets against Lincoln, thereby giving Lincoln the best chance for election. After Lincoln is elected, some Southern communities—most of them, perhaps—will refuse to let a postmaster appointed under his administration take possession of the office. Then the United States authorities will be interposed to 'enforce the laws.' Then the United States authorities will either be shot down, or they will shoot somebody down. Then the people of the community will rise up against the United States Government, and will be sustained by neighboring communities, until civil war, with all its horrid butcheries, envelops the land in blood and carnage."

(From the Cahawba [Ala.] Slave-Holder.)

"THE SOUTHERN TICKET.—We hoist to-day, as our choice for nominated candidates for the Presidency and Vice-Presidency, the names of John C. Breckinridge, of Kentucky, and Joe Lane, of Oregon.

"Our selection is made with special reference to the principles we have heretofore advocated, the most prominent and controlling of which is a union of the Southern people for the protection of our Southern institutions."

(From the Mobile Mercury, April, 1859.)

"The times are now ripe for the organization of a political movement in the slave-holding States, irrespective, of course, of all old party designations; and there are peculiar reasons why such a movement should be undertaken now and here. Indeed, we are credibly informed that conferences have already been held by leading patriotic gentlemen of this city, of all parties, and the *plans of Southern organization have been set on foot and almost matured, preparatory to action. We earnestly hope the good work may go on, and speedily.*

"*The country, we repeat, is ripe for the movement, and, if judiciously inaugurated, it will sweep over the land with a force that no opposition will be able to check.* We therefore caution our friends in the country everywhere to be prepared for it, and to keep themselves from all entangling alliances which may hinder them from joining in it untrammelled."

The Charleston *Mercury*, in April, 1859, said of the Democratic Presidential Convention of 1860, "*Unless it is limited exclusively to delegates from the South, it will be no convention of the Democratic party.*" How truly it spoke the Disunion sentiment, late events have fully shown.

(From the New Orleans Delta, April, 1859.)

"In 1860 the South and the North are to be arrayed in deadly contest; *the battle of the sections is then to be fought for the last time,* and its issues are to be decisive of our fate."

(From the Montgomery Advertiser, March, 1859.)

"It is important that we should send such men to represent us (in Congress) as possess the ability to combat the approaches of Republicanism, and the nerve to *secede from Washington in case Abolitionism should install one of its leaders in the Executive mansion of the nation.* It is important to the South, also, that her delegation should present a united front of State-Rights Democrats, for in the principles and the doctrines of the State-Rights Democracy *rests the hope of the South, in the Union* OR OUT OF IT."

(From the Eufaula [Ala.] Gazette, March, 1859.)

"Could we all think and feel alike, were our interests identical and our occupations similar, we might adopt a common government without detriment to either; *but, as we are different in all these, it becomes us to prepare for an immediate withdrawal from the alliance which has hitherto held us together;* and we hold it to be the first duty, as it should be the first object, of Southern statesmen and the Southern press, *to inaugurate a Southern Confederacy,* AND THEREBY ESTABLISH SOUTHERN INDEPENDENCE."

(From the Eufaula Spirit of the South, March, 1859.)

"The North and South, agreeing about some things and differing about others, made a Union for their benefit and a Constitution for their common government. The Supreme Court, who, according to the established creed of the North, are the final expounders of the Constitution, say that by its provisions slavery is protected in the Territories; but the greater portion of the North denounces that decision openly, while the remainder covertly repudiate it. What remains, then, but to do that which has been done in all ages and countries by sensible and right-minded people who have the misfortune to differ irreconcilably,—TO SEPARATE?"

(From the Charleston Mercury, May, 1859.)

"A revolution is, therefore, inevitable. Submission or resistance will alike establish it. The old Union—

the Union of the Constitution, of equal rights between sovereign States—is abolished. It is gone forever; strangled by consolidation, and is now the instrument of centralism to establish an irresponsible despotism of the North over the South. To break up the present Union and establish another of the South alone, is no greater revolution than that which now exists. In fact, it will be a lesser change. Let the struggle come when it may, the South, to achieve her safety, will have to trample down a Union party in the track of her political emancipation."

Knoxville Whig, Aug. 25, 1860.

This conspiracy is not complete without the following letter from Senator Yulee to one Finegan, a member of the "Sovereignty Conference" of Florida:—

"WASHINGTON, Jan. 7, 1861.

"MY DEAR SIR:—On the other side is a copy of resolutions adopted at a consultation of the Senators from the seceding States,—in which Georgia, Alabama, Louisiana, Arkansas, Texas, Mississippi, and Florida, were present.

"The idea of the meeting was that the States should go out at once, and provide for the early organization of a Confederate Government, not later than 15th February. This time is allowed to enable Louisiana and Texas to participate. It seemed to be opinion [*sic*] that if we left here, force, loan, and volunteer bills might be passed, which would put Mr. Lincoln in immediate condition for hostilities; whereas if [*sic*] by remaining in our places until the 4th of March, *it is thought we can keep the hands of Mr. Buchanan tied, and disable the Republicans from effecting any legislation which will strengthen the hands of the incoming Administration.*

"The resolutions will be sent by the delegation to the President of the Convention. I have not been able to find Mr. Mallory this morning. Hawkins [the member from Florida] is in Connecticut. I have therefore thought it best to send you this copy of the resolutions.

"In haste,

"Yours, truly,

"D. L. YULEE.

"JOSEPH FINEGAN, Esq., Sovereignty Conference, Tallahassee, Fla."

Now, it will be seen that this important letter, which breathes throughout the spirit of the conspirator, in reality lets us into the most important of the numerous secret conclaves which the plotters of TREASON then held in the national capital. It was then, as it appears, that they determined to strike the blow, and precipitate the Cotton States into secession. And yet the perjured villains resolved that it would be imprudent for them openly to withdraw from Congress, as in that case Congress might pass "force, loan, and volunteer bills, which would put Mr. Lincoln in immediate condition for hostilities."

The substance of this whole affair is, that a knot of

Senatorial traitors, *fourteen* in number, representing *seven* Cotton States, so late as January and February, 1861, sat in their seats in the Senate-Chamber, under an oath administered on the Holy Evangelists of Almighty God to support the Constitution and laws of the United States, and in good faith to act as the confidential and constitutional advisers of the President, and yet were wickedly, corruptly, and secretly plotting the overthrow of the Government. In the *daytime* they went through the forms of obeying their oaths, but *after night* they set their own swearing at defiance! The perjured scoundrels—for such they are—ought to have their foul tongues cut out, and each and all of them should be taken back to the District of Columbia, and hung by the negroes recently set free by Congress!

CHAPTER XIII.

WHICH SIDE IS THE LORD ON?—TEACHINGS OF SECESSION CLERGYMEN—PRAYER OF REV. MR. BALDWIN—PROVIDENCES OF GOD BEFORE AND SINCE THE DEVELOPMENT OF THIS GREAT CONSPIRACY—THE SOUTH HAS HAD A PREPONDERATING INFLUENCE IN THE CONTROL OF THE GOVERNMENT—GOD HAS ARRANGED THE CONDITIONS OF THIS GREAT DRAMA TO FAVOR THE GOVERNMENT OF THE UNITED STATES—UNION VICTORIES OF 1861—CITIES AND TOWNS TAKEN FROM THE SOUTH, BY DIVINE PERMISSION, IN 1862—GAMBLING-HELLS IN RICHMOND—PROFANE SWEARING AND DRINKING IN THE REBEL ARMY—WICKEDNESS OF THE SOUTHERN CLERGY—LOSS OF REBEL GENERALS.

FROM the very beginning of this WICKED REBELLION, the advocates of Secession and of a war upon the Government of the United States have arrogantly claimed that God was on their side,—pointing to the evidences of divine Providence favoring the Southern side of the GREAT CONSPIRACY. Secession clergymen, roused by the excitement of the war, have brought reproach upon religion, in many portions of the South, both by the bitterness of their sermons and the wickedness of their sentiments. It is by no means an uncommon thing to hear Secession chaplains, and other clergymen, teach soldiers from the pulpit, and assure the relatives of soldiers in the event of their death, that the *cause* in which they fall, battling for the independence of the South in opposition to the Vandal hordes of the North, constitutes a passport sufficient to introduce them to all that exceeding weight of joy at God's right hand!

On the occasion of the inauguration of *Eye-Sham G. Harris* as Governor of Tennessee, which took place in the Capitol at Nashville in October, 1861, a prayer was offered up by Mr. Baldwin, a Methodist minister, eminent as an orator and an author, though crazy upon the subject of "Southern rights," of a blasphemous character, most decidedly. He opened in these words: —"WE THANK THEE, O LORD, FOR HAVING INAUGURATED THIS REVOLUTION!" The rest of the prayer was in keeping with the opening sentence. It was blaspheming God, and reviling Him, by denying and ridiculing His perfections and word, and by ascribing to Him work base and sinful. What has been done by the agency of the devil, is ascribed to the finger of God, in this unpardonable prayer. An evil spirit, subject to the powers of Satan, influenced certain bad men in the South, evidently *possessed of devils*, to precipitate the Cotton States into this revolution. All the agency that God had in the matter was to *permit* these devils to enter into these Secessionists, just as He permitted them to enter the herd of swine and precipitate them into the Sea of Galilee! May the successors of these devils, who have entered into the

Southern leaders in this rebellion, precipitate them into the Gulf of Mexico!

When Mr. Baldwin offered up this remarkable prayer, he should have done it at one of the various very ancient altars that existed at Athens, the Greek metropolis, upon which was the inscription, "To THE UNKNOWN GOD," whom the Athenians ignorantly worshipped. An ancient sect has long since taught us that there are two Gods,—the one, the author of all good, the other, the author of all evil. It was this evil god who "inaugurated this revolution." What a calmly argumentative and sweetly persuasive prayer this, to offer up to a God of order, justice, and mercy, opposed to falsehood, plunder, and murder!

But, gentle reader, let us look calmly at the providences of God, as developed before and since the introduction of this great conspiracy. If the South had been wantonly oppressed and wickedly proscribed by the North, and if the North had "inaugurated" the war, it would have been natural to expect the God of right and justice to espouse the cause of the South. But up to 1861 the South had furnished *seven* out of the *thirteen* Presidents, and enjoyed *twelve* out of the *eighteen* terms, or *forty-eight* out of the *seventy-two* years since the adoption of the Federal Constitution; thus leaving the Presidential office to be occupied by Northern men only *twenty-four* years, or just *one-third* of the time!

And, to show the advantage the South has been allowed to enjoy over and above what she was entitled to, I subjoin a table of Electoral votes which the *fifteen* Southern States and the *nineteen* Northern States cast in the Presidential election of 1860.

SOUTHERN STATES.		NORTHERN STATES.	
Alabama	9	California	4
Arkansas	4	Connecticut	6
Delaware	3	Illinois	11
Florida	3	Indiana	13
Georgia	10	Iowa	4
Kentucky	12	Maine	8
Louisiana	6	Massachusetts	13
Maryland	8	Michigan	6
Mississippi	7	Minnesota	4
Missouri	9	New Hampshire	5
North Carolina	10	New Jersey	7
South Carolina	8	New York	35
Tennessee	12	Ohio	23
Texas	4	Oregon	3
Virginia	15	Pennsylvania	27
		Rhode Island	4
		Vermont	5
		Wisconsin	5
	120		183

Total Electoral vote 303
Necessary for an election of President 152

But another and a strong point is this. Five of the Southern Presidents each served *two terms*, or eight years; while no Northern man has ever been allowed a re-election. Besides, two Presidents, Messrs. Van Buren and Buchanan, were "Northern men with Southern principles;" and this, in effect, gives eight years more to the South,—making *fifty-six years* in which they have had almost supreme control, and leaving but *sixteen years* during which the Government has been administered, even nominally, by Northern Presidents. But during these *sixteen years* the two hundred and sixty-three thousand slave-owners of the South had a preponderating influence in the affairs of the nation, and in shaping public policy.

So long as the country was satisfied with this state of things, the political leaders of the South, of course, did not complain; but the moment the people ventured, by perfectly legal and constitutional means, to elect Mr. Lincoln,—a man who, if not representing the clearly-revealed sentiments of the majority, was at least the choice of that majority,—the Southern politicians revolted, and, in *eleven* of the *fifteen* Southern States, passed ordinances of Secession.

An able writer, in reviewing the events of the last year, in a religious periodical of high standing, together with the circumstances which preceded and prepared the way for them, develops the guiding hand of Providence, and the arguments in favor of His being on the side of the National Government. How wonderfully has God arranged all the conditions of this great drama, to favor the Government of the United States and the millions of loyal citizens adhering thereto! I present these views, and assure the reader that he will profit by their perusal:—

"I. I notice, first, the abundant cotton-crop of 1859–60, by which the wants of Europe and the world were more fully supplied than ever before:—

In 1856 the crop amounted to	3,529,841 bales.
In 1857 " "	2,939,519 "
In 1858 " "	2,113,962 "
In 1859 " "	3,851,481 "
In 1860 " "	4,600,000 "

"Of this Great Britain received,—

In 1856	1,038,886,304 pounds.
In 1857	996,318,896 "
In 1858	1,034,342,176 "
In 1859	1,225,989,072 "
In 1860	1,390,935,752 "

"These tables show the enormous yield in the last year named, and also to what extent Great Britain, by far the largest consumer in the world, was supplied. There was, in addition to this immense amount of raw material, an unprecedented stock of manufactured goods seeking a market or stored up in all the marts of the world.

"II. Next we notice the extraordinary crops of grain in this country in 1859, 1860, and 1861, which afforded not only abundance at a cheap rate for our own people during the war, but a largely-augmented amount for European consumption, and this amount all the while steadily increasing, thus turning the current of exchanges in our favor,—a financial phenomenon not before witnessed in this country for many years. The following table, showing the exportations of domestic produce, principally breadstuffs, during the last five years, will clearly demonstrate this point:—

In 1857 the exports were	$61,803,235
In 1858 "	53,949,703
In 1859 "	59,929,531
In 1860 "	95,468,296
In 1861 "	131,235,995

"III. Another most important circumstance in the work of preparing the nation was the short crop in Great Britain, France, and generally throughout Europe, during the years 1859, 1860, 1861, and 1862,—their lean years being exactly our most abundant ones. Thus, an unexpected and unheard-of increase in the demand for breadstuffs from this country sprang up just at the moment when war was involving us in extraordinary expenses, and when we had overflowing granaries to meet the timely demand.

"IV. In consequence of this happy concurrence of events, several millions of gold came back from Europe in exchange for breadstuffs and provisions in a single week, at the very commencement of our struggle; and this process went on for several months or nearly a year, by which our financial means were greatly increased, and our Government and people encouraged and sustained, while the conspirators were correspondingly depressed and disheartened. The truth of this will more readily appear from the following tables, showing the movement of specie and bullion between this and foreign countries during the last five years:—

In 1857 we exported	$44,360,174
In 1858 "	26,001,431
In 1859 "	69,715,886
In 1860 "	42,191,171
In 1861 "	4,236,250

In 1857 we imported	$12,461,799
In 1858 "	19,274,496
In 1859 "	7,434,789
In 1860 "	8,550,135
In 1861 "	44,439,859

"The cotton exported to Great Britain, in 1860, amounted to the enormous sum of *two hundred and seventy millions of dollars;* and yet, notwithstanding no cotton went forward in 1861, and the supply was thus suddenly and unexpectedly cut off, a kind Providence had so ordered events that our breadstuffs and provisions came in at that particular juncture to serve as a medium of exchange and to prevent any sudden and overwhelming revulsion in trade."

In a review of the battles lost and won in this war, it is plain to be seen which army has the approbation of Providence. I herewith give the dates and localities of these battles; and I collect them from official sources. The reader cannot but be struck with the contrast, in the successes and defeats of the respective armies:—

Union Victories, 1861.

June 3—Philippa.
June 18—Booneville.
July 11—Defeat of Pegram by Rosecrans.
July 13—Carrick's Ford, (death of Garnett, Rebel.)
August 29—Hatteras forts.
September 11—Rout of Floyd, Gauley Bridge.
October 5—Second defeat of Rebels at Hatteras.
October 9—Santa Rosa Island.
October 12—Repulse at Southwest Pass.
October 21—Jeff Thompson defeated at Fredericktown.
" "—Zollicoffer repulsed at Camp Wild Cat.
October 24—Charge of Fremont's Guard at Springfield, Mo.
October 25—Romney, (Kelley wounded.)
November 7—Port Royal.
December 13—Camp Alleghany, Virginia.
December 18—1600 Rebels captured by Pope in Missouri.
December 20—Drainesville.

1862.

Second Rebel repulse at Santa Rosa.
Humphrey Marshall's rout.
Capture of Rebel batteries in South Carolina.
Mill Spring, (Zollicoffer killed.)
Fort Henry.
Roanoke Island, 2500 prisoners taken.
Fort Donelson, 13,000 prisoners taken, besides the killed and wounded.
Island No. 10.
Pittsburg Landing.
Pea Ridge, Arkansas.
Camden, North Carolina.
Canby's, at Galeto, N.M.

Rebel Victories, 1861.

April 13—Sumter.
June 10—Big Bethel.
July 21—Bull Run.
August 9—Wilson's Creek.
September 22—Lexington.
October 21—Massacre of Ball's Bluff.
November 7—Belmont.

1862, NONE.

Union victories, 29; Secession victories, 7; ratio, *four* to *one*,—against a people *one* of whose troops can whip *five* of the enemy, and against a people and army who have the Lord on their side! In their future prayers, they should pray to be saved from their friends and be allowed to take care of their enemies!

The following-named cities and towns have, with the Lord's *permission*, been taken from the Secessionists by the Federalists, since the commencement of the present year, 1862, to May 7:—

Elizabeth City, N.C.
Edenton, N.C.
Winton, N.C.
Bowling Green, Ky.
Dover, Tenn.
Fayetteville, Ark.
Bentonville, Ark.
Martinsburg, Va.
Leetown, Va.
Lovettsville, Va.
Smithfield, Va.
Bolivar, Va.
Charlestown, Va.
Harper's Ferry, Va.
Big Bethel, Va.
Paris, Tenn.
Huttonsville, Va.
Florence, Ala.
Cedar Keys, Fla.
Springfield, Mo.
Eastport, Miss.
Columbus, Ky.
Leesburg, Va.
New Orleans, La.
Huntsville, Ala.
Stevenson, Ala.
Tuscumbia, Ala.
Fredericksburg, Va.
Paintville, Ky.
Nashville, Tenn.
Clarksville, Tenn.
Columbia, Tenn.
Savannah, Tenn.
Brunswick, Ga.
Fernandina, Fla.
San Augustine, Fla.
Jacksonville, Fla.
Manassas, Va.
Centerville, Va.
St. Marys, Ga.
Berryville, Ga.
Winchester, Va.
Occoquan, Va.
Windsor, Va.
New Madrid, Mo.
Point Pleasant, Mo.
Hickman, Ky.
Newbern, N.C.
Beaufort, N.C.
Morehead City, N.C.
Nashville, Tenn.
Baton Rouge, La.
Decatur, Ala.
Florence, Ala.
Yorktown, Va.
Williamsburg, Va.

The following Rebel forts and fortifications have also been captured since the 1st of January to May 7, 1862:

Fort Johnson, Va.
Fort Beauregard, Va.
Fort Evans, Va.
Pig's Point Battery, Va.
Shipping Point Battery, Va.
Cockpit Point Batteries, Va.
Fort Clinch, Fla.
Fort Henry, Tenn.
Fort Donelson, Tenn.
Fort St. Mark, Fla.
Fort St. Philip.
Fort Jackson.
Fort Pike.
Fort Warren, Fla.
Fort Macon, N.C.
Columbus fortifications, Ky.
Bowling Green fortifications, Ky.
Mill Spring fortifications, Ky.
Roanoke Island Batteries.
Elizabeth City Batteries, N.C.
Fortifications at St. Simons, Ga.
Fortifications at Manassas.
Batteries at Acquia Creek, Va.
Fort Pulaski, near Savannah, Ga.
Rigolette.

Do the clergymen who play at this game of Secession brag call this backing up one's friends? Besides the cities and towns, forts and fortifications, named, quite a number of forts on the Neuse River have been captured. The Federal reverses have been in New Mexico alone, where the Secessionists have occupied three or four evacuated military towns and posts, of no sort of importance, unless resorted to by a retreating foe, as they will be when these rebels take to flight!

There is now in the South a mass of corruption that would poison the atmosphere of Paradise, were it to come in contact with it. Even in Richmond, their seat of Government, if their own papers may be credited, the most abominable wickedness prevails. Drunkenness, swindling, fighting, Sabbath-breaking, and gambling are the order of the day. The correspondent of the *Nashville Union and American*, writing from Richmond, says of the gambling-"hells" in that city:—

"Richmond ought to be called Farobankopolis, so numerous are its gambling-'hells,' especially in the region of the Exchange Hotel, where the stranger may see on one side of the street a fashionable first-class establishment which towers to the skies, and on the other may enter a dozen dens of the vilest description, known to the 'fancy' as 'sweat-cloth dead-falls.' The extent to which the game is carried in Virginia is awful in the extreme. Men born and reared in the first circles of society may be seen dealing faro; and it is mentioned as a curious circumstance that nearly every one of the great faro-dealers, whose palatial houses and magnificent entertainments made them a national reputation in the late Union, were born in the counties of Campbell and Halifax in this State. The 'leading houses' from New York to New Orleans, and at all the watering-places, are owned and 'run' by Virginians. All classes and conditions of society frequent them. It is said that one of the most brilliant men in the State has lost a fortune of $200,000 at faro; and the names might be given of many talented young men who started in life under the best possible auspices, but died behind a faro-table, or are now wrecked and literally eaten by their mania for this enticing game."

What a picture of the morality of the seat of a Government having monopolized the affections and protecting care of the Almighty! True, they have brought upon the country, but recently in prosperity and happiness, the complicated miseries of war, with all its guilt, its outrages against Heaven, against all truth, honesty, justice, goodness,—nay, against all the principles of social happiness; but, then, they find an apology in the alleged fact that the Lord is on their side! With an irreligious Cabinet at Richmond, and a regiment of whiskey-bloats in the field in command of their forces, the Federal party may well envy the privilege of these "Israelites in whom there is no guile," and mourn that no land of Canaan has been promised to them and their children!

In view of the *profane swearing* in the Rebel army, and its almost universal prevalence among both officers and privates, I subjoin an extract from the original "General Order-Book" of General WASHINGTON, under date of the 29th of July, 1799. It is from the pen of a chieftain who evidently had the Lord on his side:—

"Many and pointed orders have been issued against that unmeaning and abominable custom of swearing; notwithstanding which, with much regret, the general observes that it prevails, *if possible*, more than ever. His feelings are continually wounded by the oaths and imprecations of the soldiers whenever he is in the hearing of them. The name of that Being from whose bountiful goodness we are permitted to exist and enjoy the comforts of life, is incessantly imprecated and profaned in a manner as wanton as it is shocking. For the sake, therefore, of religion, decency, and order, the general hopes and trusts that officers of every rank will use their influence and authority to check a vice which is as unprofitable as it is wicked and shameful.

"If officers would make it an invariable rule to reprimand—and, if that does not do, punish—soldiers for offences of this kind, it could not fail of having the desired effect."

I bring the charge of political preaching and praying against the great body of clergymen in the South, irrespective of sects; and I have no hesitancy in saying, as I now do, that the worst class of men who make tracks upon Southern soil are Methodist, Presbyterian, Baptist, and Episcopal clergymen, and at the head of these for mischief are the Southern Methodists. I mean to say that there are honorable exceptions in all these churches;

but the moral mania of Secession has been almost universally prevalent among the members of the sacred profession. A majority of the clergy have acted upon the principle that the kingdom of their Divine Master is "of this world;" and, as a consequence, too many of them have embarked in fighting, lying, and drinking mean whiskey. The influence and example of these men in the South have ruined the Churches and severed them into fragments, and it will take years of fasting and prayer to heal the divisions in the Churches and to reconstruct them.

But my object in this chapter is to demonstrate, by facts and figures, that God is not on the side of this rebellion, and that the evidence He affords of the part He is acting goes to show that He is on the side of the Federal Government. Look at the defeat and death of the Rebel generals:—

"The Rebel generals have had a hard time of it during the war. Garnett was killed at Carrick's Ford; Burton and Bee were killed at Manassas; Zollicoffer was killed at Fishing Creek; McCulloch, McIntosh, and Slack were killed at Pea Ridge; A. Sidney Johnston was killed at Pittsburg Landing; P. St. George Cocke killed himself at Richmond; Tilghman was captured at Fort Henry; Buckner was captured at Fort Donelson; Bushrod Johnston was captured with Buckner, and, violating his parole, escaped; Mackall, Gantt, and Walker were taken at Island No. 10; Floyd and Pillow are suspended in disgrace, for running away from Fort Donelson; Twiggs, Fauntleroy, Jackson, and Bonham resigned; Grayson died."

CHAPTER XIV.

SPEECH OF W. G. BROWNLOW, DELIVERED IN KNOXVILLE, IN OCTOBER, 1861, BEFORE THE LATE PRESIDENTIAL ELECTION, BEFORE THE BELL-AND-EVERETT CLUB—PROVES A CONSPIRACY AGAINST THE GOVERNMENT BY THE BRECKINRIDGE DEMOCRACY—CONCEDES THE ELECTION OF LINCOLN, BUT DENIES THAT TO BE A SUFFICIENT CAUSE FOR DISSOLVING THE UNION—THE SPEAKER DECLARED FOR THE UNION AT ALL HAZARDS—MY LAST INTERVIEW WITH JOHN BELL.

GENTLEMEN OF THE BELL-AND-EVERETT CLUB, AND FELLOW-CITIZENS:—

THE Bible tells us, in reference to a high and holy theme, that "day unto day uttereth speech, and night unto night showeth knowledge." This is emphatically true in regard to the Presidential election. The developments of every day and night add strength to the conviction that the Presidential contest has narrowed down to a choice between John Bell and Abraham Lincoln. Breckinridge has been *distanced* at the start; he *let down* the first heat, and it is the very madness of folly to talk about electing him. The leaders of the Democratic party who procured his nomination by a *rebellious faction* at Baltimore, took that method of accomplishing a long-cherished object,—the dissolution of this Union and the "precipitating of the Cotton States into a revolution."

Douglas, too, is out of the question—really not in the race. He *may* carry a few of the Northwestern States, and, I think, will do so; but his election is impossible. His friends desire the defeat of Lincoln, first, because he is a *sectional* candidate, as they say, running upon the Nigger issue alone; and, next, because he holds the position of a candidate for the Presidency by virtue of the prominence given to him by Buchanan, Breckinridge, and the other members of the Cabinet, who ran him against Douglas for the United States Senate, and brought the whole patronage of the Government to bear in his favor. Intelligent Douglas men see that Bell is the only man who can now defeat Lincoln. They see that Bell will carry nearly all the Southern States, if the Breckinridge party are not bent upon the dissolution of the Union, and their conservatism and devotion to the Union will finally lead them to the support of Bell.

With these preliminary remarks I will proceed to address you upon the subject, not of Mr. Bell's record, but of the record of Breckinridge and Lane, and of the merits of the party putting them forth as candidates.

I charge, first of all, that Buchanan's is the most corrupt and profligate administration ever known to this Government since its organization; nay, that ours is the most corrupt Government in the civilized world, and that this corruption and profligacy have grown up under Democratic rule; for, with the exception of four

Charles S. Douglas shot by the Rebels while sitting at his window in Gay Street, Knoxville. (Page 278.)

years under Taylor and Fillmore, the Democrats have had the control of the Government for the last twenty-four years.

In 1856, when out of power, Buchanan denounced the expenditures of $40,000,000 under Fillmore as an outrage, in an electioneering letter he put forth, and said that an honest people ought not to submit to it. *In power*, when clothed with authority to correct these abuses, he expended *double the amount;* for in one year after he was inaugurated he increased the public expenditures to $80,000,000. Here was economy with a vengeance! Nay, he found a surplus of $20,000,000 in the treasury, and not only used that for corrupt purposes, but has borrowed until the outstanding public debt is the rise of one hundred millions of dollars.

But, it may be inquired, what has all this to do with the voting for or against Breckinridge and Lane? Much, every way. Breckinridge is the *tail-end* of this miserable administration, has been connected with its Cabinet councils from the beginning, and is now its *pet candidate* for the Presidency. Old Joe Lane has stood upon the floor of the Senate for the last three years and defended its villainous measures, however monstrous they have been. Both of these men if elected will seek to hide its revolting deformities, if, indeed, they do not carry out the same lying and thieving policy. We need a change. I am sick of seeing it paraded in foreign journals that the President of the

17

United States is a *thief* and a *liar*. Mr. Buchanan has been convicted of lying and of hiding for thieves, as well as of advising them to steal from the Government, by the *sworn testimony* of various men of his own party before the Covode Committee.

As a general thing, the Breckinridge speakers pass all this over as unworthy of notice. Whilthom, the State Elector, does meet it, it is true, by charging that John Bell and Judge Douglas voted for the appropriations, and thereby placed money within the reach of Buchanan and his dishonest office-holders. This is a defence with a vengeance!

But it will be said that these are mere *assertions*. Let us, then, have the proof. Here it is; and it is high Democratic authority, and will not be called in question:—

"When I first entered Congress, in 1843, the expenses of the Government were only thirty millions per annum. The country had gone through the expensive Mexican War, with sixty-three thousand soldiers in the field, for thirty millions, and now, in time of peace, the estimates are seventy-three millions! He believed forty millions an abundance for the national expense."—*Hon. A. H. Stephens.*

"This Government, sixty-nine years of age, scarcely out of its swaddling-clothes, is making more corrupt uses of money in proportion to the amount collected from the people, as I honestly believe, than any other Government on the habitable globe."—*Hon. Andrew Johnson, of Tennessee.*

"I think it not saying too much to declare that this country has gone faster and further in ten years, in extravagance, than most other countries have gone in centuries."—*General Shields.*

"Before God, I believe this to be the most corrupt Government on earth."—*Senator Toombs.*

"From the by-ways and the highways of the Government the rottenness of corruption sends forth an insufferable stench! Why are the people so patient? Why slumbers the indignation of the Democracy?"—*Roger A. Pryor.*

But, gentlemen, I object to Breckinridge on account of his *anti-slavery* record; and, as a Southern man, I would not vote for him even if John Bell were not a candidate, and the race were between him and Lincoln! I therefore ask of you the privilege of exhibiting his record:—

Breckinridge on Intervention.

"The whole theory of Congressional intervention is a LIBEL ON OUR INSTITUTIONS."—*Congressional Globe*, vol. xxix. p. 442.

John C. Breckinridge is the nominee of a party claiming Congressional protection.

Breckinridge's Idea of the Effect on the Country of the Passage of the Kansas Bill.

"No, sir! if we reject the bill, we open up the waters of bitterness, which will be sealed again in time, but not until these agitators shall have rioted a while in the confusions of the country. We blow high the flames to furnish habitations for these political salamanders who can exist only in the fires of domestic strife. But if it passes, the question will be removed FOREVER from the halls of Congress, and deposited with the people, who can settle it in a manner answerable to their own views of interest and happiness."—*Congressional Globe*, vol. xxix.

Breckinridge's Idea of the Object of the Kansas Bill.

"Then, sir, neither the purpose nor effect of the bill is to legislate slavery into Nebraska and Kansas; but its effect is to sweep away this vestige of CONGRESSIONAL DICTATION on this subject, to allow the free citizens of this Union to enter the common territory with the Constitution and the bill alone in their hands, and to REMIT THE DECISION OF THEIR RIGHTS UNDER BOTH TO THE COURTS OF THE COUNTRY."—*Congressional Globe*, vol. xxix.

Breckinridge on Slavery in Kansas.

"Among the many misrepresentations of the Kansas-Nebraska Bill, perhaps none is more flagrant than the charge that it proposes to legislate slavery into Kansas and Nebraska. Sir, if the bill contained such a feature, IT COULD NOT RECEIVE MY VOTE. The right to establish involves the right to prohibit; and, denying both, I would vote for neither."—*Congressional Globe.*

J. C. Breckinridge on the Kansas Bill.

"Did not the non-slave-holding States (generally) insist that the true policy was the prohibition of slavery in the Territories of the Union by act of Congress, and, by consequence, insist upon applying this principle to Utah and New Mexico? Did not the slave-holding States, on the contrary, PLANTING THEMSELVES ON THE GROUND OF FEDERAL NON-INTERVENTION, RESIST THIS POLICY, and, by consequence, its adoption and application to those Territories? And, after a long and fearful struggle, did not the LATTER DOCTRINE PREVAIL?—and was it not carried into law in the Utah and New Mexico acts? Did not the public, the press, conventions, and State hail the result as a FINAL SETTLEMENT, IN PRIN-

CIPLE AND SUBSTANCE, OF THE SUBJECT OF SLAVERY?"
—*Congressional Globe*, vol. xxix. p. 441.

If this is not sufficient to establish the anti-slavery proclivities of Breckinridge, I will add a few brief extracts from his celebrated Tippecanoe speech in 1856, delivered before ten thousand Free-Soilers, whose votes he solicited for himself and Buchanan:—

"I AM CONNECTED WITH NO PARTY THAT HAS FOR ITS OBJECT THE EXTENSION OF SLAVERY, nor with any to prevent the people of a State or Territory from deciding the question of its existence with them for themselves."

The speaker continued:—

"I happened to be in Congress when the Nebraska Bill passed, and gave it my voice and vote, and because it did what it did,—viz.: it acknowledged THE RIGHT OF THE PEOPLE OF THE TERRITORY TO SETTLE THE QUESTION FOR THEMSELVES,—and not because I supposed —what I do not now believe—that it legislated slavery into the Territory. The Democratic party is not a pro-slavery party."

Now, the Southern wing of the Democratic party indignantly rejected Douglas, seceded at Baltimore, and nominated Breckinridge, because Douglas held the very doctrines herein avowed by Breckinridge! That you may see them in a still more ridiculous light, here is the resolution adopted by the Douglas Democratic State Convention of Illinois, declaring,—

"Slavery, if it exists in a Territory, DOES NOT DERIVE its validity from the Constitution of the United States, but is a MERE MUNICIPAL INSTITUTION existing in such Territory UNDER THE LAWS THEREOF."

In 1850, while Breckinridge was a member of the Kentucky Legislature, he declared, by resolution,—

"*Resolved*, By the General Assembly of the Commonwealth of Kentucky, That the question of SLAVERY in the TERRITORIES, being WHOLLY LOCAL and DOMESTIC, belongs to the PEOPLE WHO INHABIT THEM."

Will some one of the Breckinridge speakers travelling through this country, quoting garbled extracts from Bell's record and misrepresenting that able and experienced statesman's legislative course, show a shade of difference in the "squatter sovereignty" principles set forth in these two resolutions? They both declare slavery in the Territories to be *local* and only subject to the laws thereof.

But "old Joe Lane," as he is familiarly called, holds the same doctrine, and said, in one of his speeches,—

"The question of slavery is a most perplexing one, and ought not to be agitated. We should leave it with the States where it constitutionally exists, AND THE PEOPLE OF THE TERRITORIES, TO PROHIBIT OR ESTABLISH, AS TO THEM MAY SEEM RIGHT AND PROPER."

Here, then, are two rank and straight-out squatters, who have *out-squatted* Douglas, taken up by these Baltimore Disunionists and Seceders and run for the Presidency and Vice-Presidency, and Douglas unceremoniously thrust aside because he was a *squatter*.

Will some Breckinridge orator explain why it was that Douglas was set aside for this heresy, and two other gentlemen selected holding the same heresy and hugging it closer? The answer will be, "Because we wanted our rights under the Constitution." What rights? The right to secede from the Union and form a Southern Confederacy. Of this right and this unholy purpose I shall have something to say before I close.

I inquire again, why was Douglas rejected and Breckinridge selected by the *intense* Southern wing of the great harmonious? I have the true answer to this question, given on the floor of the Senate on the 24th of last May by a distinguished politician. I want you to hear it, and when you hear it ask me who he was:—

> "It is the fault of the Democratic party, in dodging truth, in dodging principle, in dodging the Constitution itself, that has brought the trouble upon the country and the party that is experienced to-day."

Who said that last May on the floor of the Senate, and is thus reported in the *Congressional Globe?* It was "OLD JOE LANE;" and I am glad that he said it, in lieu of some Opposition man; for the latter would have been charged with abusing the Democratic party!

Well might Herschel V. Johnson, of Georgia, exclaim, in a public speech at Macon but the other day,—

> "This whole Secession movement is without justification. It is not dignified by devotion to principle. It is scarcely redeemed from the odiousness of faction. Its highest attribute is that of sheer, naked, and ungenerous warfare against a great and distinguished

Democrat. Let its authors bear the responsibility and reap the coming retribution. It will come when the popular mind shall be awakened to its legitimate tendencies."

But I come now to the subject of Disunion. This is a sore subject with the Breckinridge party, and they are the more sensitive when it is named, and prone to denunciation when it is charged, because they *know* and *feel* that they are justly liable to the charge. The Breckinridge men are not all Disunionists, but all *unsophisticated Disunionists* are Breckinridge men. The States that seceded from the regular Democratic Convention had expressed themselves as favorable to Disunion before the National Convention met even at Charleston. In the debates at Charleston and Baltimore they showed that *that* was their cherished object.

Many of the leading men who supported Breckinridge, in different States, openly avow that they were in favor of Disunion in the event of the election of Lincoln, though he might be legally and constitutionally elected and by a majority of the American voters. Here are a few of their names:—

Hon. Jefferson Davis, of Miss.
Hon. L. M. Keitt, of S.C.
Hon. J. L. Orr, of S.C.
Hon. R. B. Rhett, of S.C.
Hon. Wm. L. Yancey, of Ala.
Gov. J. J. Pettus, of Miss.
Ex-Gov. McRea, of Miss.
Gov. Perry, of Florida.
Ex-Gov. McWillie, of Miss.
Hon. Mr. Curry, of Ala.
Hon. J. T. Morgan, of Ala.
Hon. D. Hubbard, of Ala.
Hon. Mr. Gartrell, of Ga.
Hon. Mr. Crawford, of Ga.
Hon. Mr. Bonham, of S.C.
Hon. Mr. Singleton, of Miss.
Hon. R. Davis, of Miss.
Hon. R. A. Pryor, of Va.

Mr. Dejarnette, of Va.	Hon. H. S. Bennett, of Miss.
Hon. L. P. Walker, of Ala.	Gov. Gist, of S.C.
Hon. Sydenham Moore, of Ala.	Hon. Mr. Boyce, of S.C.
Hon. Mr. Pugh, of Ala.	Hon. A. Burt, of S.C.

Now, hear what two of these ardent Breckinridge men have said:—

It will be remembered that Hon. Barnwell Rhett said, "The Richmond Convention *is not national: a National Convention is one based on principles common to all portions of the United States.*" The Hon. A. Burt said, "I have not an element of a National Democrat in me. I was raised a Nullifier, and should be recreant to principle if I were to apostatize and find myself in the ranks of the National Democracy."

Yancey's scheme for "precipitating" the Cotton States into a revolution you are all familiar with.

Major Polk, Douglas Elector for the State at large, is speaking with Haynes and Peyton, and at Fayetteville, August 31, stated that he was prepared to prove by a telegraphic dispatch that Breckinridge and Lane were nominated by the Richmond Seceding Convention one hour before they were at Baltimore! This *plot* explains why the letter of the Richmond Disunion Convention, notifying Breckinridge of his nomination, was never published, though his letter of acceptance was.

The St. Louis *Republican*, good Democratic authority, positively asserts,—

"The rupture at Charleston and Baltimore is seen to have been a preconcerted part of the *Disunion programme, concocted in the secret lodges of the Disunion leagues;* that the plot was deliberately hatched there for the disruption of the only national party organization, as an essential preliminary to 'precipitating the Cotton States into a revolution,' and that by a division of the Democrats in the North, and consequent election of Lincoln, the Disunionists hoped to 'fire the Southern heart' to the work of overthrowing the Constitution and the Union."

A recent issue of the Huntsville *Democrat*, a Breckinridge organ, edited by a brother of Senator Clay, says,—

"If we wait till our enemies get control of the power of the Federal Government, as they have now of the Northern State Governments, and have possession of the purse and sword, the treasury, army, navy, then we white men of the South who wield 'the power of slavery' will be 'in the course of ultimate extinction.' 'The war of extermination'—as Douglas called the 'irrepressible conflict'—predicted by Lincoln, already declared, will then have been waged."

Hon. Eli S. Shorter, Breckinridge Elector in Alabama, recently said, in a speech in Pike county,—which speech is reported in the *States Rights Advocate*,—

"He took the position boldly, that upon the election of a Black Republican, upon a sectional platform and by a sectional vote, he was for a dissolution of the Union."

The Columbia *South Carolinian*, a Breckinridge organ of recent date, says,—

"The Republicans will push forward in their work and elect their President, and, when too late to reflect or retreat, will find themselves face to face with an indignant and outraged people, *with the flag of revolution unfurled.*"

The Columbus (Ga.) *Times*, a Breckinridge-Yancey paper, thus unfurls the flag of Disunion:—

"We have not postponed the issue indefinitely. We are not going to wait for an overt act of aggression before resisting a Black Republican President. We repeat, there is no issue of dissolution in the platform of any party now before the country. We repeat that when Lincoln is declared elected we shall appeal to the 'people to redress their grievance.' We repeat all that we have ever said that means resistance to Black Republican rule, from first to last."

Hon. John Driver, of Russell county, Alabama, an ardent Breckinridge man, and a member of the Charleston and Baltimore Conventions, says, in a published card over his signature, July 23, 1860, in defence of a dissolution of the Union, "*To effect this object, we*, THE DISUNION PARTY, DISRUPTED THE DEMOCRATIC CONVENTION AT CHARLESTON, AND AT BALTIMORE INDUCED OTHERS TO JOIN US BY OUR AGREEING TO SUPPORT MEN NOT ENTIRELY OF OUR SENTIMENTS!"

James D. Thomas, the Breckinridge Elector for the Knox district, said at Maynardsville, on the 28th ultimo, that if the Judiciary, Legislative, and Executive Departments refuse protection to slave property, he and his party were for secession. He said that thing, and I presume he represents his party in Tennessee. Governor Harris is committed to the same odious and revolutionary doctrine. So are all the Disunion leaders in this State.

The Bell-and-Everett Elector in the State of Georgia, Colonel S. C. Elam, has renounced the Union ticket, and come out in a card for Breckinridge. Colonel Elam gives his reasons for the change; and I beg you to hear those reasons.

He says that Breckinridge and Lane *stand even a slimmer chance than Bell and Everett.* Then *why* does Colonel Elam leave us? He says that his "controlling reason" is that "THE BRECKINRIDGE PARTY IS PLEDGED TO DISSOLVE THE UNION IF LINCOLN IS ELECTED," and that "BRECKINRIDGE'S RUNNING RENDERS LINCOLN'S ELECTION CERTAIN." He thinks that "*Douglas might be elected if Breckinridge was out of the way,*" but "*Breckinridge couldn't beat Lincoln if Douglas was out of the way.*"

So here is the whole game of the Yanceyites. Colonel Elam has let the Disunion cat out of the bag. The Breckinridge party is pledged to dissolve the Union in a certain contingency,—the election of Lincoln. TO MAKE THAT CONTINGENCY CERTAIN, THEY ARE RUNNING BRECKINRIDGE.

Mr. Bell owns eighty-three slaves in his own right, and his wife owns just an equal number,—making in all one hundred and sixty-six,—and still he is sneeringly pointed to as unsound on the Slavery question! Mr. Douglas owns no slaves, and never did in his own right, and is a Northern man; and he has an Electoral ticket in almost all of the Southern States. Mr. Breckinridge and family live in Lexington, and board at the Phœnix Hotel, and he votes in that city, regarding it as his home. For several years past he has returned no property for taxation, either real or personal, as appears from the tax-book,—and for the best reason in the world: *he has none.* He has a *free colored woman as a nurse,* and this is all the connection he has with slavery; and yet he is the pro-Slavery candidate for the Presidency, and is supported by the slave-code, slave-trade, and Disunion party, as the only man prepared to do justice to the South upon the question of the everlasting nigger!

Now, gentlemen and members of the club, I am about through with the remarks I intended to submit to you on this occasion. Candor requires me, as the contest is rapidly drawing to a close, to admit that the chances are that Mr. Lincoln will be elected. If so, this entire Breckinridge party in the South will go in for a Southern Confederacy. If I am living,—and I hope I may be,—I shall stand by the Union as long as there are five States that adhere to it. I will say more: I will go out of the Confederacy if the rebellious party sustain itself. Nay, I will say still more: I will sustain Lincoln if he will go to work to put down

18

the great Southern mob that leads off in such a rebellion!

These are my sentiments, and these are my purposes; and I am no Abolitionist, but a Southern man. I expect to stand by this Union, and battle to sustain it, though Whiggery and Democracy, Slavery and Abolitionism, Southern rights and Northern wrongs, are all blown to the devil! I will never join in the outcry against the American Union in order to build up a corrupt Democratic party in the South, and to create offices in a new Government for an unprincipled pack of broken-down politicians, who have justly rendered themselves odious by stealing the public money. I may stand alone in the South; but I believe thousands and tens of thousands will stand by me, and, if need be, perish with me in the same cause.

I will conclude, fellow-citizens, by reading the following document, which ought to be published once a year in every newspaper in America, and read out as often from every pulpit in the land, that the real people may see *who* signed it, and *what* they pledged themselves to stand by:—

"The undersigned, members of the Thirty-First Congress of the United States, believing that a renewal of sectional controversy upon the subject of slavery would be both dangerous to the Union and destructive of its objects, and seeing no mode by which such controversy can be avoided except by a strict adherence to the settlement thereof effected by the Compromise acts passed at the last session of Congress, do hereby declare their intention to maintain the said settlement inviolate, and to resist all attempts to repeal or alter the acts aforesaid, unless by the general consent of the friends of the measure, and to remedy such evils, if any, as time and experience may develop.

"And for the purpose of making this resolution effective, they further declare that they will not support for office of President or Vice-President, or of Senator or of Representative in Congress, or as member of a State Legislature, any man, of whatever party, who is not known to be opposed to the disturbance of the settlement aforesaid, and to the renewal, in any form, of agitation upon the subject of slavery.

"Henry Clay,	H. A. Bullard,
Howell Cobb,	C. H. Williams,
C. S. Morehead,	T. S. Haymond,
William Duer,	J. Phillips Phœnix,
Robert L. Rose,	A. H. Sheppard,
H. S. Foot,	A. M. Schermerhorn,
William C. Dawson,	David Breck,
James Brooks,	John R. Thurman,
Thomas J. Rusk,	James L. Johnson,
Alexander H. Stephens,	D. A. Bokee,
Jeremiah Clemens,	J. B. Thompson,
Robert Toombs,	George R. Andrews,
James Cooper,	J. M. Anderson,
M. P. Gentry,	W. P. Mangum,
Thomas G. Pratt,	John B. Kerr,
Henry W. Hilliard,	Jeremiah Morton,
William M. Gwin,	J. P. Caldwell,
F. E. McLean,	R. I. Bowie,
Samuel Eliot,	Edmund Deberry,
A. G. Watkins,	E. C. Cabell,
David Outlaw,	Humphrey Marshall,
Alexander Evans,	Allen F. Owen."

My Last Interview with John Bell.

It will be seen from the foregoing speech that I was the zealous advocate of the Bell-and-Everett ticket in the late Presidential election. As the United States were then classed with England, France, and Russia as one of the four leading Powers of the age, so these two men were particularly referred to, on all occasions, and in all these countries, as ranking among the most illustrious and orthodox of American statesmen. There had scarcely been a debate in the American Congress, for thirty years, on any of the great and exciting topics of the day, in reference to which the country did not feel anxious to know where these two illustrious men stood.

For Colonel Bell I had battled faithfully for a quarter of a century, and adhered to his fortunes through evil and good report. Nay, I called a son after him, who is now in his twenty-second year. Imagine, then, my pain and mortification on being separated from Colonel Bell, who deserted the mild sway of the Federal Union he had so long and so ably defended, leaving the noble Everett and my humble self to battle on beneath the folds of the Star-Spangled Banner, as the only sacred shield of a common nationality!

After Colonel Bell went over to his old enemies and the enemies of his country, he performed a pilgrimage to Knoxville, with a view to cause the Union scales to fall from the eyes of his old friends. He got out a poster announcing a speech in the court-house. He sought an interview with a dozen of us, and he obtained that interview in Colonel Temple's law-office. He there made his weak argument, intended to convince us all of the error of our ways. It fell to my lot to make the Union reply; and I performed the task with great pain, but with great plainness of speech and fixedness of purpose. I told him that we would not only refuse to turn Secessionists, but that we must decline going to hear any man advocate the iniquitous cause of Secession, or who would associate with the vile men we found him in the company of, and who were prompting him to convert us from the error of our ways. We parted in tears, and have never met since. And if we never meet again to renew old friendships until we meet upon a Secession platform, we shall fix the period of our meeting to a period

"Which kings and prophets waited for,
And sought, but never found."

CHAPTER XV.

EAST TENNESSEE—POPULATION—FACE OF THE COUNTRY—CLIMATE, SOIL, AND PRODUCTIONS—RIVERS AND MINERALS—KNOXVILLE, DESCRIPTION THEREOF—THE "REGISTER" NEWSPAPER AND ITS DEGRADED EDITOR—RAILROADS AND APPROACHES TO EAST TENNESSEE—DESCRIPTION OF CUMBERLAND GAP—VOTING OUT OF THE UNION—EAST TENNESSEE LOYAL TO THE LAST!

EAST TENNESSEE—as loyal to this Government as any State in the Union—is composed of thirty large counties, and is really as separate and distinct from Middle and West Tennessee as any of the adjoining States are. It is a valley three hundred miles in length, and varying in width from fifty to seventy-five miles. It is separated from Kentucky, on the north, by the range of mountains known as Cumberland Mountains, extending westward and southwestward, and lying between the great valley of East Tennessee and the Cumberland River, one of the largest affluents—the Tennessee excepted—of the Ohio, rising among the mountains in the southeast portion of Kentucky. The Cumberland range of mountains belongs to the Appalachian chain, and extends the whole length of the great valley of East Tennessee. Over this range of mountains, through its dense groves and interminable laurel-thickets, the persecuted and oppressed Union men of East Tennessee have forced their way, travelling after night and lying up in daytime, with a view of joining the Federal army, until they are now (May, 1862) organizing the *Sixth Tennessee Regiment*, determined to fight back to their homes and families.

On the south, East Tennessee is separated from North Carolina and Georgia by the Chilhowee and Iron Mountains, and by the Alleghany Mountains, extending in a continuous chain from Virginia to Georgia and Alabama. This range of mountains forms a dividing-line between Eastern and Western Virginia, and makes East Tennessee and Southwestern Virginia one country, identical in interest, as they are one in soil, climate, and productions.

The population of East Tennessee partakes of the same parentage as that of Kentucky, the original settlers having been mostly from North Carolina and Virginia; and they are second to no people for manly frankness of character, courage, and loyalty to the Federal Government. There are fewer slaves in East Tennessee than in any other portion of the State of equal extent; and, as a general thing, the people are very much upon an equality as to their possessions.

The face of the country in East Tennessee is very agreeably diversified with mountain, hill, and plain, containing within its limits much fertility of soil, great beauty of scenery, and a delightfully temperate climate. The hills are wooded to their tops with every variety of timber, whilst on all the small rivers and large creeks there are embosomed delightful and fertile valleys of farming-lands, in a high state of cultivation. Many of the uplands are very level, and others, generally undulating, are very productive. I have resided there for more than thirty years, and have explored every one of the thirty counties. And if there lives a man, old or young, in East Tennessee who is more extensively acquainted with the inhabitants than I am, I have never made his acquaintance.

The climate of East Tennessee is mild. Considerable snow sometimes falls in the winter, which, however, is generally short, and does not allow of snow lying on the ground long. During the winter of 1861–2 there was but one light snow, and up to the time of my leaving (3d of March) there had not been a formation of ice to the thickness of half an inch! The summers are free from the intense heat of the Gulf States, and, as a consequence, many families come from the South to spend the summers at the valuable mineral springs, which are found in great abundance; and many of them are handsomely improved.

East Tennessee is not a cotton-growing country, but is favorable alone to grazing; and great numbers of live-stock—horses, mules, cattle, hogs, and sheep—are exported from thence to the Atlantic States. Indian corn and wheat are the great staples. Besides these, rye, oats, buckwheat, potatoes, (sweet and Irish,) wool, flax, and hay, are produced in great abundance. Apples and peaches, pears and plums, grow to great perfection. Maple-sugar is made of a fine quality, also superior butter and cheese. It is, in one word, the Switzerland of America; and I do not intend to be driven out of it by the more-than-savage beasts who now have it in possession.

The Holston River courses through the entire valley of East Tennessee, and is navigable for steamboats nine months in the year. Its tributaries above Knoxville are Pigeon, French Broad, Chucky, and Watauga Rivers. Below Knoxville, it receives Little River, Clinch, Hiawassee, and Tennessee, and at the confluence of this last stream loses its name, and is called the Tennessee River until its junction with the Ohio,—a distance of about seven hundred miles.

Gold has been found in considerable quantities, but the most abundant metallic minerals are iron, copper, zinc, and lead. Of the earthy minerals, coal of a superior quality is abundant in all the counties bordering on the Cumberland Mountains. There are also gypsum of a fine quality, beautiful varieties of marble, nitre, slate, and salt. The abundance of accessible iron-ore, bituminous coal, and water-power is beginning to attract the attention of capitalists. A railroad is in a forward state of construction, extending from Knoxville to the coal and iron banks at the foot of the Cumberland Mountains, and intended to connect with Kentucky and Cincinnati. Thirty miles of this road are graded, and a portion of the track is laid; and, but for this war and the blockade, it would have been in use to the foot of the mountain.

Knoxville, a flourishing city, the capital of Knox county, the great metropolis of East Tennessee, was the first seat of the State Government, where Governor Blount resided. It is beautifully situated, upon a succession of hills, on the right bank of Holston River, four miles below its confluence with the French Broad, *two hundred and sixty miles* from Nashville by railroad, and *two hundred* by the old stage-road. The town was laid out in 1794. It contains the State Asylum for the Deaf and Dumb, and is the seat of the University of East Tennessee, an institution chartered in 1807. It has a population of some six thousand, exhibits an aspect of increasing prosperity, and manufactures of various kinds are springing up in its vicinity. It has seven churches, and quite a number of stores, some of them very fine. It has three banks, and at present but *one* newspaper, and that a vile Secession journal, edited by a scoundrel, debauchee, and coward named *Sperry*, selected by a more unprincipled set of men than he is himself, because of his *adaptation* to the dirty work he is employed to do. He has really been choked down and flogged by as many as four or five different men of his own party. I seldom bestowed a notice upon him or his paper through my columns.

On the 31st of August I did publish the following notice of him:—

Sperry's Troubles Increasing.

The troubles of this poor devil, who conducts the *Register*, are multiplying on all hands, presenting a combination of shades and colors that no landscape or fresco painter, milliner or French costumer, can imitate. The fellow thinks himself badly treated by men of prominence from this and other States, visiting here, and not calling on him, while they visit the editor of the *Whig*. He complains that it is treating the Secessionists badly, and that it is an effort to get the *Whig* to supplant his miserable sheet. We wish to relieve his mind by assuring him that we are not a competitor of his. His paper is in nobody's way; it has but a limited circulation, and no character for any thing but lying,—whilst it is understood that its editor is a man of bad morals, bad associations, and the tool of the worst class of men in Knoxville. Indeed, the Secessionists speak in terms of unqualified disapprobation of his course, and regret that they have not a decent paper, in which the public can place confidence. Even the army-officers, or a portion of them, and the intelligent privates, denounce it for its tone and spirit in seeking to stir up strife whilst they are laboring to promote peace.

Decent men coming to the city *avoid*, rather than *seek*, the society and counsels of such a man. They here realize what Shakspeare meant when he called on "black spirits and white, blue spirits and gray, to mingle, ye that mingle may." They at once see that the degraded tool who fathers the slang prepared for him by men too cowardly to write over their own signatures is no associate for them. The fellow has even sunk below contempt, and in a career of six brief months gone into hateful obscurity. If he will take our advice, we will bring him into notice. Let him head a company of town-boys and small negroes,—put on a saffron-colored shirt, a yellow vest, straw-colored cap, a long-tailed coat figured and variegated generally with red, white, blue, black, green, yellow, orange, pink, cream, and straw, and many others unknown to Audubon's Ornithology or to Joseph's coat of many colors. Let him draw on a sash, belted, laced, and covered with buttons of brass, pewter, and lead. Let his pants be a deep red, with large iron knee-buckles, and long boots made of sheepskin, tanned with the wool on, and worn outside. Let him wear large wooden spurs, and a large tin sword. He must add to this an ornamental Turkish neck-tie, with a large gilt tassel hanging down in the centre, and some old negro's large brass breastpin. Let him wear a pair of green spectacles to hide his bad countenance, and style his company "Young America."

The Federal Government owes it to the loyal people of East Tennessee to send an army there and libe-

Robert B. Reynolds, the drunken Commissioner who committed Parson Brownlow to prison. (Page 295.)

rate that oppressed and down-trodden population. If it shall never accomplish any thing more, it ought at least, and at any cost of money and blood, to do that much. I have confidence in the Government doing this thing, and at no very distant day. When this is done, I desire to return to my family and former field of labor, and again edit and publish my paper.

It is the interest of the Government to take possession of that important field. The Rebel authorities have slaughtered several hundred thousand hogs there, and have a corresponding number of beef-cattle pickled up, and a quantity of wheat and flour on hand. The East Tennessee and Georgia Railroad extends from Knoxville to Chattanooga and Dalton, a distance of one hundred and thirty miles, and connects with Augusta, Montgomery, Memphis, and Nashville. Going east from Knoxville, the railroad extends to Lynchburg, and connects with Manassas, Richmond, Petersburg, and Norfolk; and from the beginning of this infamous rebellion this great line of railroad gave new impetus to the Rebel movements, pouring a stream of Secession fire into Virginia from the Cotton States. Indeed, it has been a matter of surprise that our army did not march upon East Tennessee long ago, capture Knoxville, and take possession of that great railroad. It was certainly owing to bad generalship in Kentucky, as there are several gaps through which the approach could be made. The Pound Gap is one, about a hundred miles east of Knoxville, and about opposite to Bristol, on the line between Virginia and Tennessee. Another gap is the one at Jim Town, about eighty miles northwest of Knoxville, and near where the celebrated battle of Fishing Creek was fought. After the fall of General Zollicoffer, and the disgraceful *run* made by the Rebel troops, one regiment of Federal troops could have taken and held Knoxville. And so certain were the Secession leaders that it would be done, that many of them packed up their effects and fled into Georgia.

Cumberland Gap—a very remarkable formation—is only sixty-five miles northeast of Knoxville, and only about forty miles from this great railroad. The mountain-range trends to the south, the road through the gap running nearly east-and-west. On the left of the road, looking from the Tennessee side, is a very high mountain,—I should say, more than two thousand feet above the plain,—terminating very abruptly at the gap, which is simply a depression, say about one thousand feet lower than the extreme high point. On the right of the gap the mountain rises about two hundred feet, and trends southeast, nearly four or five miles.

When I left home, the 3d of March, there were seven thousand troops there, under the command of Colonel Raines; and they, as I am informed, have been re-inforced, and are under the command of General E. Kirby Smith, late from the Potomac. But the Rebels stationed there all the fall and winter were undisciplined troops, and poorly armed with such squirrel-guns and shot-guns as were taken from the Union men. Their cannon are small, not equalling, by any means, those used by the Federal army. The position could be made very strong, but it is by no means impregnable, with men forced into the Rebel service from the Union ranks and unwilling to fight against the Stars and Stripes. The men living round about there, and for many miles up and down the valley, are on the side of the Union, and would flock to the standard of the Federal army as soon as they would appear in force.

The Federal army will cross there this spring or summer, and I shall not be at all surprised if the Rebels evacuate the place and fall back upon Knoxville. In that event, a stand and fight will be made at Knoxville.

When East Tennessee came to vote herself out of the Union, she showed her loyalty and did herself honor. The election was first held in February, under the proclamation of the Governor, and all voters were to write on their tickets *Convention* or *No Convention*, and if the Convention carried, the delegates chosen at the same time would assemble. For *No Convention* there were 70,000 votes cast as against 50,000, and but *three* Secessionists elected in the State.

The following is the vote of glorious EAST TENNESSEE:—

	Convention.	No Convention.
Anderson	137	1077
Bledsoe	190	630
Blount	450	1552
Bradley	242	1443
Campbell	71	870
Carter	55	1055
Claiborne	35	1030
Cocke	192	1332
Granger	158	1675
Greene	357	2648
Hamilton	445	1445
Hancock	100	746
Hawkins	422	1338
Jefferson	250	1999
Johnson	......	......
Knox	394	3167
Marion	108	751
McMinn	439	1457
Meigs	338	323
Monroe (in part)	685	1014
Morgan	......	......
Polk	117	1112
Rhea	79	573
Roane	67	1595
Scott	29	385
Sequatchie	50	200
Sevier	69	1243
Sullivan	1180	734
Washington	891	1353
	7550	34,000

Failing to call an election of delegates to Nashville by the people, and failing to get a Convention sanctioned, the Governor called an extra session of the Legislature; and that body, in violation of the expressed will of the people, declared an ordinance of separation on the 6th of May, submitting the questions of *separa-*

tion from the Federal Government and of *representation* in the Richmond Congress to be voted on by the people on the 8th day of June. By rushing Rebel bayonets into East Tennessee from the Cotton States, and by intimidating thousands and running rough-shod over others, the State was forced out of the Union, when a majority of her people were utterly averse to any such separation. Frauds were perpetrated at the ballot-box, timid men were kept from the polls, and thousands were allowed to vote who had no right to do so under the laws and Constitution of the State.

The vote of East Tennessee, on going out, was as follows:—

The Vote on the 8th of June.

(Official.)

EAST TENNESSEE.

	Sep.	Rep.	No Sep.	No Rep.
Anderson	97	97	1278	1278
Bledsoe	197	186	500	455
Blount	418	414	1766	1768
Bradley	507	505	1382	1380
Campbell	59	60	1000	1000
Carter	86	86	1343	1343
Claiborne	250	246	1243	1247
Cocke	518	517	1185	1185
Granger	586	582	1492	1489
Greene	744	738	2691	2702
Hamilton	854	837	1260	1271
Hancock	279	278	630	630
Hawkins	908	886	1460	1463
Jefferson	603	597	1987	1990
Johnson	111	111	787	786

	Sep.	Rep.	No Sep.	No Rep.
Knox	1226	1214	3196	3201
Marion	414	413	600	601
Meigs	481	478	267	268
McMinn	904	892	1144	1152
Monroe	1096	1089	774	775
Morgan	50	50	630	632
Polk	738	731	317	319
Rhea	360	336	202	217
Roane	454	436	1568	1580
Scott	19	19	521	521
Sequatchie	153	151	100	100
Sevier	60	60	1528	1528
Sullivan	1586	1576	627	637
Washington	1022	1016	1445	1444

For separation and representation at Richmond, East Tennessee gave 14,700 votes; and half of that number were Rebel troops, having no authority under the Constitution to vote at any election. For *no separation* and *no representation*,—the straight-out Union vote,—East Tennessee gave 33,000, or 18,300 of a majority, with at least 5000 quiet citizens deterred from coming out by threats of violence, and by the presence of drunken troops at the polls to insult them.

To aid in forcing the State out, the votes of *pretended* Tennesseeans were taken at the different military camps in and out of the State. Indeed, Governor Harris, in his proclamation on the 24th of June, records the following votes as official, and counts them on the side of Secession:—

VOTE IN CAMPS.

Camp Davis	506
Camp De Soto	15
Camp Duncan	111
Camp Jackson	622
Fort Harris	159
Fort Pickens	737
Fort Wright	3500
Harper's Ferry	575
Hermitage Camp	16
Vote in camps	6241

By such fraud and villainy as this, the great State of Tennessee was carried out of the Union. The loyal people of East Tennessee, to their great honor, had no lot or part in the work. The Union men of the State are now in the majority, and will have the State back or die in the last ditch!

CHAPTER XVI.

Candidate for Governor.

ON Saturday, the 23d of March, 1861, I issued thousands of copies of a circular declaring myself a candidate for the office of Governor of Tennessee. I give this document to the world, because it vindicates my *consistency* as a Union man, and because its doctrines will do to stand by.

I afterwards withdrew from the contest in favor of William H. Polk, a Middle-Tennesseean, who I supposed would have more strength in West Tennessee and be more likely to defeat Secession :—

To the People of Tennessee.

FELLOW-CITIZENS:—As there seems to be a tardiness on the part of aspiring men in the State to declare themselves candidates for the office of Governor at the ensuing August election, and as the people seem a little slow in moving in that direction, I take this method of informing you that I am a candidate for the office. I come before you upon my own responsibility, without solicitations from, or consultations with, the POLITICIANS of the State. To them I do not look for "aid and comfort," as they are aware that they can never control me, if in office, or use me to promote the objects of selfish cliques or factions. I look to the unbought and unterrified PEOPLE of the State to elect me, and as I purpose, if elected, to serve them and their interests only, I desire to be elected by their suffrages and influence. I have confidence in the real people of the State, and will bow to their decision as expressed through the ballot-box, without one word of complaint though that decision may be against me. I should despise myself if I could resort to any of the tricks of the demagogue to secure the votes of the honest yeomanry of the country,—such as arraying the poor against the rich, boasting of my humble origin, claiming my right to be elected upon sectional grounds or upon local issues, advocating a reduction of the salaries of public officers, and otherwise appealing to the passions and prejudices of the people. But I may be allowed to say that I have no wealth to make me prominent among the "upper tens." I have no long train of influential relatives to urge my claims. Losing my parents when a small boy, and being left without means, I went to the trade of the *house-carpenter*, and, after acquiring a knowledge of the "profession," I worked for wages long enough to enable me to acquire an "old field-school English education," adding to my store of knowledge in after-years as best I could. Whilst I do not think I ought to be supported *because of these things,* I do not think that any class of my fellow-countrymen ought to vote against me on this account. I ask for the votes of the people of Tennessee for the high and responsible office of Governor, only on account of the *political principles* I claim to represent. These I will, in brief, lay before the public, concealing nothing that ought to be made known.

1. It may be proper for me, as briefly as possible, to point out the circumstances which existed when this Confederacy and Constitution were formed. There exists now no question, political or otherwise, that did not then exist; and hence what is alleged to be the cause of the present attempt at the dissolution of this Government is a sheer fabrication, founded upon political chicanery, despotism, folly, and personal ambition. When the Constitution of the United States was formed, and was sought to be ratified by the various States which then composed the colonies, afterwards called the United States of America, there existed precisely the same elements, and many more subjects of diverse opinion and controversy than now. These were, first, the despotism and tyranny of monarchical power, that refused to grant to the colonies their just rights, for which in 1776 these united colonies waged successful war against Great Britain. *Afterwards,* for the purpose of mutual protection against invasion, it was deemed advisable to form a Confederacy,—that Confederacy to represent the *people* of the United States, and not, as is con-

tended by Secessionists, the "Sovereign States of America." Our fathers, declaring their independence, threw off the oppression of the mother-country, and summed up their grievances as "TAXATION WITHOUT REPRESENTATION." We have again in our midst a *bogus* form of Government, forced upon the Cotton States by an organized band of revolutionists, whose very foundation is that of "taxation without representation."

2. In consequence of diversity of climate, interests, and population, it was necessary to have certain *sectional* lines. Those lines already existed to a certain extent; and therefore it was deemed advisable to retain them, to prevent confusion. But the Constitution was formed by the *people* to govern the *people,* and no single individual State was called upon, as a separate "sovereignty," to sign or ratify that Constitution, but the representatives of each State were called upon to ratify it for the *people* of that State. Therefore it was that not in one, nor two, but many years of debate and controversy, as well as of amendments and substitutes, the Constitution was adopted and ratified by all the States of the then existing Union. No State, therefore, belonging to the compact, has a right to withdraw without *consulting* with the other members. Originally, the States coming in were obliged to consult their *sectional* interests; they were obliged to call in question the various political and social differences then existing;

they were obliged to question peculiar rights, to touch upon delicate points that then, more than now, bore upon the interests, welfare, and prosperity of the Union. And all who are at all acquainted with the history of our Government know that the hobby then is the bone of contention now among politicians; that it constituted not a sectional or State policy, strictly speaking, but a NATIONAL FACT; that it was considered and reconsidered; that concession after concession, plan after plan, was sought for, in order to prevent any future difficulty upon this eternal question of African slavery. I take occasion to assert that the question has not changed its relation to the General Government since then, and that, while the people of the North, then possessing slavery, desired that it should be abolished, the South clearly and distinctly understood that it was to continue here. Therefore it was made a constitutional fact that slavery should exist in every State of the Union, if the *people* of each State should so decide; and if the people of one or more States decided that it was against their interests to hold slaves, slavery should be abolished,—where not abolished, it should be protected and sustained under the Constitution. And it is known to every political historian that the patriots who formed the Constitution agreed in *secret session*, deliberating upon the welfare of the nation, that it was important to prevent any future disquiet or discussion upon the Slavery question, and that therefore it should be left as a matter of purely *sectional* interest, with which the General Government has nothing to do and for which it would not be responsible, save that it would protect the interests of all the States choosing to adhere to slavery.

3. It was the sworn duty of James Buchanan to suppress this rebellion when it first appeared, and before it grew up into its present gigantic proportions. Instead of doing his duty, he actually sat in converse with the TRAITORS engaged in the TREASON, received them into his presence, held counsel with them, and treated them with deference, instead of issuing an order for their arrest. He even consulted his Attorney-General as to the constitutionality of what was going on. An American President asks if it is constitutional to suppress rebellion or treason,—if it is constitutional to hang a traitor,—when the very spirit as well as the letter of the Constitution is death to all treason! What I advocate is this: that our Government execute its laws. If a million of lives are sacrificed, the other twenty-nine millions will have the benefits of freedom. And to the people of Tennessee I would say, in the name of your Constitution, in the name of your country, in the name of your forefathers, in the name of your children, your honors, your free institutions, I conjure you, give no ear to that insidious voice of treason which says peaceable secession will put an end to our troubles. In the same breath, I would say to the people of the

North, repeal those acts which are wrong and unconstitutional. The nation requires it; your Government requires it; children unborn, who are to represent you in the future, urge it; all your future welfare and glory among men require it; and the dictates of your holy religion require it.

4. I stand where I did in the late Presidential contest, and never can stand anywhere else; that is to say, upon the platform of the "UNION, THE CONSTITUTION, AND THE ENFORCEMENT OF THE LAWS." I do not believe that the election of Lincoln affords any sort of pretext for dissolving this Union; I deny the right of secession; I regard the States that have gone out of the Union as guilty of TREASON; and I view the leaders of the Secession party as TRAITORS. If elected Governor, I would refuse to convene the Legislature or take any step that would advance the cause of Secession, and treat them as men guilty of breaches of good faith and common honesty.

5. I endorse the Inaugural Address of Lincoln, and I commend it for its temperance and conservatism and for its firm nationality of sentiment. From it I infer that we shall have no war *unless* it be forced upon the country by the Seceding States. If Lincoln should attempt to inaugurate oppressive and unconstitutional measures, and Congress shall sanction or adopt these measures, either in reference to the Slavery question or any other subject, we of the South should await the

decision of the Supreme Court, and if the Executive, Legislative, and Judicial departments of the Government all sanction such iniquitous measures and unite in attempts to carry them out, then, and in that case, I would advocate resistance "at all hazards and to the last extremity." But, until this is apparent, it is the duty of this patriotic State to stand firm, and not entangle herself with the extremes of either the North or South, and to act upon the sound maxim that *Disunion* is not a remedy for any wrongs whatever.

6. The leaders in this movement to dissolve this Union, the great citadel of our liberties, and the depository of the hopes of the human race, will go down to their graves without any halo of glory surrounding their brows, while on their heads will be gathered the hissing curses of all generations, horrible as the forked-tongued snakes of Medusa. Their ghosts will stand on the highest and blackest eminence of infamy, the detestation of mankind. Having met a traitor's death, they will each and all fill a traitor's grave, over which there will be no requiem but the groans of the oppressed and the execrations of the good. Their monuments will be of human bones upon foundations slippery with human blood. However high may have been their elevation in office, their fall will be like that of Lucifer. And whilst from their bad eminence they shall turn from beholding the glories of that Constitution and Union against which they rebelled in the year

of grace 1861, to survey the barren waste, the boundless and bottomless pits, of Secession, they will exclaim, like Lucifer, their "illustrious predecessor,"—

> "Farewell, happy fields! where joy forever dwells!
> Hail, horrors! hail, infernal world! and thou,
> Profoundest hell! receive thy new possessor!"

7. I claim to have had no lot or part in bringing upon the country the terrible crisis that is now upon us. The late Chief Magistrate, James Buchanan, was inaugurated into office under auspices of general peace and prosperity,—strong in the confidence of a mighty, united, and triumphant Democracy. Possessed of every aid and inducement to an honest, a patriotic, a brilliant, and a vigorous and successful administration of the Government, he has retired from power amid general execration and disgrace, carrying into his retirement the official brand of public condemnation upon his forehead, and leaving to history, as the only trophies of his administration, the national treasury depleted, the country loaded with an incubus of debt, that great national and conservative party, to whose generous and confiding suffrages he owes all his fortunes, demoralized and dismembered, the perpetuity of the republic a doubtful and an appalling problem, and his own name a by-word of infamy and derision throughout the civilized world. And in this State the men are in power, wielding its patronage, who travelled all over the State defending this corrupt Administration after

the proof of its infamy was before the world, both clear and unquestionable.

The policy of the new Administration is not yet fully developed. Taking the nomination of that great and good man, Mr. Crittenden, to the Supreme Court as an example, it has manifested thus far only conservative tendencies, and it has afforded proof that it does not seek to abolitionize the Judiciary. It would be more reasonable, more prudent, and infinitely safer for the people of the South patiently to await the developments of the policy of the new Administration, than to fly from the ills they have to others that they know not of, and which are already creating so much discontent in the new Confederacy. That I may be fully understood, I repeat that I am for the Union as it came to us from our fathers,—the most glorious legacy of modern times. I believe it ought to be preserved. It should be maintained by *peaceable* means,—and this can be done; but if the property belonging to the General Government and now in its possession, and costing the common people of all the States millions of dollars, cannot be held except by force and against the assaults of the Rebels going out of the Union, I say, boldly, let the gates of the temple of Janus open; let a national blow be given which will resound—like the shouts of Michael's host hurling treason over the ramparts of heaven—through all the avenues of unrecorded time.

8. I protest against a surrender of the navigation of

the Mississippi River, and would not, if elected to the office of Governor, agree to relinquish the right Tennessee has to the free navigation of that great "inland sea," if even the General Government should basely surrender its rights and the rights of the several Western and Northwestern States. Nor am I willing to recognize the act of Secession on the part of Florida, Louisiana, and Texas in any other light than that of *dishonesty* and *treason*, meriting the scorn and contempt of the civilized world. I say this because of the vast amount of money paid by our Government, to say nothing of the sacrifice of human life, for the exclusive benefit of these three States. Louisiana, (purchased of France,) $15,000,000; interest paid, $8,385,353; Florida, (purchased of Spain,) $5,000,000; interest paid, $1,430,000; Texas, (boundary,) $10,000,000; Texas, (for indemnity,) $10,000,000; Texas, (for creditors, last Congress,) $7,750,000; Indian expenses of all kinds, $5,000,000; to purchase navy, pay troops, $5,000,000; all other expenditures, $3,000,000; Mexican War, $217,175,575; soldiers' pensions and bounty-lands, $100,000,000; Florida War, $100,000,000; soldiers' pensions, $7,000,000; to remove Indians, $5,000,000; paid by treaty for New Mexico, $15,000,000; paid to extinguish Indian titles, $100,000,000; paid to Georgia, $3,082,000; total cost, $617,822,928.

Ought these three rebellious States to be tolerated in their mad schemes of plunder and treason, after costing the people of the other States *six hundred and eighteen millions of dollars?* I say, No; and, as the Executive of this State, I could never do an act that would in the remotest degree tolerate this wholesale robbery.

9. The President of the new Confederacy has confined his Cabinet appointments to the old Democratic party,—appointing none but Breckinridge Disunionists, although the Bell and Douglas men were a majority in some of their States. The provisional Government is, therefore, a revival of corrupt Southern Democracy, and is a lawless mob banded together for the purpose of perpetuating that exploded, hateful, and God-forsaken organization. It is not *a government of the people,* and it will not long be tolerated by the people. The people, *who ought to be the source of power,* have been refused the privilege of passing upon any one of their ordinances of Secession, and now they are to be refused the privilege of passing upon their Constitution. I would sooner go into the worst form of European monarchy than into this *bogus* Confederacy. And if elected Governor of this State, I will oppose, to the bitter end, any fellowship with such Confederacy by the State of Tennessee.

10. I take the ground steadfastly to support the General Government in the exercise of every constitutional power, to enforce the execution of the Federal laws, and to sustain in all their integrity the Constitu-

tion and the Union. In other words, I do not propose to sit quietly by and peacefully surrender our country, ourselves, our children, our peace and happiness, to the wicked schemes of *treason*. We hear much said about "coercing" a State, and about the tramp of hostile armies to conquer and subdue a State Government. Coercion of a State is an adroit form of expression, coined in the school of Secession to give dignity to treason. The American Constitution nowhere contemplates such a thing as war upon a State, either by the General Government or by a foreign Power. If a foreign nation attack or invade any State of the Union, it is not, in the theory of the Constitution or of international law, an act of war upon the State, but upon our General Government. Nor does the Constitution, operating as it does only upon individuals, recognize such a thing as war against the Government by a State, or an association of States. It treats resistance to its authority as *rebellion*, and those who join in such resistance as a MOB; and when any number of its own citizens band together for treasonable purposes, and levy war upon the General Government, it holds them individually responsible, and hangs them as traitors to this country. The founders of the Government avowed that it afforded the needful physical means to execute its powers. History gives us memorable examples of the use of those means for their purpose.

I repeat that the word "coercion" is one in very common use in these days, and it is very offensive to all advocates of Disunion. Like many other *catch*-words, it serves a purpose. Any thing looking to the enforcement of the laws, or the preservation of the public property in seceded States, or States about to secede, is called *coercion,* and the honest and confiding people are warned against it as a fearful despotism! This *trick,* like every thing else, will, in some quarters, serve its purpose. I deny the right of any State or number of States to secede, and I insist upon it that the seceded States, one and all, are *constitutionally* as much in the Union as they were six months ago. While laws exist in reference to them, it is the duty of the Government to enforce them. If this cannot or ought not to be done, why, let them be repealed. This the public good and the national honor alike require. A State cannot be *coerced,* but *individuals* in it can, and *ought* to be, who violate the laws and plot treason.

And although I look upon the withdrawal of the troops from Fort Sumter as an act of humiliation on the part of the Government, I approve the act, under all the circumstances which surround us, and I consider that it removes all danger of civil war. It is a master-stroke of policy, and by it the rabid Disunionists have been disarmed, and deprived of all their thunder,—leaving them nothing to cavil at, nothing to attack, nothing over which they can pretend to get in a passion. While this evacuation of Fort Sumter removes all danger of immediate collision, it will disabuse the minds of deluded Southerners as to the alleged aggressive character of the Administration, and will do more than all that has been proposed towards suppressing Disunion, and recalling the masses of our countrymen in the South to their sober senses, and to their rightful allegiance to the Union and the Constitution, and the Stars and Stripes by which they are represented. Every man, woman, and child, in every locality of our once happy land, should devoutly labor for the peaceful solution of our unfortunate political difficulties. With peace, we may anticipate happiness and plenty; with war, crime, poverty, wretchedness, weeping, lamentation, and sorrow all over the land.

11. As it regards State policy, I am the advocate of establishing a branch of the penitentiary in the Western District, and another in East Tennessee. The cost of building to the State would be saved in twenty-five years in the single item of conveying the convicts to prison. Besides this, it would open up a cash-market to the citizens in each end of the State for provisions to sustain, and raw material to keep, the convicts employed in manufacturing,—such as lumber, marble, iron, leather, &c. This would furnish employment, and cash wages, to quite a number of mechanics in each division of our State; and, as there are several salaried offices in each, it would distribute the patronage of the State in her three natural divisions.

12. The Governor has the control of a heavy patronage in the railroads and banks of the State; and this is all now in the hands of Secessionists, who must be swept from office, or the public interests will suffer, and the State treasury will bleed at every pore, as it has been doing in several of the banks! It would be my duty, if elected, to turn these men out; and I would take the greatest pleasure in removing them. Neither the bank of the State, nor any of its *dozen* branches, are under the control of farmers, mechanics, and laboring-men; but they are, each and all, controlled by political partisan leaders, county-court lawyers, and street-loafers. If I am elected, the iniquitous reign of these pampered bank-officers and recipients of bank-favors is at an end!

The condition of the Bank of Tennessee and branches, officially set forth at Nashville on the 1st instant, shows that they have bills and notes in suit amounting to $822,224 12. Here is a million of the people's money squandered; and this showing does not include what the politicians and partisans have, upon which, from considerations of *favoritism*, no suits have been instituted! The same showing sets forth that they hold in real estate $246,863 58. This must prove a ruinous loss to the people. They show of notes discounted $2,497,829 90. This is in the hands of *one party*, as a general thing.

In most of these branch banks, men have been refused discounts, when they have presented well-endorsed paper, on account of their politics, although the State has recently declared against the politics of these same bank-officers by a majority of SEVENTY THOUSAND VOTES! Thus the banks of the people are used against their owners by a mere faction who have them in charge. The Secessionists also have the arms of the State in their possession, distributed by the present Governor.

The Disunionists of Tennessee ought to, and I suppose will, long remember the ever-memorable 9th of February, 1861. On that day the freemen of the State were called upon to vote for and against a Convention, for and against Disunion. The vote stood thus, in eighty-one counties in the State:—

No Convention	69,675
Convention	57,798
Majority against Convention	11,877

This was a decided vote against the first step of the Disunionists to drag Tennessee into a detestable Confederacy, and out from under the protection of the Stars and Stripes. But when the people came to elect delegates, the Disunionists received a majority in only *four* counties, the vote footing up thus:—

Union	88,803
Disunion	24,749

Thus the Union party received a majority, after a thorough canvass, of 64,054 in the State, with six other counties to hear from, which will increase the majority to 70,000. Never was such a victory achieved in any State! Ought a *faction*, therefore, representing twenty-five thousand out of one hundred and twenty thousand votes polled, to hold the offices of the State and control her patronage, when that faction is seeking to destroy the Government? I say, most emphatically, No! And if the people think proper to elect me, I will see that they cease to control the patronage of the State.

13. I am frank to confess that I desire the position on account of its honor, and as a means of rebuking my numerous Southern calumniators, who are unrelenting in their abusive war upon me because of my Union sentiments and of my opposition to their treason. I shall, of course, if elected, hope to serve the interests of the people of the whole State, irrespective of parties. But, not being rich, I would like to fill the office for two years, for the sake of the THREE THOUSAND DOLLARS PER ANNUM. Candor requires these avowals.

14. If voted for, and elected, it must be done without my canvassing the State, or speaking to the people otherwise than through a circular. Though my general health is good, and constantly improving, I have suffered for two years past from *bronchitis*, or a disease of the throat, rendering it impossible for me to

speak loud enough to be heard ten steps. Now that I am able to speak in moderation for one hour, I dare not do this more than once in a week; and I would fear to do even this many weeks in succession. The people of the State know me, and they know my politics. I have edited a WHIG paper in East Tennessee for the last twenty-two years. I still edit that paper, and it circulates in every county in the State, and there can really be no necessity for my canvassing.

The demand made upon the standard-bearer in this State, for the last quarter of a century, of all parties, to canvass the whole State, at an outlay of several hundred dollars, and an amount of labor and fatigue ruinous to the constitution, has caused many of our best men to decline the position of candidate for Governor, and to remain in private life. The present is a suitable time to abandon the practice of stumping the State; and I propose to lead the way in this *reform.* If any candidate, of any party, running in opposition to me, shall think proper to arraign me upon *personalities*, and to *denounce* me in my absence, and attribute my declining to canvass the State to *cowardice*, I will make one appointment to meet him at some prominent point, and, from the same stand, meet his assaults with *personalities* and *denunciations*, publish my speech to the world, distribute it over the State, and let the people settle the dispute as to personal courage.

15. If the real people, who constitute the great Union party in the State, shall prefer some other candidate to me, and shall make that fact known by a distinct and legitimate expression of their will, uninfluenced by leaders and wire-workers, I will not be the man to disturb the harmony of the Union organization: I will at once fall into line, and enter most heartily into the support of their choice,—*provided*, always, that the standard-bearer avows *substantially* the doctrines I have herein enunciated. A time-serving man, and a trimmer, cannot get my support, though he run as the representative of the principles of the great Union party and succeed in obtaining the nomination by a State Convention. The progressive exigencies of our country imperatively demand of a man aspiring to an office of such honor and trust, that he *show his hand in unmistakable terms!*

In this I do not mean to dictate to the party or their candidate their political creed, or to set up my standard as one of political perfection. I simply mean to say that a candidate falling short in the political articles of faith I enunciate cannot receive my vote; though, if nominated, I will not make war upon him, or give him any factious opposition. And this circular, in lieu of the hastily-sketched address I put forth last week, is the PLATFORM upon which I propose to run this race; and if I have not clearly defined my position, it is because I am not capable of expressing my opinions.

16. From the press of the State I ask that courtesy and consideration which it is accustomed to extend to new candidates for popular favor,—that of copying this circular entire; each paper reserving to itself the universally conceded right to condemn each and every part. Such papers as do not think proper to yield so much of their space to my service will do me the simple act of justice not to give garbled extracts and in that way misrepresent my sentiments.

I have the honor to be,

Very respectfully, &c.,

W. G. Brownlow.

March 23, 1861.

CHAPTER XVII.

EXHORTING THE SECESSION LEADERS TO VOLUNTEER—GOVERNOR HARRIS CALLS FOR THIRTY THOUSAND VOLUNTEERS—THE BRAVE SECESSIONISTS TRY TO ENLIST UNION MEN—TAKE OFFENCE AT OUR IRONICAL ARTICLES, AND STOP OUR PUBLICATION—OUR FAREWELL ADDRESS TO OUR PATRONS.

THE Secession leaders in East Tennessee refusing to turn out as soldiers, or to let their sons turn out, I called upon them through my paper, and *tauntingly* and *ironically* called upon them to volunteer. These articles, short and to the point, exasperated them, and they had my paper suppressed immediately thereafter. I give these articles now entire, believing they will prove both refreshing and instructive:—

To Arms! To Arms! Ye Brave!!

Come, Tennesseeans! ye who are the advocates of Southern rights, for separation and for Disunion,—ye who have lost your rights, and feel willing to uphold the glorious flag of the South in opposition to the Hessians arrayed under the despot Lincoln,—come to your country's rescue! Our gallant Governor, who led off in this State in the praiseworthy object of breaking up the old rickety Government in the hands of the Black Republicans, calls for thirty thousand volunteers, in addition to the fifty-five thousand already in the field. Shall we have them? If they do not volunteer, we shall have our State disgraced by a *draft*, and then we must go under compulsion. Come, gentlemen! Many of you have promised that "when it becomes necessary" you will turn out. That time has come, and the *necessity* is upon us. Let us show our *faith* by our *works*. We have talked long and loud about fighting the Union-shriekers and the Vandal hordes under the despot Lincoln. Now we have an opening. Some of us have even said we were willing for our sons to turn out and fight Union men. We have a chance at a terrible array of Unionists in Kentucky: let us volunteer, and General Sidney Johnston will either lead us on to victory, or something else! Come, ye braves, turn out, and let the world see that you are in earnest in making war upon the enemies of the South! Many of you have made big speeches in favor of the war; not a few of you have sought to sell the army supplies; and thousands of you are willing to stoop to fill the *offices* for the salaries they pay, and you have been so patriotic as to try to get your sons and other relations into offices. Some of you have *hired yourselves out as spies, under-strappers,* and *tools* in the glorious cause, at two to four dollars per day. Come, now, enter the ranks, as there is more honor in serving as a private. Come, gentlemen, *do* come, we insist, and enter the army as volunteers. You will feel bad when *drafted*, and pointed out as one who had to be *driven* into the service of your country! Let these Union traitors submit to the draft, but let us who are true Southern men *volunteer*. Any of us are willing to be judges, attorneys, clerks, Senators, Congressmen, and camp-followers for *pay*, when out of danger; but who of us are willing to shoulder our knapsacks and muskets and meet the Hessians? Come, gentlemen: the eyes of the people are upon you, and they want to see if you will pitch in. This is a good opening!

Knoxville Whig, Oct. 12, 1861.

Who will Volunteer?

We hope that our Secession neighbors will not become vexed at us for urging them to the discharge of a most serious obligation. The Governor of their choice, who has led the way in precipitating this State into rebellion, has called for an addition of thirty thousand volunteers. The men who ought to lead the way, who have been most noisy in the defence of a Southern Confederacy and of a war for independence, stand back, refuse to move a peg, and even allow those who have entered the army to come from the field of battle, where their services are actually needed, to raise companies. This is a shame! We have not less than a half-dozen gentlemen in this town, besides some in the county, who are willing to serve as members of the Confederate Congress; but not one of them proposes to raise a company or regiment, or even to serve as a private in the grand army of the South, struggling for independence! These men, moreover, are in comfortable circumstances, and could leave their families enough to live on. Not so with the poor laborers and mechanics they are urging to turn out. Their wives and children during a hard winter would be obliged to suffer.

We have several citizens who have actually been appointed to offices by the Confederate Government—say *four* of them—in this town, civil offices, that pay good salaries. Now, if these will lay aside their offices and enter the army, we shall in all time to come give them credit for a proper amount of patriotism. Let them undergo the privations of camp-life and the dangers and exposures of the battle-field, and, our word for it, the people of all parties will say they are in earnest. What do you say, gentlemen,—you who hold offices, and you who are seeking offices? Let the strife and struggle for the accumulation of fortunes and posts of honor subside until this war is brought to an end. Let us show our "*faith* by our *works;*" let us moderate our desires to make money and to fill positions of honor removed from all danger, and contribute to the general weal by the *example* of entering the service. Our ostentatious display of large subscriptions to the cause will make no lasting impression in our favor, as long as we refuse to submit to personal exposures where armies meet.

Come, gentlemen; we must insist upon your entering the service, and upon your doing it *now*. Hundreds are standing off to see if you will make good your promise to turn out "*whenever it became necessary*." It is necessary now, and the call is made from head-quarters. If your section is not more prompt, not a single regiment will be made up under this last call, and a *draft* will be resorted to, which the whole South will regard as a disgrace to the "Volunteer State."

Knoxville Whig, Oct. 19, 1861.

Closing the Knoxville Whig.

This issue of the *Whig* must necessarily be the last for some time to come: I am unable to say how long. The Confederate authorities have determined upon my arrest, and I am to be indicted before the Grand Jury of the Confederate Court, which commenced its session in Nashville on Monday last. I would have awaited the indictment and arrest before announcing the remarkable event to the world, but, as I only publish a weekly paper, my hurried removal to Nashville would deprive me of the privilege of saying to my subscribers what is alike due to myself and them. I have the fact of my indictment and consequent arrest having been agreed upon for this week, from distinguished citizens, legislators, and lawyers at Nashville, of both parties. Gentlemen of high positions, and members of the Secession party, say that the indictment will be made because of "some treasonable articles in late numbers of the *Whig*." I have reproduced those two "treasonable articles" on the first page of this issue, that the unbiased people of the country may "read, mark, learn, and inwardly digest" the treason. They relate to the culpable remissness of these Knoxville leaders in failing to volunteer in the cause of the Confederacy.

According to the usages of the court, as heretofore established, I presume I could go free, by taking the oath these authorities are administering to other Union men; but my settled purpose is not to do any such thing. I can doubtless be allowed my personal liberty, by entering into bonds to keep the peace and to demean myself toward the leaders of Secession in Knoxville, who have been seeking to have me assassinated all summer and fall, as they desire me to do; for this is really the import of the thing, and one of the leading objects sought to be attained. Although I could give a bond for my good behavior, for one hundred thousand dollars, signed by fifty as good men as the county affords, I shall obstinately refuse to do even that; and if such a bond be drawn up and signed by others, I will render it null and void by refusing to sign it. In default of both, I expect to go to jail, and I am ready to start upon one moment's warning. Not only so, but there I am prepared to lie in solitary confinement until I waste away because of imprisonment or die from old age. Stimulated by a consciousness of innocent uprightness, I will submit to imprisonment for life, or die at the end of a rope, before I will make any humiliating concession to any power on earth!

I have committed no offence. I have not shouldered arms against the Confederate Government, or the State, or encouraged others to do so. I have discouraged rebellion, publicly and privately. I have not assumed a hostile attitude toward the civil or military authorities of this new Government. But I have committed grave, and, I really fear, unpardonable offences. I have refused to make war upon the Government of the United States; I have refused to publish to the world false and exaggerated accounts of the several engagements had between the contending armies; I have refused to write out and publish false versions of the origin of this war, and of the breaking up of the best Government the world ever knew; and all this I will continue to do, if it cost me my life. Nay, when I agree to do such things, may a righteous God palsy my right arm, and may the earth open and close in upon me forever!

The real object of my arrest and contemplated imprisonment is to dry up, break down, silence, and destroy the last and only Union paper left in the eleven seceded States, and thereby to keep from the people of East Tennessee the facts which are daily transpiring in the country. After the Hon. Jeff Davis had stated in Richmond, in a conversation relative to my paper, that he would not live in a Government that did not tolerate freedom of the press,—after the judges, attorneys, jurors, and all others filling positions of honor or trust under the "permanent Constitution," which guarantees *freedom of the press*,—and after the entire press of the South had come down in their thunder tones upon the Federal Government for suppressing the Louisville *Courier* and the New York *Day-Book*, and other Secession journals,—I did expect the utmost liberty to be allowed to one small sheet, whose errors could be combated by the entire Southern press! It is not enough that my paper has been denied a circulation through the ordinary channels of conveyance in the country, but it must be discontinued altogether, or its editor must write and select only such articles as meet the approval of a pack of scoundrels in Knoxville, when their superiors in all the qualities that adorn human nature are in the penitentiary of our State! And this is the boasted liberty of the press in the Southern Confederacy!

I shall in no degree feel humbled by being cast into prison, whenever it is the will and pleasure of this august Government to put me there; but, on the contrary, I shall feel proud of my confinement. I shall go to jail—as John Rodgers went to the stake—for my *principles*. I shall go, because I have failed to recognize the hand of God in the work of breaking up the American Government, and the inauguration of the most wicked, cruel, unnatural, and uncalled-for war

District Attorney J. C. Ramsey (the man who swore out the warrant for the arrest of Parson Brownlow) drummed out of Zollicoffer's camp. (Page 302.)

ever recorded in history. I go, because I have refused to laud to the skies the acts of tyranny, usurpation, and oppression inflicted upon the people of East Tennessee for their devotion to the Constitution and laws of the Government handed down to them by their fathers, and the liberties secured to them by a war of seven long years of gloom, poverty, and trial! I repeat, I am proud of my position and of my principles, and shall leave them to my children as a legacy far more valuable than a princely fortune, had I the latter to bestow!

With me life has lost some of its energy: having passed six annual posts on the western slope of half a century, something of the fire of youth is exhausted; but I stand forth with the eloquence and energy of right to sustain and stimulate me in the maintenance of my principles. I am encouraged to firmness when I look back to the fate of Him "whose power was righteousness," while the infuriated mob cried out, "Crucify him! crucify him!"

I owe to my numerous list of subscribers the filling out of their respective terms for which they have made advance payments, and, if circumstances ever place it in my power to discharge these obligations, I will do it most certainly. But if I am denied the liberty of doing so, they must regard their small losses as so many contributions to the cause in which I have fallen. I feel that I can with confidence rely upon the magnanimity and forbearance of my patrons under this state of things. They will bear me witness that I have held out as long as I am allowed to, and that I have yielded to a military despotism that I could not avert the horrors of or successfully oppose.

I will only say, in conclusion,—for I am not allowed the privilege to write,—that the people of this country have been unaccustomed to such wrongs; they can yet scarcely realize them. They are astounded for the time-being with the quick succession of outrages that have come upon them, and they stand horror-stricken, like men expecting ruin and annihilation. I may not live to see the day, but thousands of my readers will, when the people of this once prosperous country will see that they are marching by "double-quick time" from freedom to bondage. They will then look these wanton outrages upon right and liberty full in the face, and my prediction is that they will "stir the stones of Rome to rise and mutiny." Wrongs less wanton and outrageous precipitated the French Revolution. Citizens cast into dungeons without charges of crime against them, and without the formalities of a trial by jury; private property confiscated at the beck of those in power; the press humbled, muzzled, and suppressed, or prostituted to serve the ends of tyranny! The crimes of Louis XVI. fell short of all this, and yet he lost his head! The people of this country, down-trodden and oppressed, still have the resolution of their illustrious forefathers, who asserted their rights at Lexington and Bunker Hill!

Exchanging, with proud satisfaction, the editorial chair and the sweet endearments of home for a cell in the prison or the lot of an exile,

I have the honor to be, &c.,

WILLIAM G. BROWNLOW,

Editor of the Knoxville Whig.

Knoxville Whig, Oct. 24, 1861.

CHAPTER XVIII.

GENERAL ZOLLICOFFER'S CORRESPONDENCE—HIGHLY IMPORTANT REVELATIONS MADE BY THE REBEL LEADERS—UNION FEELING IN EAST TENNESSEE—THE PEOPLE OF EAST TENNESSEE TO BE CRUSHED OUT.

A LARGE mass of correspondence was found in General Zollicoffer's camp after his army was routed and his head-quarters were captured, portions of which contain important admissions as to the prevalence and extent of the Union feeling in East Tennessee. I have found this correspondence since I came North, and I desire to have it preserved in a permanent form, and to see that it gets back into East Tennessee, that the Union men there, and their children after them, may see the signatures, and *hold the guilty and murderous authors in everlasting remembrance!*

I am sorry to find in this correspondence letters from General Zollicoffer breathing the spirit that his do, and giving the advice he did. It only proves that when the disease of Secession takes hold of a man, he is at once given over to hardness of heart and reprobacy of mind! From the turn-coat Methodist *Hopkins*, the pious Presbyterian elder *C. Wallace*, and the *Parson Colonel Wood,* I was prepared to hear all that they have said. These men are the regular descendants of the families of *Baron Munchausen, Lemuel Gulliver,* and *Captain Riley,* and rank among the first families in "Dixie," combining all the marvellous faculties of their ancestry. The dark tide, turbid as the waves of hell, that has engulfed and swept over every thing South for the last twelve months, looms up in this rich and racy correspondence; and none need wonder that it should have carried with it a venal press and a debauched and time-serving *pulpit.* When preachers, elders, and class-leaders write out such letters and dispatches and engage in such work, what could we expect but that the watchmen on the walls of Zion would turn active traitors, and dwindle down to "dumb dogs who would not bark"?

This correspondence suggests several important facts; and I must remind the reader of them, to secure an attentive perusal of the letters.

First. That an overwhelming number of the East Tennesseeans were devoted to the Union, and intended to die by it. This is true; and I am proud to have it in my power to say that this Union sentiment has never given way in the least degree.

Second. That the Rebel leaders were resolved to subjugate them at the point of the bayonet, and have, ever since the date of these letters, been executing their hellish plans, thus deliberately agreed upon!

Third. That all the Union men were to be *disarmed,* and their property used to carry on the war. This thieving resolve they have carried out in good faith, even doing more and going further than they bargained for!

Fourth. That "no prisoners were to be released, even on taking the oath of allegiance to the Jeff Davis Government." The time for such conciliatory measures with them had passed, even at the date of these *infamous* letters. Read the correspondence carefully, and see how these incarnate devils unmask themselves, and disclose the deep and damning depravity of their sin-clad hearts and souls.

Rebel Correspondence.

"ATHENS, TENN., NOV. 10, 1861.

"COLONEL WOOD, Knoxville, Tenn.:—

"I have reliable information that some 1500 Lincoln men are under arms in Hamilton county, ostensibly for Jamestown. Their destination is more probably Lowden Bridge.

"C. WALLACE, *President.*"

"LOWDEN, EAST TENN., NOV. 10, 1861.

"COLONEL WOOD:—

"DEAR SIR:—Captain Canood's company arrived here at six P.M. yesterday, and are pitching their tents to-day at the northern end of the bridge, while Captain Eldridge is encamped at the southern end. Extra pickets and sentinels were posted during the night, but no demonstration was made from any quarter, and the night was passed in quiet.

"*The Union feeling of this county is exceedingly bitter, and all they want, in my opinion, to induce a general uprising, is encouragement from the Lincoln armies.* They have a great many arms, and *are actually manufacturing Union flags* to receive the refugee Tennesseeans when they return. They are getting bold enough. If I had one or two more companies, a great many arms could be procured here in this neighborhood,—I mean, if we had the force to spare from the bridge.

"Very respectfully,

S. SLASSON, *Major commanding.*"

"JACKSBORO, Nov. 9, 1861.

"COLONEL W. B. WOOD, Knoxville, Tenn.:—

"SIR:—Your dispatch is just received, informing me of the burning of Hiawassee bridge, and other bridges on the railroad, and asking me for reinforcements. Colonel Powell's regiment being five miles from here, on the Knoxville road, I have sent him an order to march at daylight for Knoxville, making a forced march. He is instructed to communicate with you immediately on his arrival. You will be in command, and may make such disposition of the forces as you may think advisable. Brigadier-General W. H. Carroll's three regiments have been ordered to report to me, but have not reported, and I have no knowledge where they are. I have expected them by now at Knoxville. Have you any knowledge where they are?

"Very respectfully,

"F. K. ZOLLICOFFER,

"*Brigadier-General.*"

[Telegram.]

"CHARLESTON, NOV. 10, 1861.

"COLONEL WOOD:—

"A reliable messenger informs me that (75) seventy-five Union soldiers were to-day near Harrison. They had knapsacks, and were going to Captain Clift's. It is believed that he has fifteen hundred (1500) men organized.

"J. D. STOUT."

[Telegram.]

"TO WM. H. SNEED, J. T. CROZIER, MAJOR C. WALLACE, GENERAL ZOLLICOFFER, COLONEL WOOD:—

"About nine hundred men, part of them from Bradley county, leave Clift's, in this county, to-day, in squads, either to organize for operations against this place and Lowden Bridge, or to meet Union forces from Kentucky. They have some wagons, and are partly armed. The regiment is formidable. Send word to General Zollicoffer, that he may catch them.

"JOHN L. HOPKINS."

[Telegram.]

"CHARLESTON, TENN., NOV. 12, 1861.

"TO GILLESPIE AND KEY:—

"Jeff Mathis is within twelve miles of this place; has one hundred men. We can disperse them. Shall we do it? I expect help from you immediately.

"SMITH AND MCKANEY."

[Telegram.]

"CHATTANOOGA, Nov. 12, 1861.

"TO GENERAL GILLESPIE:—

"They have formed a camp at Bower's, near Smith's Cross-Roads. They may return to this place or to Lowden. They calculate to organize one thousand men. Reliable.

"J. L. HOPKINS."

"BRIGADE HEAD-QUARTERS, JACKSBORO, Nov. 12, 1861.

"COLONEL W. B. WOOD, Knoxville:—

"SIR:—The express-man reached me this evening at nine o'clock, with two letters from you, both dated November 11. You say the tory force at Papaw Hollow is augmenting from the adjoining counties. Please state what county Papaw Hollow is in. You say you enclose me a dispatch from John L. Hopkins, Chattanooga; but no dispatch is enclosed.

"I have two cavalry companies under Captain Rowan, near Oliver's, on the road from Knoxville to Montgomery, and two near Huntsville, on the road from Chetwood's to Montgomery. But your omission to send the dispatch of Hopkins, and only incidental allusion to cutting off somebody near Kingstown, leaves me at a loss what orders to send there. Please give me all the information you have which will enable me to intercept any body of tories attempting to pass toward Montgomery, Jamestown, Huntsville, or Post Oak Springs. I rejoice that you have caught six of the bridge-burners. I am yet unadvised what precise bridges are actually destroyed, or whether my intended telegrams are really transmitted over the wires. . . . I will to-morrow send dispatches to the forces near Jamestown, the cavalry near Huntsville, that near Oliver's, and start out the cavalry here *to commence simultaneously disarming the Union inhabitants.* You will please simultaneously send orders to all detachments under your command to inaugurate the same movement at the same time in their various localities. Their leaders should be seized and held as prisoners. The leniency shown them has been unavailing. They have acted with duplicity, and should no longer be trusted.

"F. K. ZOLLICOFFER, *Brigadier-General.*"

"KNOXVILLE, Oct. 28, 1861.

"GENERAL:—The news of your falling back to Cumberland Ford has had the effect of developing a feeling that had only been kept under by the presence of troops. It was plainly visible that the Union men were so glad that they could hardly repress an open expression of their joy. This afternoon it assumed an open character, and *some eight or ten of the bullies or leaders made an attack on some of my men near the Lamar House, and seriously wounded several.* Gentlemen who witnessed the whole affair say that my men gave no offence, and were not at all to blame. The affair became directly general, and couriers were sent to apprize me at my camp of its existence. I immediately marched Captain White's cavalry and one hundred of my men into the town to arrest the assailants; but they made their escape.

"*The Southerners here are considerably alarmed,* believing that there is a preconcerted plan for a united action among the Union men if by any means the enemy should get into Tennessee. Lieutenant Swan told me to-night that he heard one say this evening, as Captain White's cavalry rode through town, that 'they could do so now; but in less than ten days the Union forces would be here and run them off.' I cannot well tell you the many evidences of disaffection which are manifested every day, and the increased boldness that it is assuming.

"Very respectfully,

"W. B. WOOD, *Col. com'g Post.*

"Brigadier-General ZOLLICOFFER."

"HEAD-QUARTERS, KNOXVILLE, TENN., Nov. 1, 1861.

"HON. J. P. BENJAMIN, *Secretary of War*:—

"SIR:—I have to-day written to General Cooper in reference to the state of affairs in East Tennessee, and the necessity of reinforcements being sent immediately. But, as there is a misapprehension in reference to the feeling of the late Union party, I have requested Mr. Walker, of Richmond, now on a visit here, to call on you and give you fuller information than I can write.

"In addition to what I have written to General Cooper, I will say that there can be no doubt of the fact that large parties, numbering from twenty to a hundred, are every day passing through the narrow and unfrequented gaps of the mountain into Kentucky to join the army. My courier, just in from Jamestown, informs me that a few nights since one hundred and seventy men passed from Roane county into Kentucky.

"*I do not believe that the Unionists are in the least reconciled to the Government, but, on the contrary, are as hostile to it as the people of Ohio,* and will be ready to take up arms as soon as they believe the Lincoln forces are near enough to sustain them. . . .

"Yours, respectfully,

"W. B. Wood, *Col. com'g Post.*"

"Knoxville, Tenn., Nov. 10, 1861.

"General Zollicoffer:—

"Sir:—Information has been received that Mr. Hodges, member of the Legislature, has been making a treasonable speech over in Lewis county. He is also suspected of having a knowledge, if not an instigator, of the bridge-burning.

"He was here yesterday morning, and we could have arrested him; but he made his escape, and will probably try to get through the lines.

"Five of the incendiaries that burned the Lick

Creek bridge have been arrested. The bridge at Union has been destroyed, one at Charleston, two on the Western and Atlantic Road, below Chattanooga. *I had a company at Lick Creek; but the incendiaries deceived them, and, getting possession of their guns, took them prisoners and accomplished their ends.* . . .

"Respectfully,

"W. B. WOOD."

"KNOXVILLE, TENN., NOV. 11, 1861.

"GENERAL S. COOPER, *Adjutant-General, &c.*:—

"SIR:—My fears expressed to you by letter and dispatches of the 4th and 5th inst. have been realized by the destruction of no less than five railroad-bridges. The indications were apparent to me; but I was powerless to prevent it.

"*The whole country now is in a state of rebellion.* A thousand men are within six miles of Strawberry Plains Bridge, and an attack is contemplated to-morrow. I have sent Colonel Powell there with two hundred infantry, one company of cavalry, and about one hundred citizens armed with shot-guns and country rifles.

"Five hundred Unionists left Hamilton county today,—we suppose, to attack Lowden Bridge. I have Major Campbell there, with two hundred infantry and one company of cavalry.

"I have about the same force at this point, and a cavalry company at Washington bridge. An attack was made there on yesterday. Our men succeeded in beating them off; but they are gathering in large force, and may secure it in a day or two.

"They are not yet fully organized, and have no subsistence to enable them to hold out long. A few regiments and vigorous means would have a powerful effect in putting it down. A mild or conciliating policy will do no good: they must be punished, and some of the leaders punished to the extent of the laws.

"I have arrested six of the men who were engaged in firing the Lick Creek bridge, and I desire to have instructions from you as to the proper disposition of them. The slow course of civil law in punishing such incendiaries, it seems to me, will not have the salutary effect which is desired.

"I learned from two gentlemen just arrived that another camp is being formed about two miles from here, in Sevier county, and already three hundred are in camp. They are being reinforced from Blount, Roane, Johnson, Greene, Carter, and other counties.

"I feel it to be my duty to place this city under martial law, *as there were a large majority of the people sympathizing with the enemy and communicating with them* by the unfrequented mountain-paths, and to prevent surprises and the destruction of public property. *I need not say that great alarm is felt by the few Southern men here.* They are finding places of safety for their families, and would gladly enlist if we had arms for them. I have had all the arms in the city seized, and authorized Major Campbell to impress all he can find in the hands of Union men.

"Very truly,

"WM. B. WOOD."

Letter from Wood to Benjamin.

"KNOXVILLE, November 20, 1861.

"To HON. J. P. BENJAMIN, *Secretary of War:*—

"SIR:—The rebellion in East Tennessee has been put down in some of the counties, and will be effectually suppressed in less than two weeks in all the counties. Their camps in Sevier and Hamilton counties have been broken up, and a large number of them made prisoners. Some are confined in this place, and others sent to Nashville. In a former communication, I inquired of the Department what I should do. It is a mere farce to arrest them and turn them over to the courts. Instead of having the effect to intimidate them, it really gives encouragement and emboldens them in their traitorous conduct. Patterson, the son-in-law of Andrew Johnson, State Senator Pickens, and several other members of the Legislature, besides others of influence and distinction in their counties,—these men have encouraged the rebellion, but have so managed as not to be found in arms. Nevertheless, all their actions and words have been unfriendly to the Government of the Confederate States. Their wealth and influence have been exerted in favor of the Lincoln Government, and they are the parties most to blame.

"They really deserve the gallows, and, if consistent with the laws, ought speedily to receive their deserts. But there is such a gentle spirit of conciliation in the South, and especially here, that I have no idea that one of them will receive such a sentence at the hands of any jury. I have been here at this station for three months, half the time in command of this post; and I had a good opportunity of learning the feeling pervading this country. *It is hostile to the Confederate Government. They will take the oath of allegiance with no intention to observe it. They are the slaves of Johnson and Maynard, and never intend to be otherwise. When arrested, they suddenly become very submissive,* and declare they are for peace, and not supporters of the Lincoln Government, but yet claim to be Union men. At one time, while our forces were at Knoxville, they gave it out that a great change had taken place in East Tennessee, and that the people were becoming loyal.

"*At the withdrawal of the army from here to the Gap, and the first intimation of the approach of the Lincoln army, they were in arms, and scarcely a man but was ready to join it and make war upon us.* The prisoners we have all tell us that they had every assurance that the enemy was already in the State and would join them in a few days. I have requested at least that the prisoners I have taken be held, if not as traitors, as prisoners of war. To release them is ruinous. To convict them before a court is next to impossibility. But if they are kept in prison for six months, it will have a good effect.

"The bridge-burners and spies ought to be tried at once.

"Very respectfully, yours,

"W. B. WOOD."

Benjamin's Reply.

"WAR DEPARTMENT, RICHMOND, November 25, 1861.

"COLONEL W. B. WOOD:—

"SIR:—Your report of the 20th instant is received, and I now proceed to give you the desired instruction in relation to the prisoners of war taken by you among the traitors of East Tennessee.

"*First.* All such as can be identified in having been engaged in bridge-burning are to be tried summarily by *drum-head court-martial,* and, if found guilty, *executed on the spot by hanging. It would be well to leave their bodies hanging in the vicinity of the burned bridges.*

"*Second.* All such as have not been so engaged are to be treated as prisoners of war, and sent with an armed guard to Tuscaloosa, Alabama, there to be kept imprisoned at the depot selected by the Government for prisoners of war.

"Whenever you can discover that arms are concentrated by these traitors, you will send out detachments, search for and seize the arms. *In no case is one of the men known to have been up in arms against the Government to be released on any pledge or oath of allegiance.* The time for such measures is past. They are all to be held as prisoners of war, and held in jail to the end of the war. Such as come in voluntarily, take the oath of allegiance, and surrender their arms, are alone to be treated with leniency.

"Your vigilant execution of these orders is earnestly urged by the Government.

"Your obedient servant,

"J. P. BENJAMIN,

"*Secretary of War.*

"COLONEL W. B. WOOD, Knoxville, Tenn.

"P.S.—Judge Patterson, (Andy Johnson's son-in-law, Rem. Corresp.,) Colonel Pickens, and other ringleaders of the same class, must be sent at once to Tuscaloosa to jail as prisoners of war."

INCIDENTS

CONNECTED WITH THE GREAT SOUTHERN REBELLION IN TENNESSEE;

TO WHICH IS ADDED

A Sketch of Prison-Life,

AND THE SUBSEQUENT RELEASE AND JOURNEY OF THE AUTHOR.

CHAPTER XIX.

MUCH of what now follows was written down by the author in small blank-books, with a pencil, in the Knoxville jail, and in a private room, while the outer doors were guarded with Rebel bayonets. That portion given in the form of a *journal* will be transmitted to posterity just as it was written down at the time, and without any attempt at polish. When most of these sketches reach the eyes of my prison-companions in the Knoxville jail, they will recall to them our mutual sufferings, and they will readily attest the truthfulness of my narrative. They will at once bear testimony as to the fidelity of my descriptions and the accuracy with which I have stated facts, although they will regret that I have not gone more into detail.

Whilst I desire to let the world see what the real *spirit* of Secession is in the South, and to expose the guilty leaders to the scorn and contempt of all coming generations, I wish to enlist the interests and sympathies of all who may find leisure to peruse these pages. I have known, during my darkest hour of trial, that I had the sympathies of all good citizens in the loyal States, and did not doubt that thousands of devout prayers were offered up for my preservation and ultimate release, and for the safety and release of the innocent Union men confined with me and in other jails. If in these pages I can vindicate my consistency and satisfy the public that their sympathies have been merited, I will have accomplished all that is desired or aimed at by the publication of them.

When the storm arose in the South,—say a little over twelve months ago,—and the current set in seemingly favorable to Secession, vast numbers rushed into their ranks, actuated by the worst motives that ever governed the actions of as many bad men,—the daring and improvident, the indolent, the thoughtless, the bankrupts of the country, and the thousands indebted to Northern merchants, debauched members of the churches, apostate preachers, and the intemperate,—all the loose elements of society in the towns and villages,—those who were reckless of consequences, and to whom no change could be productive of injury,—men who really had every thing to gain and nothing to lose, even by so violent and destructive a revolution.

And whilst many of the substantial men of the country entered the army,—for the most part as officers, contractors, wagon-masters, and furnishers of supplies in various forms,—a much greater number entered the service who were pusillanimous and worthless, lazy and sensual, having no visible means of support. Many of these were known to me in East Tennessee and other portions of the South; and I can safely say that when they entered the service, and were fitted out with suits of coarse jeans and supplied with army-rations, they were better dressed and fed than they ever had been before. Not a few of these entered the Rebel service with a view to get rid of their wives and children, who were looking to them for a support, and whose bréad and meat were guaranteed by those who urged them to volunteer, but who, after they were goné, left their families to shift for themselves.

It was a common thing to hear men of this class, dressed in uniform, and under the influence of mean whiskey, swearing upon the streets that they intended to have their rights, or kill the last Lincolnite north of Mason & Dixon's line! Ask one of them what rights he had lost and was so vehemently contending for, and the reply would be, the right to carry his negroes into the Territories. At the same time, the man never owned a negro in his life, and never was related, by consanguinity or affinity, to any one who did own a negro! Nay, I have heard captains of Rebel companies bluster in this way, who could not get credit in a Secession store for a pair of shoes or a pound of coffee.

And, as if resolved to keep up a show of consistency and carry out the same spirit, society was disjointed, and was everywhere thrown into the loosest state in which it could exist, upon the inauguration of Secession. There were no regular magistrates, no laws, no judges, no tribunals to protect the weak and innocent or to punish the guilty. Take for example the case of a Union man in Knox county, who was tied upon a log, his back stripped bare, and cut all to pieces with hickories, as one of my engravings will show. When he was brought into the court-house, and his back exhibited, he was told that these were revolutionary times, and that he had no remedy. Every man had to assert his own rights and avenge his own wrongs, or, as most were compelled to do, submit to insult and injury. Squads of six and ten Rebel troops, upon their own responsibilities, scoured the country, arrested whom they chose, and treated them as their malice and beastly habits of life suggested. Take the case of Captain *Bill Brown*, of Bradley county, who, at the head of a company of cavalry, arrested Union men, and forced from them sums of money to pay him for their release, until he boasted of having two thousand dollars. This charge was brought before the military authorities at Knoxville, and again dismissed without a reproof to this robber.

As a general thing, these outlaws, who were operating all over East Tennessee, were neither restrained by a sense of shame, the dictates of humanity, nor the fear of God. Hence, many innocent persons fell victims to their malevolence, and had their property either shamefully abused or recklessly destroyed. Tennessee is a greatly-damaged State,—thousands of the men having escaped into Kentucky, leaving their homes and crops, all of which have since been destroyed by the Rebel troops. This is especially so in the several counties along the south side of the Cumberland Mountains. Kentucky and Missouri will both feel the effects of this devastating war,—a war which the Cotton States artfully contrived to transfer to the border States, but which, thanks to the energy of the heads of the Federal army, is falling back to where it ought to have begun, and where it should end.

Virginia is a ruined State. Poor old Virginia! her children yet unborn will feel the effects of this wicked revolution. Indeed, I pause in the midst of my labors to moralize upon the condition of my native State, which but yesterday

> "might have stood against the world;
> Now none so poor to do her reverence."

Mother of heroes and statesmen, the birthplace of Presidents, the burial-place of the greatest American,—it seems but yesterday that she had the strongest claims upon the great Republic, on account of her dignity, her retrospect of noble labors, her frontier position,—holding as it were the balance of power,—and the noble future which hung upon the expected assurance of her loyalty. But, urged and incited by her maddened and vile leaders, such as Wise, Mason, Pryor, and a host of desperate men whose names can never be mentioned but with disgust, she was hissed on until she was out of her senses, and she fell from her high estate into the disgraceful ranks of rebellion. New dominions must arise upon her ruins, a new race of men must people her soil, and the "Old Dominion" be but a historic cognomen in all time to come. What a fate, and what a retribution! Let loyal Maryland legislate for a part, let New Virginia control the West, let East Tennessee teach the extreme southwestern counties loyalty, and to little Delaware let Accomac and Northampton be annexed!

This may seem to be a terrible fate; but such would be a merited degree of punishment for the leading demagogues of Virginia, and for the masses who followed them to perdition. The way of transgressors may be hard, but the retribution is none the less logical and their punishment none the less just.

All these evils were brought upon the country by

Parson Brownlow entering the Knoxville Jail. (Page 308.)

the Southern Senators and Representatives going out of Congress and urging their States to secede. Pryor at one time telegraphed, "We can get the Crittenden Compromise." But Douglas overheard Mason say in the Senate, "No matter what compromise the North offers, the South must find a way to defeat it." The Congress of the United States would have given any compromise wanted. In the Senate, had the Southern States remained, they would have had a majority of SIX, and in the House, a majority of THIRTY-SIX, over the entire Republican party.

Early in the spring of 1861 a stream of Secession fire began to pour through East Tennessee, along the great Tennessee & Virginia Railroad, and troops were rushed along the road in greater numbers than the rolling stock upon the road would afford facilities for transporting. These regiments, coming from the Cotton States, and many of them *vagabonds* and *wharf-rats* from New Orleans, Mobile, and Texas, were brimfull of prejudice against me and my paper. These prejudices were increased and their malice inflamed by the falsehoods related to them by unprincipled citizens and cowards whom I had denounced for years, and by certain railroad-employés on their way to Knoxville. Hence, after they would arrive in Knoxville and pay a visit to the whiskey-shops, they would forthwith swarm around my printing-office and dwelling-house, howl like wolves, swear oaths that would blister the lips of a sailor, blackguard my family, and threaten to demolish my house, and even to hang me. This was kept up the entire summer and fall, and increased in violence until my paper was suppressed and my office seized upon and occupied by the Rebel military authorities,—which was in November last.

While General Zollicoffer remained at Knoxville in command, I was protected, and so were all other Union men and their families. Previous to his coming, however, certain officers of Vaughn's regiment of East Tennessee Volunteers commenced personal violence on Union men, and occasioned a row in the street, shooting down a *Mr. Ball,* and firing several shots at *Charles S. Douglas,*—the man who ran up the Union flag on Gay Street and protected it with a double-barrel shot-gun,—one shot slightly wounding him in the neck. The next day certain of these officers came into town from camps, in a close carriage, entered the hotel at the ladies' entrance, and watched for Douglas from a window until he appeared at his window on the opposite side of the street, when they took deliberate aim at him and shot him through the breast with a large musket-ball. Thus was Douglas murdered in a most cowardly and brutal manner, while the State was a member of the Federal Union; and the circuit court judge and the State's Attorney were both in town, but, being Secessionists, no bill was sent against the murderers of Douglas, nor was one word said in court on the subject; but his widow and one small child were left to take care of themselves. Nor is this all. The Episcopal minister, Mr. Hames, was proscribed for daring to attend the funeral and officiate, at the request of the widow. This is the *spirit* which has characterized this rebellion throughout the South!

After the departure of General Zollicoffer to Cumberland Gap, I soon became convinced that I was in danger of personal violence from the soldiers left there under the command of one *Rev. Colonel W. B. Wood*, of Alabama, a hypocrite, who preached in the Methodist Church on Sunday and the next day encouraged his men to do acts of violence. Certain of these troops were in the habit of coming daily to my residence, or passing by it, flourishing their large knives, pointing their guns at the windows, and threatening to take my life. They were incited to act in this manner by my bitter personal enemies and by the cowardly miscreant who conducted the rebel organ in Knoxville, and who desired me and my paper out of their way. They were also encouraged by this unmitigated villain, *Parson Colonel Wood.* My enemies seeking to make the military the instruments of their private revenge, and my condition becoming more and more perilous each day, my family became convinced that my life was in danger, as did other friends, and all believed that my presence at home imperilled instead of securing the safety of my wife and children. I therefore yielded to the entreaties of my family and friends to leave home for a time, and I consented to do so the more readily as I had debts owing to me in the adjoining counties of Blount, Sevier, Cocke, and Granger, for advertising. I accordingly left home the first week in November, on horseback, in company with Rev. James Cumming, and whilst I was still in Blount—less than thirty miles from home—the bridges on the railroad were destroyed by fire. My absence at the time was seized upon as evidence of my complicity in the matter, although I was not nearer than one day's ride of the railroad, and on Sunday, the day after the burning, I preached to a large congregation in Sevierville.

But the most intense excitement prevailed in the country after the news was circulated; harangues were delivered in the towns and military camps, and the passions of the Secession citizens and of the soldiers were inflamed; and my knowledge of the history of mankind in the past taught me that in such seasons of high excitement the innocent and the guilty would suffer together. Meanwhile, I learned, by express-riders friendly to me, that this vile man Wood had sent out scouts of cavalry after me in different directions, with instructions, publicly given them on the street, not to take me a prisoner, but to shoot me down upon sight. Military law was declared in Knoxville; the city was guarded, and those who escaped from the city to give me word had to cross the river after night in a canoe. In this state of things, prudence dictated that I should for a time conceal myself from the gaze of these bloodhounds and authorized murderers, so that no occasion should occur for violence to my person. Quite a number of us—among whom were members of the Legislature, preachers, and planters—retired into the Smoky Mountains, separating North Carolina from Tennessee, and quite beyond the precincts of civilization. Amidst the high summits of this range of mountains, and in one of their deep gorges where no vehicle had ever penetrated, we struck up camp, and for days and nights together we stayed there. Our friends from Wear's Cove conveyed provisions to us, and in the mean time one of our party killed a fat bear, which supplied us with meat. In the cove below us there was a company of "Home-Guards,"—Union men,—well armed, who kept a watch for our pursuers, who failed to learn our whereabouts. We were high up on the east fork of Little River, and there was but one gap through which we could have been approached, and in that event it would have required a large force to take us.

Scouts were multiplied to search for us, and we were made acquainted with that fact; and, as it was known that we were in Tuckaluchee Cove and in Wear's Cove, we deemed it prudent to disperse, and to secrete ourselves in different places, two-and-two together. I resolved upon going within six or eight miles of Knoxville, where I had Union friends who would take care of me; and, accordingly, the Rev. W. T. Dowell and myself mounted our horses at dark, having previously come down out of the mountains, and, riding something less than forty miles through the deep gorges, daylight brought us to the comfortable lodgings of a friend. Here we tarried for a time, and were put in secret communication with Knoxville, distant six miles, having removed our horses to another point. Learning that the murderous scouts of the still more bloodthirsty and despicable Wood were still after me, I addressed the following note to Brigadier-General Carroll:—

Friday, Nov. 22, 1861.

GENERAL W. H. CARROLL:—

Having understood that you are to be placed in command of the military post at Knoxville in a few days, I desire to lay a statement of facts before you. I left home on the 4th of this month to attend the Chancery Court in Maryville, Blount county, and to go from there to Sevierville, to collect fees due me for advertising, and in part I have succeeded. I have not been concerned in getting up an armed force to war upon your troops, as falsely reported.

I left home, and have remained absent for eighteen days, at the earnest and repeated solicitations of my family, who insisted that they would be more secure in my absence. Certain troops came daily on my portico, and, in front of my dwelling, drew out and flourished side-knives, and sometimes presented muskets, threatening my life. I was told that they were under the command of an Alabama officer by the name of *Wood,* and that he was arrayed against me.

As it regards the bridge-burning, I never had any intimation of any such purpose, from any quarter. I condemn the act, and regard it as an ill-timed measure, calculated to bring no good to any one or any party, but much harm to innocent men and to the public. When I, together with fifteen or twenty other leading Union men, signed a communication to General Zollicoffer, proposing to counsel peace, I acted in good faith; and I have kept that faith. That address has been published in all the Tennessee papers; and, had any purpose to fire the bridges been made known to me, I should have felt bound to disclose the fact to the officers of the road.

I am ready and willing at any time to stand a trial upon these or other points before any civil tribunal; but I protest against being turned over to *any infuriated mob of armed men* filled with prejudice by my bitterest enemies.

This communication will be handed to you by my friend Colonel John Williams, a man favorably known to you and the country.

I am, respectfully, &c.,

W. G. Brownlow.

"HEAD-QUARTERS, KNOXVILLE, Nov. 28, 1861.

"REV. DR. BROWNLOW:—

"It is my business here to afford protection to all citizens who are loyal to the Confederate States; and I shall use all the force at my command to that end. You may be fully assured that you will meet with no personal violence by returning to your home; and, if you can establish what you say in your letter of the 22d inst., *you shall have every opportunity to do so before the civil tribunal, if it is necessary,*—PROVIDED YOU HAVE COMMITTED NO ACT THAT WILL MAKE IT NECESSARY FOR THE MILITARY LAW TO TAKE COGNIZANCE.

"I desire that every loyal citizen, regardless of former political opinions, shall be fully protected in all his rights and privileges; and to accomplish which I shall bend all my energies, and have no doubt I shall be successful. Respectfully, &c.,

"WM. H. CARROLL,

"*Brig.-Gen. Com.*"

THURSDAY, December 4, 1861.

GENERAL W. H. CARROLL:—

Your letter of the 28th ult. did not reach me until the 1st inst., and I return, for an answer to the slanderous charges whispered into your ears by my cowardly enemies, touching myself and others, as the correspondents of men in Kentucky, and as *knowing* the bridges were to be burned, the following documents:—

"The undersigned, being charged with having and reading a letter in Maryville, during the fourth and fifth days of November past, purporting to say that the railroad-bridges were to be burned, take this method of testifying to the public that there is not one word of truth in the entire statement; that we have neither seen, handled, read, or heard read, any letter on that subject, from any quarter whatsoever. We further state, upon our oaths, that neither of us has received from, or addressed or conveyed to, any person in Kentucky, or connected with the Federal army, during the entire summer and fall, any private letter touching the war or the troubles growing out of the war. We also testify, upon our oaths, that we had no knowledge whatsoever of any purpose or plot, on the part of any persons or party, to burn the bridges: had we been apprized of such a movement, we should have protested against it as an outrage. Subscribed and sworn to this 2d of December, 1861.

"James Cumming,
"W. G. Brownlow,
"W. T. Dowell.

"Personally appeared before me, an acting Justice of the Peace in and for the County of Blount and State of

Tennessee, this 2d of December, 1861, James Cumming, W. G. Brownlow, and W. T. Dowell, and made oath, in due form of law, that the allegations set forth in the foregoing statement, and subscribed by them, are true.

"SOLOMON FARMER,
"*Justice of the Peace for Blount County.*"

Mr. Cumming is now in his seventy-seventh year, has all his life long sustained an unblemished character, has been a Methodist itinerant preacher for the last *forty* years, and previous to that served two campaigns under General Jackson, associated with your venerable father, General Coffee, and other patriots, in defending our *whole* country—not a part of it—against the combined assaults of our British and savage foes,—undergoing the hardships of camp-life among the inhospitable swamps of Mobile and New Orleans. Indeed, he was a major in Colonel Williams's regiment of Tennessee Volunteers; and that gallant officer, afterwards a Senator in Congress, bore witness to the courage and fidelity of Mr. Cumming. His character and services ought to shield him in his declining years from such slanders as are now heaped upon him, and would do it were he living anywhere else than in this so-called Southern Confederacy. But he is a Union man, opposed to the disruption of the Government he has suffered and fought for; and this is the head and front of his offending.

Mr. Dowell is a native of Alabama, but has lived nearly all his life in East Tennessee, sustaining the character of an honest man, in the counties of Anderson, Carter, Sevier, Knox, and Blount, where he is now a respectable merchant and an acceptable local preacher in the Methodist Church. But he is a Union man, loyal to the Government of the United States, and opposed to the heresy of Secession; and this is the reason why he is assailed.

So far as I am concerned, I have labored for years, in my humble way, to help build up this great line of railroads, and I can have no desire to see them destroyed. If the Federal Government succeed in recovering this country, it will need the facilities these roads afford; but if the Confederates hold the country, the roads are alike important to the citizens of all parties. No good can come to anybody from the destruction of these roads, but much harm to individuals and to the public at large.

No candid man of any party believes that I am even remotely connected with the recent burning of these bridges; but to charge it upon me, and raise a clamor through the country, affords a pretext, though flimsy it be, for seizing upon my property, as has been done, by a military mob, and appropriating it to the use of your so-called Confederacy. It was not enough that I should be refused the privilege of publishing my paper, but my press, engine, and type have been seized upon, and I am refused the privilege of selling them to procure the means of supporting a helpless family of children. Nay, my office-building has been taken from me, and is occupied by your military authorities, without fee or reward to me. Is this the liberty and justice offered to men by this new and better Government you are setting up? Are these the blessings of Southern Rights so much talked of? If so, God deliver me and my children from their benign influences! But, sir, what better could I expect from a bogus Government, that originated in fraud and falsehood, perjury and theft?

I have now been absent from home one month,—not because I have committed any crime, but because I have desired no collision between me and the drunken and infuriated troops, urged to assault me by the cowardly villains who throng the town, and whose frauds, bad morals, and revolting crimes I have held up to public gaze. I cannot feel safe in returning, for I am not sure that your letter offers protection to me. You say it is your "business here to afford protection to *all citizens who are loyal to the Confederate States.*" If you mean by *loyalty* faithfulness and fidelity, I can scarcely hope for protection. I am loyal to the Government of the United States, and that is the only Government I consider as having an existence in this country. I have studied the Bible for many years, and I have great respect for the lessons it has taught me. One

Removing Prisoners from Knoxville Jail to Tuscaloosa, Alabama. (Page 309.)

of these lessons is, that I must not attempt to serve TWO MASTERS. I am therefore a Union man, and I must adhere to the Federal Government until that is destroyed,—which I hope and trust may never be done, —and then I will turn to the next best Government I can find.

I am not in arms against your Confederacy. I have not encouraged rebellion on the part of Union men, but the reverse; and I am quietly awaiting the result of the contest going on. In this *neutral* condition I feel that I ought to be let alone, and left to the quiet enjoyment of opinions I honestly entertain and cannot conscientiously surrender. *You*, but a few months ago, entertained the same opinions I do, and acted with me in opposition to Secession. Toward me, personally, I think you would entertain none but kind feelings, were you not associated with the men you are. I understand that your daily associates are *John H. Crozier*, *J. Crozier Ramsey*, and *W. H. Sneed.*

Crozier blames me for driving him into private life. He is a corrupt demagogue, a selfish liar, and an unmitigated coward. I have held him up to public gaze, in this threefold capacity, from the stump and through the press, before his face and behind his back, and he has never had the spirit to resent it until recently, and then only by hiding behind your volunteers and seeking to hiss them on me. He also feels *sore* under my exposure of his brother, *A. R. Crozier*, who was connected with the great swindle practised by the Bank of East Tennessee, and, after making his pile by that operation, packed up bag and baggage and cut out for Texas! The records of our Chancery Court will give you the facts in the case.

Ramsey is but a few degrees removed from an idiot. He is the nephew of the Croziers and the son of one of the directors of this villainous bank, against whom I instituted and recovered an important suit, exposing the *father*, the *uncle*, and the entire *Democratic* swindle. Young Ramsey is smarting under the part I took in helping to defeat him for the United States Congress, when he was beaten two thousand votes by Horace Maynard. Somebody once said, "That in the kingdom of the blind the one-eyed are monarchs;" and I suppose it was upon this principle, if we give the maxim a literal construction, that young Ramsey, with his "one talent," was elevated to such a pitch as to be made a Confederate Attorney by Jeff Davis!

Sneed is a noble specimen of the physical man. Corpulent, swaggering, a giant in his own estimation, his form looms up in the distance, and when he is on the street he makes the whole town know it! His whole figure exhibits a majesty of proportion, a majesty of combination, sometimes seen in the liquor-shop statues with whom he associates. His eyelashes are nearly scorched off by alcoholic fire; and nature, to keep up appearances, in a fit of desperation is substituting in their stead a binding of red, which looks like two little rainbows hanging upon a storm, such as he often passes through in the domestic circle! This man has been a candidate for all the offices of honor and profit that have come up during his long residence in East Tennessee, and never was successful but once, when he was elected to the Congress of the United States. The people then complained that he was elected through the influence of my press, for I entered heartily into his support, as he was a *Whig* and his competitor a *Democrat.* In Congress his associates were *Disunionists* and his votes were *sectional.* He was not again a candidate. Indeed, a press like mine in each of the ten counties in the district could not have re-elected him. When Secession turned up, he pitched in, and became a candidate to represent Knox county in the Convention. Out of four thousand votes polled in a single-handed contest he obtained two hundred and thirty. Since then he has been travelling in search of his rights, and swears that he will follow them on to the other side of sundown!

Whenever the Federal army shall approach Tennessee in force, Crozier, Ramsey, Sneed, and others of the same clique, will fall back into the Cotton States, and call upon the mountains and hills to hide them from the wrath of the Union men in East Tennessee whom they have persecuted, insulted, and sought to have murdered by your drunken and infuriated troops. These are certainly accomplished and erudite reformers of our National Government! Mark my prediction: these men will take to their heels upon the approach of one regiment of Federal troops. I know the men and have studied their characters. I may not be living when a Federal army enters East Tennessee, but if I am living next spring, I expect to enjoy the luxury. If this be treason, make the most of it!

As this letter to you is private, General, and as you were until recently a Union man, you must allow me to deal candidly with you. I have no idea that you approve this Secession movement, but feel certain that in your heart you despise the whole affair. As long as I see the *spirit* of the rebellion acted out by your leaders, and as long as I bear in mind the *characters* of the men who originated it, I can but despise the whole concern and desire its overthrow. I may not be gratified with seeing this rebellion put down, but my children will; and, if I am not assassinated by the hired tools of some of your new associates, I will live to see the rebellion closed out, and not be more than *one year* older than I now am!

I am, sir, &c.,
W. G. BROWNLOW.

My friend, who was in charge of the foregoing letter, withheld it from General Carroll, on account of the following epistles, intended for me, and of the existence of which I had no knowledge at the time I wrote the one of the 4th of December:—

"HEAD-QUARTERS, KNOXVILLE, TENN., Dec. 4, 1861.

"W. G. BROWNLOW, ESQ.:—The Major-General commanding directs me to say that upon calling at his head-quarters, within twenty-four hours, you can get a passport to go into Kentucky, accompanied by a military escort, the route to be designated by General Crittenden.

"I am, sir, very respectfully, your obedient servant,

"A. S. CUNNINGHAM,

"*Acting Adjutant-General.*"

The following letter, a copy of which I was furnished with on the day and date of the foregoing, seems to have been withheld, or, at least, not acted upon, for ten days:—

CONFEDERATE STATES OF AMERICA,
"WAR DEPARTMENT, RICHMOND, Nov. 20, 1861.

"TO MAJOR-GENERAL CRITTENDEN:—

"DEAR SIR:—I have been asked to grant a passport for Brownlow, to leave the State of Tennessee. He is said to have secreted himself, fearing violence to his person, and to be anxious to depart from the State.

"I cannot give him a formal passport, though I would greatly prefer seeing him on the other side of our lines, *as an avowed enemy*. I wish, however, to say that I would be glad to learn that he has left Tennessee; and I have no objection to interpose to his leaving, if you are willing to let him pass.

"Yours, truly,

"J. P. Benjamin,

"*Secretary of War.*"

It turned out, upon examination, that Colonel Baxter, of Knoxville, a moderate Secessionist, was in Richmond at the time Mr. Benjamin wrote to General Crittenden, and made this application without my knowledge. He was doubtless influenced by two motives,—one of friendship to me and my family, and a conviction in his mind that I would be assassinated if I remained.

Relying upon this promise of passports into Kentucky and of the protection of a military escort, I reported myself in person to General Crittenden before the twenty-four hours had expired, and was accompanied by Colonel Baxter. I there and then obtained from General Crittenden a renewal of his promise. This was on the 5th; and the morning of the 7th was agreed upon for me to start, and Captain Gillespie was designated as the man to put me through with his company of cavalry. Before that time arrived, I was arrested upon a warrant for treason, issued by Robert B. Reynolds, the Confederate Commissioner,—a third-rate county-court lawyer, a drunken and corrupt *sot*, who had been kicked out of a grocery a few days before by a mechanic, and who was afterwards taken up from the pavements of the street, in a beastly state of intoxication, by Rebel troops, and lodged in the guard-house! See a drawing of this beautiful specimen of a judge,—a fit representative of the morality and integrity of the Confederate Government!

Here follows the warrant, issued upon the application and *false swearing* of that *corrupt scoundrel* and most unprincipled knave, *J. Crozier Ramsey*, Confederate Attorney for the State of Tennessee:—

"CONFEDERATE STATES OF AMERICA,
"DISTRICT OF TENNESSEE.

"TO THE MARSHAL OF SAID DISTRICT:—

"J. C. Ramsey, Confederate States District Attorney for said district, having MADE OATH before me, that he is informed and believes that William G. Brownlow, a citizen of said district, and owing allegiance and fidelity to the Confederate States, but, being moved and seduced by the instigation of the devil, and not having the fear of God before his eyes, did wilfully, knowingly, and with malice aforethought, and feloniously, commit the crime of TREASON against the Confederate States, by then and there, within said district and *since the 10th day of June last*, publishing a weekly and tri-weekly paper, known as 'Brownlow's Knoxville Whig,' said paper had a large circulation in said district, and also circulated in the United States, and contained, weekly, divers of editorials written by the said Brownlow, which said editorials were treasonable against the Confederate States of America, and did then and there commit treason, and prompt others to commit treason, by speech as well as publication; did as aforesaid commit treason, and did give aid and comfort to the United States, both of said Governments being in a state of war with each other. You are therefore commanded to arrest the said Brownlow, and bring him before me, to be dealt with as the law directs.

"R. B. REYNOLDS,
"*Commissioner, &c.*

"J. C. RAMSEY,
"*C.S. Dist. Att'y.*

"December 6, 1861."

I was arrested by the marshal, refused a trial, and refused bail, though my friends voluntarily offered a bond of ONE HUNDRED THOUSAND DOLLARS. While in the hands of the marshal, I addressed the following note to General Crittenden, and sent it by Colonel Williams:—

KNOXVILLE, Dec. 6, 1861.

MAJOR-GENERAL CRITTENDEN:—I am now under an arrest, upon a warrant issued by Commissioner Reynolds, at the instance of J. Crozier Ramsey, upon a charge of treason, founded upon sundry articles published in the Knoxville Whig since the 10th of June last.

I am here, as you will recollect, upon your invitation and the instructions of your Secretary of War to give me passports into the old Government. Claiming your protection, as I do, I shall await your early response.

Very respectfully, &c.,
W. G. BROWNLOW.

No response was made to this note until the next day, and I was cast into prison. This gross breach of faith, both by the War Department at Richmond and the general in command at Knoxville, is a disgrace to the Confederate Government,—if such a Government, originating as it did in fraud, falsehood, and perjury, can be disgraced!

The next day I received from a self-conceited member of General Crittenden's staff—a fellow late from California—the following note. After receiving this note, I gave up the chase, and felt that the whole concern, civil and military, were alike unreliable, having no regard for their pledges:—

"KNOXVILLE, Dec. 7, 1861.

"W. G. BROWNLOW:—

"SIR:—Your note, stating that you were under an arrest upon a warrant upon a charge of treason, &c., has been handed to General Crittenden.

"He desires me to say, in reply, that in view of all of the facts of the case, (which need not be recapitulated here, for you are familiar with them,) HE DOES NOT CONSIDER THAT YOU ARE HERE UPON HIS INVITATION IN SUCH MANNER AS TO CLAIM HIS PROTECTION FROM AN INVESTIGATION BY THE CIVIL AUTHORITIES OF THE CHARGES AGAINST YOU, which he clearly understood from yourself and your friends you would not seek to avoid.

"Respectfully, yours, &c.,

"HARRY I. THORNTON,

"*A.D.C.*"

This corrupt man Ramsey, after issuing this warrant, accompanied it with a part of one of the editorials he had falsely sworn was issued since the 10th of June, 1861, at which time the State voted out. He only gave that part of the article relating to the railroads, commencing with the words, "Let the railroad on which," &c.; and, although he swore in his warrant, and published the falsehood in the paper, that the article appeared since the 10th of June, the truth is it appeared on the 25th of May, and *before* the State voted out! One of the reasons why he refused me a trial was that he knew I would produce a file of my papers and convict him of *false swearing*. Here is, however, the entire article:—

"Murder Will Out."

A secret of some importance has been cautiously communicated to this city from Alabama, by a man not likely to be deceived. The same facts, in substance, have been intrusted to a most estimable individual here, under the solemn injunction of secrecy for a specified time. There are now three other gentlemen besides ourselves, and they are men of high positions, who know the facts and have the evidence of them. This stupendous and appalling conspiracy amounts to this: Johnson, Nelson, Baxter, Temple, Trigg, Maynard, Brownlow, and George W. Bridges, are to be arrested after the election in June, by a military force, and taken in irons to Montgomery, and either punished for *treason*, or held as hostages to guarantee the quiet surrender of the Union men of East Tennessee!

The facts of this conspiracy against the rights of American citizens, together with the names of those concerned in urging it on, will all be left in the hands of reliable, bold, and fearless men, who will make them public at the proper time. The thousands of Union men of East Tennessee, devoted to principle and to the rights and liberties of those who fell at the hands of these conspirators, will be expected to avenge their wrongs! Let the railroad on which Union citizens of East Tennessee are conveyed to Montgomery in irons be eternally and hopelessly destroyed! Let the property of the men concerned be consumed, and let their lives pay the forfeit, and the names will be given! Let the fires of patriotic vengeance be built upon the Union altars of the whole land, and let them go out where these conspirators live, like the fires from the Lord, that consumed Nadab and Abihu, the two sons of Aaron, for presumption less sacrilegious! If we are incarcerated at Montgomery, or executed there or even elsewhere, all the consolation we want is to know that our partisan friends have visited upon our persecutors—certain Secession leaders—a most horrible vengeance! Let it be done, East Tennesseeans, though the gates of hell be forced and the heavens be made to fall!

In disclosing this bold and deep-laid plot against the liberties of freemen, we have not intended a *sensation* article. Some may smile at its alleged senseless absurdity, but we are not alone in putting forth these facts. We most solemnly implore our friends throughout East Tennessee, as they regard our welfare and as they cherish the principles for which we are alike battling, not to molest any person or property in advance of an attack upon any of us, but to hold themselves in readiness for *action*, ACTION, ACTION! As

Hanging of Fry and Hensie near the railroad, by Colonel Leadbetter. (Page 311.)

yet the conspiracy is only partially revealed,—the *murder* partly *out:* the mask will be taken off in due time! We are not in possession of the names of any confederates and abettors outside of the limits of East Tennessee, though some have been closeted with East Tennesseeans and the details of their plans agreed upon. Again, in the name of every thing sacred, we ask for ourselves, and those threatened with us, that no move shall be made by our friends towards injuring the person or property of any living man or existing corporation, until further developments are made; and then let every brave man act, and let all act together. Thanks be to God for the vigilance of some true men, and for their promptness in making communications! A Union man, of high character, who will disguise himself and travel hundreds of miles at his own expense to serve true men to him personally unknown, deserves to be immortalized, and to live forever!

This man Ramsey, in swearing a lie with a view to injure me, was influenced by his deep-seated malice. He is the son of the vain old *historian of Tennessee*, against whom I brought and sustained a suit for a nefarious *bank-swindle*, and to avoid the damages of which, the old rebel has put his property out of his hands, making this corrupt son the trustee!

Besides, this Attorney for the Commonwealth of the Confederacy attempted to get up a company of volunteers, but never was able to muster more than *thirty* men; and, being detected in drawing rations and clothing for sixty-five, he was, under General Zollicoffer's reign at Knoxville, drummed out of the service. Let the reader turn to the drawing of this man, and look at his hang-dog countenance as he "retires" to the tune of the Rogues' March!

CHAPTER XX.

BEING refused a trial and refused bail, as good and as strong as East Tennessee could afford, I was confined in the common jail of the county. And for what? For *treason* growing out of newspaper editorials! The warrant sued out by this judicial functionary contains within itself no charge of treason, though he afterwards brought out a garbled extract from the foregoing editorials, and alleged that therein lay the treason. Every man of legal knowledge will see that the publication of a newspaper, however objectionable its matter may be, does not amount to treason. The object of this hardened villain, and the numerous cowardly scoundrels associated with him, was to subject me to close confinement in a crowded and most uncomfortable jail. In this these vile conspirators succeeded; but the reader will agree, after perusing these pages, that they have made but little by the operation. And when the whole affair is done with, they will have made still less.

I became satisfied, after I went into jail and had slips of newspapers conveyed to me, that General Carroll had not acted in good faith towards me. Take, for instance, the following dispatch, on the day I was committed. It is from the pen of young *Mr. Brett*, whom I found to be in some way connected with General Carroll's staff, and who visited my prison frequently, and treated me and my family with the courtesy and kindness of a gentleman.

[Special Dispatch to the Memphis Appeal.]

"KNOXVILLE, Dec. 6.

"Dr. W. G. Brownlow, late editor of the Knoxville Whig, was arrested to-day by order of Brigadier-General Carroll, and committed to jail to await his trial on the charge of treason. General Carroll is pursuing a determined and vigorous policy, which is exercising a salutary effect upon the traitors in this section. The arrest of Brownlow will do much to quell their insurrectionary spirit.

"There has been some little skirmishing between straggling squads of Lincolnites and our troops above this place, but no outbreak of importance has occurred.

"The rebellion in East Tennessee may now be regarded as completely quelled.

"J. B."

A note of later date, from this same *walking groggery*, Carroll, addressed to his corrupt associate, *Attorney Ramsey*, and afterwards published in the Secession organ at Knoxville, goes to confirm my suspicions that he was acting the part of a two-faced man:—

"HEAD-QUARTERS, KNOXVILLE, Dec. 29.

"C. S. DISTRICT ATTORNEY J. C. RAMSEY:

"SIR:—In answer to your note of the 28th, I state that, though not aware of Dr. Brownlow's plan of concealment, his letter dated November 22d (enclosed a copy and my reply) induced me to believe that he was not very distant from this city, and could have been arrested. You will also see by his letter that he seemed only to dread violence, but was entirely willing to be tried before the civil tribunals for any offence of which he might be charged.

"Respectfully,
"WM. H. CARROLL,
"*Brigadier-General.*"

The only apology I can offer for Carroll in his deceptive course is that of his habits of drunkenness, his villainous associates in Knoxville, and the fact that he occupied as his quarters the house of the most unmitigated scoundrel in Knoxville, *John Hooper Crozier*,—a man whose baseness and villainies I have held up to public gaze for years. Such cowards and malicious rascals as this surrounded Carroll, took possession of him, drenched him in liquor, and used him to do their dirty work!

But I was thrown into this jail, a drawing of which is herewith submitted, where I found *about one hundred and fifty* Union men, old and young, representing all professions. The jail was so crowded that on the lower floor we had not room for all to lie down at one time. The prisoners took rest by turns, a portion standing while the others slept. There was not a chair, bench, stool, block, table, or any other article of furniture, in the building, save a dirty wooden bucket and a tin cup, used for watering the occupants of the room. A bucketful would not go round, as the weather was at times warm and many of the prisoners were feverish. To supply them with water, a hogshead was placed by the side of the jail, and a boy with a cart hauled water through the day. One prisoner at a time was allowed to go out with the bucket and draw it full, under an escort of bayonets. About twenty-four men were kept around the jail in arms, and on the inside at the windows, which were allowed to be up in daylight only to give us fresh air. Through the windows we could see these dirty, sweating, insulting, and abusive Rebel soldiers go to the hogshead and wash their hands and faces in it. I remonstrated, telling these ill-bred fellows that this water was our only dependence for drinking-water. The reply was, "By G—d, sir, we will have you know that where a Jeff Davis man washes his face and hands is good enough for any d——d Lincolnite to drink!" We, of course, had no remedy but to submit.

The food given the prisoners to eat was not fit for a good and trusty dog to devour. It was composed of the scraps and leavings of a dirty hotel kept by the jailer and deputy-marshal of the Confederacy,—the meat and bread sometimes half raw, sometimes burned, and always a scanty supply. I never tasted a particle of it, but was allowed the privilege of having my meals sent from home three times each day, an officer examining my basket as it came in and went out, to see that there was no correspondence between me and the Unionists out-of-doors. As this vile treatment and loathsome food produced disease, and, added to colds, often fell upon the bowels, the Rebel brutes who guarded us were furnished with additional opportunities for offering us personal indignity.

*   *   *   *   *

Blackguard songs were sung for our benefit, and we were all cursed and denounced both day and night. In marching us out and into the prison, we were ordered to "walk faster," and threatened with the bayonet if we did not obey. The most insulting of these sentinels were those from the Cotton States, men heralded to the world as the "flower of the Southern youth" and the "best blood" of the Confederacy.

There was one gentleman who visited us either daily or every other day: he was a gentleman and a humane man. I allude to Dr. Gray, Brigade Surgeon. He did all he could to prevent this sort of treatment, and had some benches made for the prisoners to sit on, and a sort of table upon which to place their scanty meals. But the feeling was, as a general thing, that any sort of treatment and fare were "too good for a set of d——d Union-shriekers and bridge-burners," as they styled all the prisoners.

Here my jail-journal commences, written in prison, with a lead-pencil, in small blank-books I kept in my side pocket. I will give it, without any polish or the slightest improvement, just as it was sketched,—written amidst the crowd and clamor of so many men, some sick, others impatient and tired, but all respectful to me and kind to each other.

Friday, (sunset,) Dec. 6.—I was committed to the jail of Knox county this evening upon a warrant sued out by the Confederate Attorney, *J. C. Ramsey,* upon a false oath he swore before a drunken commissioner, *Reynolds,* charging me with treason in the editorials of my paper. The only editorial cited was written in May, before Tennessee separated from the Federal Government.

I have found many old acquaintances here and long-tried friends; and whilst some were glad to see me in no worse condition, and in expectation of hearing the current news of the day, as well as from their families, others shed tears upon taking me by the hand, grasping it in silence. As a general thing, I have found them down in spirits and expecting the worst results. Some of them have been here since October, some since November, and others were committed but recently.

Some of them have said to me that they "never expected to come to this,"—that they had "never before looked through the grates of a jail." I have cheered them up as far as I have been able to do. Having them around me, I addressed them in this language:—

"Gentlemen, don't take your confinement so much to heart. Rather glory in it, as patriots, devoted to your country and to your principles. What are you here for? Not for stealing; not for counterfeiting; not for murder; but for your devotion to the Stars and Stripes, the glorious old banner under which Washington conquered, lived, and died. You will yet enjoy your liberties, and be permitted to die beneath the folds of the old Star-Spangled Banner, the sacred emblem of a common nationality. The Federal Government will crush out this wicked rebellion and liberate us, if we are not brutally murdered; and if we are, we die in a good cause. I am here with you to share your sorrows and sufferings, and here I intend to stay until the Rebels release me or execute me, or until the Federal army shall come to my rescue. You may take a different view of the subject, but I regard this as the proudest day of my life."

Saturday, Dec. 7.—This morning, *forty* of our number, under a heavy military escort, were sent off to Tuscaloosa. Thirty-one others arrived to take their places, from Cocke, Greene, and Jefferson counties. They bring us tales of woe from their respective counties, as to the treatment of Union men and Union families by the drunken and debauched cavalry in this rebellion. They are taking all the fine horses they can find, and appropriating them to their own use; they are entering houses, breaking open drawers and chests, seizing money, blankets, and whatever they can use.

The dirty organ of the mob who have placed me here —the Knoxville *Register*—has opened upon me; and, now that I have no paper in which to reply, shut up in solitary confinement, it will keep up a regular fire upon me. The following notice comes out this morning:—

"ARREST.—William G. Brownlow was arrested yesterday upon a charge of treason on a warrant ordered by the Confederate States Commissioner and drawn up by the District Attorney. He was committed to jail. His trial will come up in due course before the Confederate Court,—perhaps next week. The rumor of an order from the War Department for his safe-conduct to the North, in the last two days, has created intense excitement throughout this country, especially among those who have friends and relatives now languishing in prison on account of his teachings."

Sunday, Dec. 8.—Three others arrived from Cocke county, telling us tales of horror as to the treatment of Union men by the ruffian troops of Jeff Davis. Self-styled Vigilance Committees are prowling over the country like wolves, and military mobs, armed to the teeth, are arresting men upon suspicion of hostility to their new Government, and shooting others down in the field. They speak of the case of poor *Pearce,* a quiet man, a Methodist class-leader, shot down in his own field with a musket-ball,—not for any offence he had ever committed, but simply for being a Union man. I knew him personally, and know him to have been a harmless man. A brother of this villainous attorney, Ramsey, was in the crowd that murdered Pearce.

Monday, Dec. 9.—More prisoners arrived this evening. Twenty-eight are in from Jefferson and Cocke counties. Some of the Jefferson county prisoners have given us the particulars of the hanging of Hensie and Fry upon the same limb of an oak-tree over or close by the railroad-track. The bloody scoundrel who tied the knot was one Colonel Leadbetter, a native of Maine, who, after serving fifteen years in the United States army, married a gang of negroes at Mobile, and has become the great champion of Southern Rights. He ordered these two men to hang four days and nights, and the trains to pass by them slowly, so that the passengers could see, and kick, and strike with canes their dead bodies, from the front and rear platforms of the cars, as they passed,—which was actually done. I shall illustrate the scene with an engraving if I ever live to get out of this prison. And I propose, if ever the Federal army shall capture East Tennessee,—as I believe it will,—and with it this murderer, *Leadbetter*, that he shall hang on the same limb, and that Fry's widow shall tie the knot around his infernal neck.

Tuesday, Dec. 10.—The tedium of prison-life has rather oppressed us all to-day. It has been relieved a little by our coming in contact with some insolent

Southern negroes. One in uniform, from Alabama, has been guarding us with a double-barrelled shot-gun, and has been insulting and abusive. Another negro came into the jail and threw slugs of lead through the grates into the iron cage of one of our prisoners. We have all to submit to this sort of treatment. When we are put here, we are deprived of our weapons, pocket-knives, and money, and all are confiscated, leaving us helpless. Some of our men had several hundred dollars in their pockets, and all had more or less money.

One of the scoundrels who took an active part in having me put here is *Colonel W. M. Churchwell*, the great bank-swindler, whose dishonesty I brought to light in a suit in chancery, all of which is now on record. One of the privates in Churchwell's regiment, by the name of *Barker*, is now here a prisoner for having knocked down his captain. Barker was run against Churchwell for colonel, and actually beat him one hundred and eighty votes; but Carroll gave the certificate in favor of Churchwell. Churchwell afterwards had Barker chained to a tree, and more recently he had Captain Jackson arrested for heading a petition to C. to resign on the score of *incompetency*.

Wednesday, Dec. 11.—C. A. Haun, a man about twenty-seven years of age, was taken out to-day and hung, on a charge of bridge-burning. He had but a short notice of his sentence, having been condemned

C. A. Haun parting from his Family before his Execution. (Page 313.)

without any defence allowed him by a drum-head and whiskey-drinking court-martial. I think that he was notified of his coming death about one hour in advance. I know he desired a Methodist preacher sent for to sing and pray with him, and this was refused him: so that he was forced to exchange worlds without the "benefit of clergy." They drove up a cart with a coffin in it, surrounded by a hardened set of Rebel troops, displaying their bayonets and looking and talking savagely. It is stated to us that one of the Rebel chaplains officiated at the hanging, and stated that Haun desired him to say that he had been misled by the Union leaders and papers and was sorry for his conduct, whereupon Haun contradicted him, and said that he had admitted no such thing. Haun leaves a young wife and two or three little children. I had, myself, sooner be Haun than any one of his murderers.

Fifteen more prisoners came in to-day from Greene and Hancock counties, charged with having been armed as Union men and accustomed to drill, which I have no doubt is true. What their fate will be, God only knows. These savage beasts of the Southern Confederacy are prepared to hang a man for saying that Secession is wrong or unconstitutional, although John C. Calhoun admitted this much himself.

Thursday, Dec. 12.—Fifteen of our prisoners were

started to Tuscaloosa this morning, to remain there as prisoners of war. They had no trial, but were sent upon their admission that they had been found in arms, as Union men, preparing to defend themselves against the murderous assaults and highway-robberies daily committed by the so-called Confederate cavalry. Poor fellows! They hated to go; and no wonder, for they are treated like dogs on the way, as well as after they get there!

Friday, Dec. 13.—Three more prisoners in to-day, from Hancock and Hawkins counties. Charge, as usual, Union men, attached to a company of Home-Guards. The *Register* has been handed to me, in which I find the following cowardly attack from some one of the many hypocrites who have gone over to Secession or been bribed by the leaders of this rebellion:—

(For the Register.)

Brownlow.

"Why is this ringleader of all the toryism and devilment in East Tennessee dealt with so leniently, and others, not half so guilty, punished extremely? We insist upon it that all who have been apprehended and are now in prison ought to be released without further trouble. They have only done what Brownlow, Johnson, Nelson, Maynard, Fleming, Trigg, and others, who were leaders in trying to ruin the country, told them to do. And now why keep any others in custody? Why weary the troops in hunting them out and bringing them to justice? Justice should be meted out to all alike; and if the principal leader is not only released, but furnished a safe escort, it should so be exercised to others. We should invite Johnson and Maynard home, and promise them safety while they may be disposed to remain among us and learn all the details of the Southern movement.

"The brave men who see that Brownlow gets safely out could certainly see that Johnson and Maynard came safely in!

"But, seriously, we have no desire to see any man—not even Mr. Brownlow—pull Tennessee hemp, or that of Missouri, nor yet that of Kentucky. But we do think that the least punishment that should be inflicted ought to be a residence at Tuscaloosa until the war closes, and then the enviable gentleman can go over by himself and see Abe Lincoln, and abide with him forever.

"Can it be that any officer or soldier will be pleased to carry out such a tormentor as Brownlow,—conduct him safely out who has all the time been seeking the ruin of every Secessionist and the whole Southern Confederacy,—who would 'rather be in hell than with such a bogus Government'? Can it be that those brave men who have left all that is dear to them to defend the country will feel themselves honored by safely conveying their most inveterate enemy over to Lincoln to do them still more damage? or will they not rather feel like they have lost more than half they have been fighting for in this State? East Tennessee has been a heavy expense to the State and to the Confederate Government, in consequence of the teaching and leading of Brownlow and others; and now to let him go in peace seems to be the height of folly, or we cannot see right. It will cool the ardor of many a soldier, and cause the community to lose confidence in the hope they entertained of the speedy independence of the South.

"We have nothing to controvert with those at the helm of affairs, but we think we can safely say that our friends at Nashville and Richmond have been led astray and badly hoodwinked by those from East Tennessee, who are better friends to Unionism or Toryism than to the Southern interests.

"It has been said in the ears of authority that Brownlow was so secreted that he could not be found. But no true Southern man believes a word of that in this part of the country. He could have been picked up in three days, at any time during his absence, by a deputation of ten soldiers. The only wonder is that it was not done.

"It may be well said that enemies with fair faces have dictated, and have been heard and listened to, instead of those who have been faithful to the cause of the South through thick and thin.

"The enmity and trouble amongst Union men in East Tennessee is not rooted out: it is only covered up; while the heat, with some honorable exceptions, is increasing, and waiting and hoping for Lincoln to send over his army, and they will 'pitch in.'"

Saturday, Dec. 14.—Three more prisoners from the upper counties were brought in to-day. They speak of the outrages perpetrated by these Rebel troops, and of their murderous spirit. Three officers visited me to-day. Lieutenant-Colonel Golladay stated to me that, whilst he was not informed as to what they would do with me, he was in favor of sending me to Nashville, boarding me at a hotel, giving me the privileges of the city until the war was over, but confining me to its limits. I told him that his mode of punishment was not severe, but that I preferred his Government should carry out its stipulations with me and send me beyond their limits.

General Carroll visited me, but was, as I supposed,

more drunk than usual. He thought that I ought to be out of this, but that I ought to be willing to swear allegiance to the Confederate Government. I told him that I would lie here until I died with old age before I would take such an oath. I did not consider that he had a Government; I regarded it as a big Southern mob. It had never been recognized by any Government on earth, and never would be!

Sunday, Dec. 15.—Started thirty-five of our lot to Tuscaloosa, to be held during the war. Levi Trewhitt, an able lawyer, but an old man, will never get back. His sons came up to see him, but were refused the privilege. Dr. Hunt, from the same county of Bradley, has also gone. His wife came sixty miles to see him, and came to the jail-door, but was refused admittance. Dr. Hunt's offence is twofold. First, his wife is my wife's only sister; and, next, he holds the clerkship of the Chancery Court, and *Tom Campbell,* the judge-advocate on the court-martial, has a brother-in-law whom he desires to put in the office. I have told the doctor that as soon as his office could be declared vacant he would be turned out, and McMillan, the brother-in-law of Campbell, put in his place.*

* Trewhitt has since died, Hunt has been turned out, and McMillan appointed Clerk of the Chancery Court! Campbell has been ordered to go to his command; but, not having joined to fight, he refused, and resigned. His resignation was not accepted, and he was driven out of camps in Middle Tennessee.

Monday, Dec. 16.—Brought in Dr. Wells and Colonel Morris, of Knox county, two clever men and good citizens. Their offence is that they are Union men, first; and, next, as old Whigs, they voted and electioneered against this scoundrel Ramsey, the Confederate Attorney, when he was beaten for the United States Congress, about two years ago. He now has a chance of paying these gentlemen back!

I have this day mailed the following letter to the Secretary of War at Richmond:—

KNOXVILLE JAIL, Dec. 16, 1861.

HON. J. P. BENJAMIN:—

You authorized General Crittenden to give me passports and an escort to send me into the old Government, and he invited me here for that purpose; but a third-rate county-court lawyer, acting as your Confederate attorney, took me out of his hands and cast me into this prison. I am anxious to learn which is your highest authority,—the Secretary of War, a major-general, or a dirty little drunken attorney such as *J. C. Ramsey* is!

You are reported to have said to a gentleman in Richmond that I am a bad man, dangerous to the Confederacy, and that you desire me out of it. Just give me my passports, and I will do for your Confederacy more than the devil has ever done,—I will quit the country!

I am, &c.,

W. G. BROWNLOW.

Knoxville Jail, Dec. 16, 1861.

Hon J. P. Benjamin

You authorized Gen. Crittenden to give me passports, and an escort to send me into the old Government, and he invited me here for that purpose. But a third rate County Court Lawyer, acting as your Confederate Attorney, took me out of his hands and cast me into this prison. I am anxious to learn which is your highest authority, the Secretary of War, a Major General, or a dirty little drunken Attorney, such as J. C. Ramsey is!

You are reported to have said to a gentleman in Richmond, that, I am a bad man, dangerous to the Confederacy, and that you desire me out of it. Just give me my passports, and I will do for your Confederacy, more than the Devil has ever done, I will quit the country!

I am, &c,

W. G. Brownlow

Tuesday, Dec. 17.—Brought in a Union man from Campbell county to-day, leaving behind six small children, and their mother dead. This man's offence is holding out for the Union!

Two more carts drove up with coffins in them and a heavy military guard around them. This produced in our circle of prisoners great consternation, for we did not know certainly who were to hang. They, however, came into the jail and marched out Jacob Harmon and his son Henry, and hung them up on the same gallows! The old man was a man of property, quite old and infirm, and they compelled him to sit on the scaffold and see his son, a young man, hang first; then he was ordered up and hung by his side. They were charged with bridge-burning, but protested to the last that they were not guilty. I know not how this was; but the laws of Tennessee only send a man to the penitentiary for such offences.

To-night, two brothers—named Walker—came in from Hawkins county, charged with having "*talked Union talk.*"

Wednesday, Dec. 18.—Discharged sixty prisoners to-day, who had been in prison from three to five weeks,—taken through mistake, as was said, there being nothing against them. Business suffering at home, unlawfully seized upon and thrust into this uncomfortable jail, they are now turned out by the corrupt, wicked, God-defying, and hell-deserving authorities of this usurped, bogus, and truly infamous Confederacy. We are getting our number reduced, but these devils will replenish our prison as long as they can find Union men in East Tennessee; and that will be until they kill them all off!

Thursday, Dec. 19.—I have now only been fourteen days in this *Union Hall,* but I am feeling the effects of the cold nights and confinement. My old disease. *bronchitis,* is troubling me. So well am I satisfied of the inflammation of the bronchi, or ramifications of the windpipe, that I have called in a physician and had him insert a silk cord in my breast just below the chin, so as to bring the inflammation to the surface.

To-night twelve more Union prisoners were brought in from lower East Tennessee, charged with belonging to Colonel Clift's regiment of Union men, arming and drilling to go over to Kentucky and join the Federal army.

Friday, Dec. 20.—General Carroll, hearing of my indisposition, came in to-day and offered to remove me to their dirty hospital. I declined the offer,—did not want passports to where I would likely be poisoned in twenty-four hours. I told him I was ready to receive passports to go beyond the limits of the Confederacy. If these could not be had, I desired to remain where I was. This is a terrible night! The sentinels are all drunk,—howling like wolves,—rushing to our windows with the ferocity of the Sepoys of India, and daring prisoners to show their heads,—cocking their guns and firing off three of them into the jail, and pretending it was accidental. Merciful God! how long are we to be treated after this fashion?

Saturday, Dec. 21.—Took out five of the prisoners brought here from the Clift expedition,—liberated them by their agreeing to go into the Rebel army. Their dread of Tuscaloosa induced them to go into the service. They have offered this chance to all, and only sent off those who stubbornly refused.

The troops in town are on a general spree, for as many as twenty-five of them have been thrust into prison with us. I suspect they are made drunk and put into jail to get up a row with the Union prisoners. They are yelling all night like savages,—some cursing Lincoln and the Union men, some cursing Davis and his Confederacy, and all swearing that they are sick of the war. I write this at midnight.

To-day I succeeded in having mailed to Nashville the following letter, written yesterday, which I feel confident the *Patriot* will do me the justice to publish:—

KNOXVILLE JAIL, Dec. 20, 1861.

EDITORS OF THE NASHVILLE PATRIOT:—

In your issue of the 17th instant you say, "We learn that W. G. Brownlow, imprisoned at Knoxville, refuses to eat any thing, *desiring to starve himself to death.*"

I have no doubt, Mr. Editor, that you have learned such a thing, but it is wonderful intelligence! And, but for the fact that I do not wish to be understood as trying to commit suicide, I would not care to correct the erroneous statement. The truth in my case is, that I have now been in jail two weeks, and I have eaten too much every day, my family, with the permission of Brigadier-General Carroll, furnishing me with three meals each day. But for taking cold, and suffering from a sore throat, I could boast of usual health. As it is, I claim to be the most cheerful of more than one hundred prisoners I found here on my arrival.

But, sir, I will now give you an additional item or so, which many of your readers will peruse with interest if you are allowed to publish them. I left home about the 5th of November, with a view to collect some claims due my office for advertising, and to relieve the fears of my family, who were daily annoyed with drunken soldiers, calling before my house and flourishing their side-knives and pistols and making threats of violence. The last week in November I received a letter from Brigadier-General Carroll, inviting me to return and promising me protection from personal violence. On the 5th of December I received a brief letter from Major-General Crittenden, inviting me to his head-quarters in Knoxville, promising me passports

Execution of Jacob Harmon and his son Henry. (Page 319.)

into Kentucky and a military escort to conduct me safe. At the same time I was furnished with the copy of a letter to the major-general from J. P. Benjamin, Secretary of War, advising him to give me passports and a safe-conduct beyond the Confederate lines.

Supposing the head of the War Department and the major-general commanding here to be acting in good faith, I reported myself in person and accepted the offer of passports. I agreed to start on Saturday, and the general designated Captain Gillespie's company of cavalry for an escort.

But on Friday evening, just before sundown, I was arrested for *treason,* founded on certain *editorials* in the *Knoxville Whig* since June last, the warrant being signed by Commissioner Reynolds and Attorney Ramsey. I am, therefore, in jail,—in close confinement,—perfectly contented, and making no complaints against any one. I am waiting patiently to see which is the highest power,—the War Department at Richmond associated with the major-general in command here, or the Commissioners' Court for Knoxville. Nay, I am anxious to know whether the high authorities inviting me here were acting in good faith, or were only playing off a *trick* to have me incarcerated. I am not willing to believe that the representatives of a would-be great Government struggling for its independence, and having in charge the interests of twelve millions of people, intend to act in bad faith to me. The *chivalrous* people of the South, and all the journals, have denounced the high-handed measures of the United States Government in suspending the *habeas corpus* act, suppressing public journals, and incarcerating citizens upon *lettres de cachet;* and I will not allow myself to believe that the Confederate Government will resort to similar tricks.

I am, sir, very respectfully, &c.,

W. G. BROWNLOW.

Sunday, Dec. 22.—Brought in old man Wamplar, an old Dutchman seventy years of age, from Greene county, charged with being an *Andy Johnson man,* and "talking Union talk." Sentinels are stationed in our rooms to watch us,—cursing us all for d——d thieves, Tories, and scoundrels, to even guard whom is a disgrace, they allege. One of them carried the matter so far that one of our prisoners, *Tucker,* pitched into him and flogged him without arms, and in defiance of his musket.

Monday, Dec. 23.—Officer of the day in charge of the sentinels furnished liquor to a portion of the prisoners, such as came out of the ranks of Secession. They got drunk. A general row was threatened. Union prisoners and Rebel sentinels played cards, and the former won the money.

Tuesday, Dec. 24.—White's regiment, some of whom have been guarding us, left to-day for Kentucky to join Zollicoffer's army. Many of them seemed to regret it,—told our prisoners that they felt like going to their graves. Officer of the day came into the jail and demanded all the cards. They were handed over to him, and he burned them. We have but three men who play cards. To-night they brought in one of their "Texas Rangers," who had deserted from Manassas. He looks but little like killing Yankees. Various troops put in jail during the day for drunkenness.

Wednesday, Dec. 25.—The Union ladies in and around Knoxville applied to General Carroll for leave to send in a Christmas dinner. He granted leave, and stated that he regarded it as an act of humanity. The supply was abundant and sumptuous, and was most thankfully received.

It affords me great pleasure to know that I have been able, out of my basket of provisions and coffee-pot, to furnish several very old men, and very sick, who could not eat what comes from the greasy inn. Two of them are Baptist ministers, Messrs. Pope and Cate, each as much as, or more than, *seventy* years of age. The first-named was sent here for praying, in his pulpit, for the President of the United States. The latter is here for cheering the Stars and Stripes as the banner neared his house, borne by some men on horseback.

Thursday, Dec. 26.—Some twelve Confederate troops,

beastly drunk, have to-day been confined in our jail for outraging all the decencies of life. They make our jail a hell on earth. What an affliction it is to be cursed with confinement in such a place and with such brutes as these are! I am sick, without an appetite, and I fear I am taking the fever. Several of our men are now sick, stretched out upon the floor; and some of them, I have reason to believe, will never survive this confinement.

Friday, Dec. 27.—Harrison Self, an industrious, honest, and heretofore peaceable man, a citizen of Greene county, was notified this morning that he was to be hanged at four o'clock P.M. His daughter, a noble girl, modest, and neatly attired, came in this morning to see him. Heart-broken and bowed down under a fearful weight of sorrow, she entered his iron cage, and they embraced each other most affectionately. My God, what a sight! What an affecting scene! May these eyes of mine, bathed in tears, never look upon the like again! The weeping of prisoners who beheld this scene brings to my mind the verses I subjoin:—

"Did Christ o'er sinners weep?
And shall our cheeks be dry?
Let floods of penitential grief
Burst forth from every eye.

"The Son of God in tears,
Angels with wonder see!
Be thou astonished, O my soul:
He shed those tears for thee."

But her short limit to remain with her father expired, and she came out weeping bitterly, and shedding burning tears. Requesting me to write a dispatch for her and sign her name to it, I took out my pencil and a slip of paper, and wrote the following:—

"KNOXVILLE, Dec. 27, 1861.

"HON. JEFFERSON DAVIS:—

"My father, Harrison Self, is sentenced to hang at four o'clock this evening, on a charge of bridge-burning. As he remains my earthly all, and all my hopes of happiness centre in him, I implore you to pardon him. ELIZABETH SELF."

With this dispatch the poor girl hurried off to the office, some two or three hundred yards from the jail; and about two o'clock in the afternoon the answer came to General Carroll, telling him not to allow Self to be hung. Self was turned out of the cage into the jail with the rest of us, and looks as if he had gone through a long spell of sickness. But what a thrill of joy ran through the heart of that noble girl! Self is to be confined, as I understand, during the war. This is hard upon an innocent man; but it is preferable to hanging.

Self stated that when he expected to hang, and only a few hours before Davis's dispatch came, the marshal and jailer, Fox, told him that he was authorized to say to him that if he would confess his guilt as a bridge-burner, under the gallows, and would state that BROWNLOW, TRIGG, BAXTER, and TEMPLE had put him up to it and furnished money to burn the bridges, he would be reprieved! He replied to the wicked, malicious, and infernal offer that he could not say so, as it would not be true. What an effort to involve innocent men! And what a temptation to the man about to hang! The men who authorized this bribe deserve the lowest and hottest apartments in the infernal regions.

Upon the jail-floor, in one corner, lies Madison Cate, low with fever, and upon a bit of old carpeting, with some sort of bundle under his aching head to serve as a pillow. I feel confident that he will die. Poor fellow! He is an honest man,—a man who stays at home and attends to his own business. He has a little farm in Sevier county, a wife and six small and helpless children, and is here for being a Union man and mustering with a company of Union Guards. This is the head and front of his offending.

We have all just witnessed a thrilling scene. The wife of poor Cate came and presented herself in front of the jail, neatly attired, with an infant at her breast, of five or six weeks old,—born, I think, since her husband's confinement! She asked leave to see her dying husband, but was refused at the door, by some one claiming to act upon authority. I put my head out of the window and remonstrated, telling them that it was a sin and a shame to refuse this poor woman, after coming so far, the liberty of seeing her husband, and seeing him for the last time! They allowed her to enter, but limited her stay to twenty minutes. She came in. And, oh, my soul! what a scene! Seeing the emaciated form of her husband on the floor, pining with sorrow and severe affliction, and destitute of every comfort, she approached with faltering step, and sank down upon his heaving breast, bathed in tears of anguish. I asked her to give me the babe as she ventured up; for I saw that she was unconscious of having it in her arms. In that condition, without a word, they remained until her twenty minutes expired, of which being notified, she rose up and retired. I hope I may never look upon such a scene again. Oh, what oppression! And yet this is the *spirit* of Secession! I find some consolation in the following verses:—

"Oppression shall not always reign:
There dawns a brighter day,
When freedom, burst from every chain,
Shall have triumphant sway.

"Then right shall over might prevail,
And truth, like hero armed in mail,
The hosts of tyrant wrong assail,
And hold eternal sway!"

CHAPTER XXI.

THE outside pressure against me I knew was very great, and the clamor for my blood, or rather for my *neck*, was to be heard among the Secession citizens on the street, and among the infuriated troops in camp and in the liquor-shops of the town. I really supposed, at one time, that they would hang me, and I made up my mind to meet the occasion like a man. In view of this fate, I sketched off a brief speech, which I intended to ask the privilege of delivering on the scaffold. I think they would have granted the request, from an intense curiosity to hear what I had to say in such a trying moment; and I believe I could have stood forth and said it in the face of ten thousand people. I give the speech just as I prepared it in pencil-writing, at intervals, in prison. I began writing it when they commenced hanging our prisoners:—

Intended Speech under the Gallows.

FELLOW-COUNTRYMEN:—I have often addressed many of you, upon different topics, but never under circumstances like those which now surround me, as I feel that I am speaking for the last time. I suppose I have been sentenced to hang by a court-martial sitting in this city: I say I *suppose* so, for I have never had any trial, or even a notice of a trial being in progress. So it has been with those who have been executed before me. It is alike a matter of indifference whether I was tried by *that* court-martial in my absence and in the absence of witnesses and counsel, or whether I had been present; the result would have been death. The judge advocate, THOMAS J. CAMPBELL, is a perfidious man, as destitute of real honor and purity of purpose as he is of true courage and manly virtue. Associated with him is JAMES D. THOMAS, a man who was expelled from the Methodist ministry for whipping his wife and slandering his venerable old father-in-law! This man Thomas has advocated on the bench, in open court-martial, the sending of the Union masses of East Tennessee to Alabama and Mississippi, and working them in the field, under negro overseers, and the hanging of the Union leaders here! Justice at the hands of such a set of men is the last thing I would expect. Indeed, there is more glory in being put to death by such men than in being acquitted, after going through the forms of a trial.

It is known to many of you that I had left home to avoid personal violence, and was out of the reach of the mob, who could not find me, after repeated efforts by squads sent out, armed, by that arch-hypocrite and would-be murderer, W. B. Wood, of Alabama. In my concealment I was informed by a letter from Major-General Crittenden, in command at this place, that he was instructed by the Secretary of War at Richmond, Mr. Benjamin, to give me passports and a military escort to conduct me out of this bogus Government into the Federal Government; and I was invited to appear at his head-quarters in twenty-four hours, where he promised me that I should be furnished with said passports. I was there within the time specified, accompanied by Colonel Baxter, the arrangement was made, and the company of Captain Gillespie designated as my escort. But that evening, just before sundown, I was arrested upon a warrant issued by that disgraceful specimen of our nature, *Commissioner Reynolds*, upon the false oath of *Attorney Ramsey*, a corrupt man, for whom no decent Secessionist entertains any respect. The charge against me was *treason*, founded upon editorials, one of which has been published, in part, by Ramsey, in the Knoxville *Register;* and although the miserable man swore that the editorial was published *since the* 10*th of June*, at which time the State voted out, my files will show that it was published on the 25th of May.

Thus I was taken out of the hands of a major-general and of his Secretary of War by a worthless little Confederate lawyer, and thrown into the common jail of this county; refused bail, when the best the county affords was offered; and, up to this eventful hour, I have been denied a trial, and an opportunity to defend myself before the court condemning me to an ignominious death. The proof of all that is here charged will be found in the correspondence cited, which I have placed in the hands of a friend for publication. It will show that these parties, one and all, have acted a treacherous part towards me, and have violated their pledges and faith. Their perfidy and treachery are absolutely disgraceful to their bogus Government, if indeed such a Government can be disgraced.

Some hostile reminiscences of the past, as between other cowardly, mean, and murderous men of this city and myself, will appear in the documents I leave behind; and I request my sons to publish them, even at the cost of their lives. I desire to bear my testimony, even in a dying hour, to the perfidy, double-dealing, and cowardly course toward me of that prince of hypocrites and great embodiment of human deceit, Campbell Wallace, the president of the railroad, and one of the great lights of Secession. I warn all men present, and all who may hear of this statement, never to confide in that man. He is supremely selfish, notoriously insincere, and would sell his interest in his God—which, I fear, is not a very large one—for money!

I must also bear witness to the treachery and insincerity of William G. MacAdoo, who, while meeting me with a smile and professing friendship, stated to John Black that I ought to be kept in prison during this war. This man was on the verge of starvation, and without credit, when I took it upon myself to attend the sitting of our Legislature, some years ago, and help make him District Attorney. He since lost one wife and married a second owning a gang of negroes and a rice-plantation in Georgia, and has turned over to Secession. I warn my family and friends never to confide in him.

Fellow-countrymen, I am shortly to be executed,—not for any crime punishable with death, but for my devotion to my country, her laws and Constitution. I die for refusing to espouse the cause of this wicked rebellion; and I glory in it, strange as you may think it. I could have lived, if I had taken an oath of allegiance to this so-called Confederacy. Rather than stultify myself and disgrace my family by such an oath, I agree to die! I never could sanction this Government, and I trust that no child of mine will ever do it. Look at the past history of the leaders and originators of this rebellion. There is not a man of unstained character to be found among them. Yancey is a convicted murderer, who killed his uncle, (Dr. Earl, of South Carolina,) and, instead of going to England to intrigue against this Government, he would have been in prison had he not been pardoned by the Governor of that State. Wigfall, a Confederate Senator and a

Interview of W. H. H. Self with his daughter in Knoxville Jail. (Page 326.)

general, fled from his native State of South Carolina to Texas to escape the horrors of assassination, became a collecting attorney for large amounts, and then swindled his employers out of their dues, murdering as many as two men in Texas. Floyd, while Governor of my native State, was guilty of swindling the State out of some thirty thousand dollars of the Washington Monument Fund intrusted to his care; while in Buchanan's Cabinet, in violation of his oath, he stole, besides large amounts of bonds, the guns, forts, and ammunition of the Federal Government, to aid in carrying on this infamous rebellion. Slidell, another intriguer, who never had an honest emotion of soul in his life, assisted, while in the United States Senate, to pass through Congress that great swindle of the age, the "*Houmans Land Grant*,"—a swindle so gigantic and a cheat so enormous that the next Congress revoked the grant. Benjamin, your Secretary of War, and one of the men engaged in deceiving me, was expelled from a New England college for stealing money and jewelry out of the trunks of his fellow-students: he afterwards got into the Senate from Louisiana by turning from a Whig to a Democrat, and became the partner of Slidell in the Houmans swindle. Thompson, the Mississippi member of Buchanan's Cabinet, while Secretary of the Interior, was a partner in stealing some Indian Trust Bonds, and, when about to be dismissed for the offence, fled from the Federal capital by night, to avoid a prosecution. Cobb, the Georgia member of Buchanan's Cabinet, speculated in stocks, using Government money, and was detected in it; and all this was at a time when he was acting under oath, as the head of the Treasury Department. Davis, your President, after his State had borrowed millions, led the way in the work of repudiation and in defrauding Mississippi's honest creditors. Toombs, the big man of your Government at Richmond, was the confederate of Keitt and Brooks in their attempt to assassinate Sumner. Swan, your Congressman from this district, and an original Secessionist, is the forger of the Johnson letters to Lawrence, with a view to swindle the latter out of ten thousand dollars. These, and a host of others like them, are the men who originated and are carrying on this Southern Rebellion. Ought not any honest man to prefer to hang rather than act with *such* men in a wicked crusade against the mild sway of the best Government on earth?

But I must close. Solemn thought! I die, with confidence that the United States Government will crush out this rebellion during the coming spring and summer. Mark my prediction! I would like to be living when that is done; but I must resign myself to my fate.

I have a word to say as it regards my family. I leave a wife and seven children to the mercies of a cold-hearted world. I hope the Union men of the country will be kind to them, and seek to impress their minds with what is true,—that they are not disgraced, but honored, by my death. Let me be shrouded in the sacred folds of the Star-Spangled Banner; and let my children's children know that the last words I uttered on earth were,—

> "Forever float that standard sheet!
> Where breathes the foe but falls before us,
> With Freedom's soil beneath our feet,
> And Freedom's banner streaming o'er us!"

January 1, 1862.—For the last four or five days I have been very sick, and I am now *salivated* from an excess of mercury. I have, therefore, not made any note of what has passed. Captain Monserrat, late of Nashville, is in charge of this post at present; and I will do him the justice to say that he has treated me and my family with great kindness, and as I would expect to be treated by a gentleman. Upon the testimony of Dr. Hill, one of my family physicans, Captain Monserrat has had me brought to a private room, on my own lot, and guarded as at the jail. It was upon the faith of this certificate that I was removed:—

"KNOXVILLE, TENNESSEE, Monday, Dec. 30, '61.

"CAPTAIN MONSERRAT:—

"SIR:—For a day or two past I have been in attendance upon Mr. Brownlow at the jail, and have much regretted that greater quiet could not be secured to him, and have little hopes of his recovery without it; injuries of his skull, received years since, complicate his sickness, and render this imperatively necessary for a rapid recovery.

"Very respectfully, &c.

"O. F. HILL."

Upon learning that I was about to be removed, and upon getting a letter from the War Department to the effect that I ought not to have been imprisoned, the miscreant Ramsey went into court and ordered my release upon the civil arrest; but an officer of the army, who accompanied the notice of my release to my bedside, re-arrested me under the military authority, and placed an armed guard at my door.

The following document appeared in the *Register*, and shows two things,—that the villainous attorney withheld the letter of Benjamin for a week after receiving it, and that the military authorities were acting with Reynolds and Ramsey from the first. The article herewith presented is from the Richmond *Dispatch*:—

Trial of Brownlow—His Release—Letter from the Secretary of War.

"The Knoxville *Register* of Saturday says that the cause of Parson Brownlow, arrested for the publication of incendiary articles against the Confederate Government, was called up in court on last Friday.

"The Deputy Marshal, Fox, having been ordered to bring from jail W. G. Brownlow, reported that Brownlow was too unwell, as he represented himself, to appear at the court-house. Very few spectators were present. The Commissioner ordered the District Attorney to proceed; whereupon the District Attorney arose and read the following letter, which he had just received from Mr. Benjamin, Secretary of War at Richmond:—

"CONFEDERATE STATES OF AMERICA,
"WAR DEPARTMENT, RICHMOND, Dec. 22, 1861.

"SIR:—Your letters of the 17th and 19th inst. have been received. In relation to Brownlow's case, the facts are simply these. Brownlow, being concealed somewhere in the mountains, made application to General Crittenden for protection against what he called a military mob or military tribunal, if he came to Knoxville, professing his willingness to undergo a civil trial,—*i.e.* a trial before the civil court, as distinguished from court-martial; and, as I understand, General Crittenden promised to protect him from any violence and from any trial before a military tribunal.

"In the mean time Mr. Baxter came here, and represented that Brownlow, who was entirely beyond our power and so concealed that no one could get possession of his person, was willing to leave the country and go into exile, to avoid any further trouble in East Tennessee, and proffered that Brownlow would come in and deliver himself up to be conveyed out of East Tennessee, if the Government would agree to let him do so and to protect him in his exit.

"If Brownlow had been in our hands, we might not have accepted this proposition; but, deeming it better to have him as an open enemy on the other side of the lines than as a secret enemy within the lines, authority was given to General Crittenden to assure him of protection across the border if he came into Knoxville.

"It was not in our power, nor that of any one else, to

prevent his being taken by process of law; and I confess it did not occur to me that any attempt would be made to take him out of the hands of the military authority. This has been done, however, and it is only regretted in one point of view,—that is, color is given to the suspicion that Brownlow has been *entrapped*, and has given himself up under promise of protection which has not been firmly kept. General Crittenden feels sensitive on this point; and I share his feeling. Better that any, the most dangerous enemy, however criminal, should escape, than that the honor and good faith of the Government should be impugned or even suspected. General Crittenden gave his word only that Brownlow should not be tried by the court-martial, and I gave authority to promise him protection if he would surrender, to be conveyed across the border. We have both kept our words as far as was in our power; but every one must see that Brownlow would now be safe, and at large, if he had not supposed that his reliance on the promise made him would insure his safe departure from East Tennessee.

"Under all the circumstances, therefore, if Brownlow is exposed to harm from his arrest, I shall deem the honor of the Government so far compromitted as to consider it my duty to urge on the President a pardon for any offence of which he may be found guilty; and I repeat the expression of my regret that he was prosecuted, however evident may be his guilt.

"J. P. BENJAMIN,
"*Secretary of War.*

"J. C. RAMSEY, ESQ.,
"*C.S. Dist. Att'y, Knoxville.*

"Upon the reading of the foregoing letter, the Attorney remarked that the arrest of Brownlow had been made after consultation with the military authorities, who had given assurances that if Brownlow should be arrested by civil process the military would in no manner interfere in his behalf, except to protect him from personal violence; that this arrest had been made because of the following and similar articles which had been published in Brownlow's paper:—

"'Let the railroads on which Union citizens of East Tennessee are conveyed to Montgomery in irons be eternally and hopelessly destroyed. Let the property of the men concerned be consumed, and let their lives pay the forfeit, and the names will be given!'

"District Attorney Ramsey then proceeded to say that he would enter a *nolle prosequi* only upon the ground that the good faith of the Confederate States Government should be carried out in this case, and Brownlow be transported beyond our lines. This he did that no imputation whatever should be made against the authorities at Richmond of bad faith, no matter what might be the circumstances which led the authorities to such a conclusion. For himself, he believed that Brownlow could have been arrested; but as a different impression prevailed at Richmond, and the authorities acted upon that, from the information they had, he could not do otherwise than enter a *nolle prosequi.*

"Judge Reynolds, having heard the letter of the Secretary of War, remarked that, under the circumstances, he could not hesitate as to the discharge of Brownlow, and so ordered."

It is not true that I made application to General Crittenden; but he applied to me to come in. He first sent General Cazwell to my house, to ask my family to send me word to come in. Although General Cazwell is much of a gentleman, and I did not doubt the truth of his message, yet I desired to have the request from General Crittenden in writing, which I got, and which will be found in the preceding pages. Colonel Baxter's application was without my knowledge. But the rebuke of Ramsey and his clique, I apprehend, was occasioned by a trip to Richmond by General Crittenden.

And although I was instantly re-arrested by the military and surrounded by a strong guard, and there kept through the months of January and February, the *clique* raved like savages to think that I should be released from one arrest, and taken to a private room, where my family could furnish me with a feather-bed. The *Register* brought out the following, no doubt the joint production of the civil and military authorities:—

"THE RELEASE OF W. G. BROWNLOW.

"We do not desire to be understood as attaching an undue or extravagant importance to the discharge of Brownlow from the custody of the Confederate authorities. The writer of this has known this individual for years. He is, in few words, a diplomat of the first water. Brownlow rarely undertakes any thing unless he sees his way entirely through the millstone. He covers over his really profound knowledge of human nature with an appearance of eccentricity and extravagance. If any of our readers indulge the idea that Brownlow is not '*smart*,' in the full acceptation of the term, they should abolish the delusion at once and forever. Crafty, cunning, generous to his particular friends, benevolent and charitable to their faults, ungrateful and implacable to his enemies, we cannot refrain from saying that he is the best judge of human nature within the bounds of the Southern Confederacy.

"In procuring from the Confederate authorities a safe-conduct to a point within the Hessian lines, he has exhibited the most consummate skill. Absenting himself from the immediate vicinity of Knoxville,—hiding at a point where he was concealed from the observation of any one, save his particular friends,—with easy communication with the military commanders at the Knoxville post,—he succeeding in foiling the Confederate authorities at every point. By a hypocritical appeal to Southern generosity against what he chose to term '*mob-law*,' he succeeded in concealing his real whereabouts just long enough to accomplish his real purposes. *Time* was all he wanted.

"Cajoling the authorities here with the idea that 'he was doing nothing,' his emissaries were dispatched to Richmond. By a species of diplomacy and legerdemain, Secretary Benjamin is induced to believe that Brownlow, forsooth, is quite a harmless individual. The move was made, the blow was struck, and the shackles fall from the person of Brownlow. Brownlow was triumphant, and Benjamin outwitted. In fact, we do not know whether to laugh or get mad with the manner in which Brownlow has wound the Confederate Government around his thumb. That Brownlow is now laughing, like the king's fool, in his sleeve, we doubt not for a moment.

"The pledge to convey Brownlow within the Hessian lines has been made by the head of the War Department of the Confederate States; and even if this promise was procured by *fraud* and *misrepresentation*, as we have heard intimated, yet it must be fulfilled to the exact letter. In giving Brownlow the promise, the Confederate authorities have committed, in our opinion, what has been so often characterized as 'worse than a crime,—a *blunder*.' That all the authorities, in this case, acted in perfect good faith, we do not and will not doubt; that they have been outwitted and overreached diplomatically, we can affirm with equal truth.

"Brownlow! God forbid that we should unnecessarily magnify the importance of this name; but there are facts connected with the character of the man which a just and discriminating public would condemn in us did we not give them due notice.

"In brief, Brownlow has preached at every church and school-house, made stump-speeches at every cross-road, and knows every man, woman, and child, and their fathers and grandfathers before them, in East Tennessee. As a Methodist circuit-rider, a political stump-speaker, a temperance-orator, and the editor of a newspaper, he has been equally successful in our division of the State.

"Let him but once reach the confines of Kentucky, with his knowledge of the geography and the population of East Tennessee, and our section will soon feel the effect of his hard blows. From among his own old partisan and religious sectarian parasites he will find men who will obey him with the fanatical alacrity of those who followed Peter the Hermit in the first Crusade. We repeat again, let us not underrate Brownlow."

CHAPTER XXII.

THROUGHOUT January and February, whilst I lay sick, and much of the time very low, the very old devil seemed to have been turned loose. The reverses the Rebels met with after this year set in seemed to fill them with all the malice of hell! Every little upstart of an officer in command at a village or cross-roads would proclaim *martial law*, and require of all going beyond, or coming within, his lines, to show a pass, like some negro slave! A singular and persistent error seems to cling to the minds of all Secessionists in regard to the power of military officers to declare martial law. It is certain that, by the law of the land,—in force in war as well as in peace,—military officers have no right to establish and exercise over persons not in the military service a law inconsistent with, or in violation of, or paramount to, the common, universal civil law of the land.

The legislative authorities alone have power to declare and establish martial law. In England, a contest between the king and the people, as to this power, resulted in favor of the people, and wrung from Charles the First a pledge that the king and his officers would no more attempt its exercise. And now in England

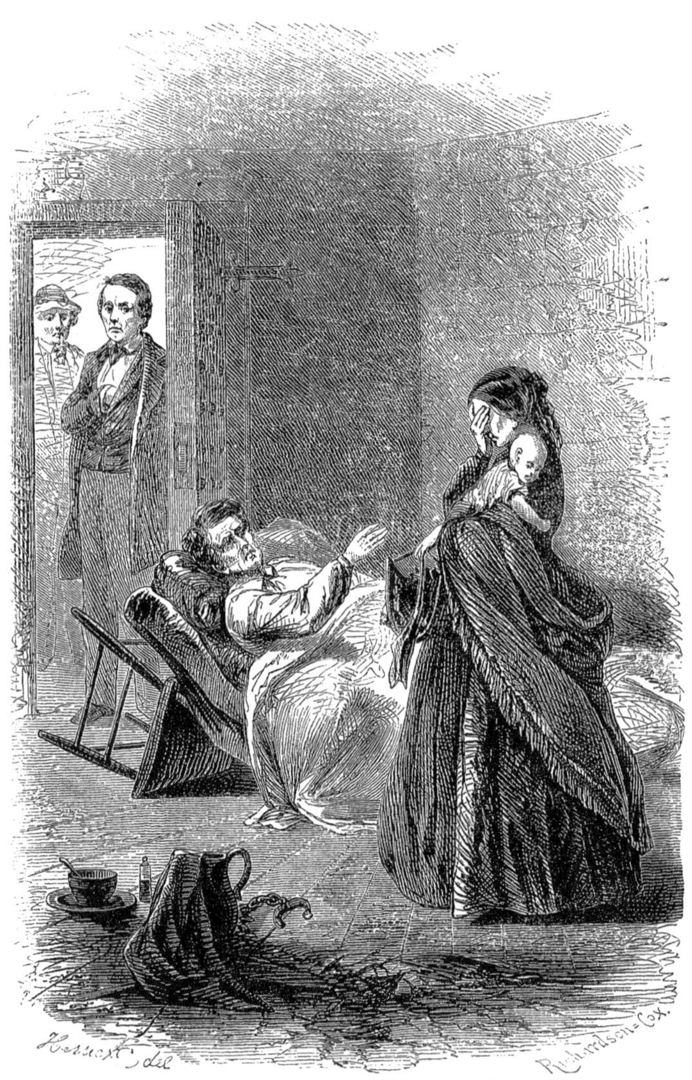

Interview of Madison Oate with his Family. (Page 329.)

no principle of liberty is better understood and more surely guarded than that no other authority than the Parliament can declare or establish martial law. In America the same law prevails, for the principle of law is here the same as in England. This was decided in the Borden case, which grew out of the Dorr Rebellion in Rhode Island. That decision sets forth that it is alone competent to the Legislature of a State, by public act, to declare martial law. In the case of General Jackson at New Orleans, in 1815, the question subsequently got into the Supreme Court of Louisiana, an able bench and profoundly learned in the law; and that tribunal decided that no military officer, no matter of how high a grade, could lawfully arrest or suspend the action of the regular courts of the country. (See the case reported by Martin.)

But in Knoxville that bad man and tyrant, Leadbetter, alone presided in his military court, declared martial law, and refused to obey the writ of *habeas corpus* when issued by Judge Brown.

But to return to the wicked *spirit* of Secession, as displayed in the South. I take the following from the Columbus (Ga.) *Times* of January:—

"OLD BROWNLOW.—This poor devil is leading a checkered, if not a very pleasant, life. Being tired of viewing mountain-scenery, to which romantic business the fear of justice had driven him, he proffered to surrender himself to the Confederate military authorities on condition that he be protected in his exit from the country to a more congenial latitude. The condition was accepted by Secretary Benjamin, and the old sinner accordingly surrendered himself to the military authorities. Upon his release therefrom, he was arrested under a civil process and lodged in jail to answer for his crime against the laws of Tennessee. His case being brought up in the Commissioners' Court at Knoxville on the 27th December, a letter was read from Secretary Benjamin, stating that, in order to maintain the integrity and good faith of the Government, he should feel it his duty to advise the President to pardon the Parson for any offence of which he might be found guilty. Under the circumstances, the District Attorney entered a *nol. pros.* in the case, and Brownlow was again released. On the same day, however, he was re-arrested and remanded to jail by the military authorities. Now, this hoary-headed and persistent traitor is occupying too much of the time and attention of the country. HE DESERVES DEATH, AND WE VOTE TO KILL HIM."

And next comes a specimen of Secession literature in the shape of a resolution passed by the Rebel Legislature of Tennessee. The author of the resolution is one *General Lane*, of the county of McMinn; and I doubt not that the climate there will soon be too hot for his comfort:—

"*Resolved, by the General Assembly of the State of Tennessee,* That the conduct and treasonable movements of Andrew Johnson, Horace Maynard, Emerson Etheridge, and such others of our public men as have expatriated themselves from our State, are regarded as alien enemies of our people, and the infamy and turpitude of whose offences win the sovereign contempt and perfect indignation of all good and loyal citizens, as well also as the just punishment of the law in such cases made and provided."

The Nashville *Gazette*, of as late a date as February, gave this mild and humane order to the lamb-like saints of the Nashville Vigilance Committee:—

"It is said there are still some Union men in Nashville. If it be possible that such WHITE-LIVERED SCOUNDRELS are really in our midst, our citizens CANNOT BE TOO VIGILANT IN WATCHING THEIR MOVEMENTS. WATCH them! WATCH them! WATCH them!"—*Feb.* 13.

The authors of this bull are a pretty set to call for clemency, liberality, humanity, and compassion at the hands of Governor Johnson or the provost-marshal of that city.

In the Memphis *Appeal* the following advertisement appears, going forth from two Rebel officers in East Tennessee:—

"BLOODHOUNDS WANTED.—We, the undersigned, will pay five dollars per pair for fifty pairs of well-bred hounds, and fifty dollars for one pair of thorough-bred bloodhounds that will take the track of a man. The purpose for which these dogs are wanted is to chase the infernal, cowardly Lincoln bushwhackers of East Tennessee and Kentucky (who have taken the advantage of the bush to kill and cripple many good soldiers) to their haunts and capture them. The said hounds must be delivered at Captain Hanmer's livery-stable by the 10th of December next, where a mustering-officer will be present to muster and inspect them.

"F. N. MCNAIRY.
"H. H. HARRIS.

"CAMP CRINFORT, CAMPBELL CO., TENN., NOV. 16.

"P.S.—Twenty dollars per month will also be paid for a man who is competent to train and take charge of the above dogs."

Here is a specimen of the vaunted chivalry of the Southern army. They first disarm Union men, and then advertise for "bloodhounds" to run them down. What barbarity! In New Orleans they have a regiment of negroes; and under the notorious Albert Pike they have Indians, who have been *scalping* Federal soldiers. Before this war is over, these savage beasts will have other employment than that of hunting Union men with "bloodhounds," drilling negroes, or bringing Indians into the field with their scalping-knives.

On the 1st of February last, the Nashville *Patriot* used the following atrocious language in regard to the Union men of West Tennessee:—

"We trust that the name of each and every one of these vile Tories will be taken down and sent to us. We want to keep them for future reference. *We will put their names as high on the roll of infamy* AS THEIR DESPICABLE BODIES OUGHT TO BE ON THE GALLOWS."

In Chattanooga, a hell-born and hell-bound Vigilance Committee resolved to put to death fifteen or twenty of the prominent Union men of that place if the Federal army should dare to approach there. This was done to induce the army to stay away; but the device will utterly fail. The Federal forces are destined to be there this summer, and there, too, in force. I append the names of this committee as I find them in a Nashville paper:—

VIGILANCE COMMITTEE OF CHATTANOOGA, TENNESSEE.

Israel J. Browning,	R. M. Hooke,
William D. Fallton,	Malone Johnson,
John W. Hoyl,	Edward Marsh,
J. Swim,	William Moore,
S. R. McCamy,	W. B. Whiteside,
Jesse Thompson,	James C. Owner.

Here is the call of the *Richmond Examiner*, of February 21, 1862, upon the chivalry of the South. They have grown desperate from the many floggings they have received from the Yankees, five of whom could not stand before a Southern man:—

"But if the inhabitants of the South have any real manhood, these reverses will inspire them with determination. They will cease to palter between the laws of peace and the measures of war. They will enrol their names, and compel the enrolment of all over whom they have any control. They will silence traitors with the halter or the pistol. They will force their Government and their generals to energy, their troops to fight; devote to resistance the last man, the last dollar, the last gun; support defeat after defeat without murmurs; ravage their fields and burn their crops on the advance of the foe; pluck victory from despair, and deserve the future prosperity and security with which Providence has never yet failed to reward a downright endeavor for independence."

Ramsey, the villainous and corrupt attorney who had

me arrested, swore out a warrant against Mr. Fleming, of Knoxville, a Union member of the Legislature, and followed him to Nashville and arrested him. He was tried before Judge Humphreys, of the Confederate Court, and in the *Patriot* for February 10 this report of the case is given:—

"THE CASE OF HON. JOHN M. FLEMING.—This case came up for consideration in the Confederate Court on Monday. Mr. Fleming was arrested in December last on a charge of having 'harbored, secreted, and concealed' Dr. R. H. Hodsden, who was charged with treason. After a full investigation, we understand that the court decided:—

"1st. That Dr. Hodsden had committed no treason.

"2d. That the defendant (Fleming) did not harbor, secrete, and conceal Dr. Hodsden.

"3d. That there is nothing in the conduct of said Fleming that would warrant the court in requiring any obligation on his part to be a loyal citizen.

"4th. That the defendant be unconditionally discharged, and that the Confederate States pay the costs of this prosecution."

As far back as April, 1861, the vilest spirit characterized the movements of these incarnate devils. See the following correspondence from the Memphis *Avalanche*:—

"TRENTON, TENNESSEE, April 16, 1861.

"TO J. D. C. ATKINS AND R. G. PAYNE:—

"Etheridge speaks here on Friday. Be here to answer him Friday or next day. ——."

The following is the answer to the above:—

"MEMPHIS, April 16.

"TO MESSRS. ——:—

"I can't find Atkins. Can't come at that time. If Etheridge speaks for the South, we have no reply. If against it, *our only answer to him and his backers must be cold steel and bullets.*

"(Signed) R. G. PAYNE."

Jan. 28, 1862.—For days and nights I have been very sick, and have ceased to keep up my regular journal. A strong guard has been kept around my house, and my friends and neighbors have been denied the privilege of visiting me. That prince of villains, tyrants, and murderers, *Colonel Leadbetter*, has come rushing into my room, and insultingly demanded to know when I would be ready to *leave the Confederacy*,—adding that "very many persons were anxious that I should be sent out of the country." I replied to him that I was improving, but utterly unable to travel, as I could not sit up, but assured him that I would go as soon as I could travel, and that I was more anxious to leave than his "many persons" could be for me to go. He insultingly rose up, started out, and told me to let him know when I felt able to travel.

Jan. 30.—One *Burch Cook*, the captain of a company, and the drunken tool of this Leadbetter, came in and read me an order requiring my instant removal to the hospital, where I could be guarded more effectually and be prevented from plotting treason with Union leaders. I protested against being dragged out of my room, when unable to sit up, and placed in a cold room without fire, to vacate a feather-bed and go upon such a mattress as I would find in the hospital. He spoke in an abrupt and insulting manner to my wife,—as only a coarse, vulgar man, a profane swearer, and a common drunkard, such as he is, would do. He pretended to doubt the reality of my sickness, and said he was instructed to bring in one of the hospital-surgeons to examine me. Accordingly, Dr. Love was called in: he examined me thoroughly, and gave a certificate to Cook to the effect that my removal at that time to the place designated would jeopardize my life. This seemed to defeat their hellish schemes to get me out where they could poison me or have me assassinated, and they at once placed a *double guard* around me, with orders not to allow any one to enter the house but my family physician. Cook came in and directed that a sentinel should stand in each of the doors leading into my room, with a loaded musket, and also stationed guards around the house. This was the order of the scoundrel *Leadbetter;* and *Cook* was a suitable instrument to execute such an order.

Saturday, 8th February.—Leadbetter this day refused James R. Cocke, one of my lawyers, the privilege of visiting me, although Cocke is one of the moderate but decided Secessionists of the town. He denounced me to Cocke, and insultingly told him that he had no business to visit such a man!

Sunday, 9th February.—This day was celebrated, in part, by a gang of these Rebel troops congregating in my office and library, and in my back yard, playing cards and swearing. No remedy for a man in such cases! F. S. Heiskell, an old citizen of this county, and a friend of mine, made application to *Leadbetter* for leave to visit me, but was insultingly refused. He was told that I was a bad man, and that he ought not to contaminate himself by visiting me. Major Heiskell controverted the statement,—told him that he had known me for years, and that he knew me to be a clever and an honorable man. Angry words were exchanged, and the parties separated.

Wednesday, 12th February.—The Rebel mob seized upon the hall in East Knoxville—used in part as a Methodist church, where a Union congregation worships—and placed in it a portion of one of their regiments. The representatives of the congregation remonstrated, saying that it had been fitted out at considerable expense by a poor congregation of Methodists, mostly mechanics. Major Burleson replied that he had ordered it to be taken because he understood it was "the property of old Brownlow." The members told him that it was not,—that Brownlow was indeed one of the largest contributors towards building it and fitting it up, but that it was conveyed to trustees for the three-fold purposes of worship, education, and temperance. They told him that Brownlow held his membership there, and that but for him it never would have been built,—but that he was not even one of its trustees.

This man was urged to destroy the hall by a hardened villain, *John H. Crozier*, whose nomination has just been rejected by the Legislature, in secret session, by an overwhelming vote. Governor Harris had nominated him as a commissioner to settle the war-claims. Only *one* East Tennesseean voted to confirm his nomination. There is half a million of dollars involved in the settlement. Crozier is a scoundrel, and a brother of the man lately involved in swindling the State out of her bonds through some banking-operations.

Thursday, Feb. 14.—The *Register*, the Secession organ, contains a call for a meeting of the citizens of the town and county to organize a regiment for home-defence, in view of the approach of the Federal army. Procession formed and marched to the court-house, Confederate flag flying, and drum and fife in operation. Crozier and Sneed headed the procession,—men who were never known to resent an insult, and whose families have packed up their goods to leave.

These two men addressed the crowd, and they adjourned to meet again.

Friday, Feb. 15.—War-meeting reassembled at the court-house. *Rev. Isaac Lewis* presided,—an old Locofoco Secessionist, who has three grown sons, neither of whom can be induced to go into the service, but all are candidates for civil offices. Colonel Baxter made a speech, and killed off, very properly, their meeting; reviewed their treatment of Union men. Rev. Richard O. Curry, a Presbyterian, made a violent speech against Union men. Disgraceful assault upon Union men, and a slander against their patriotism!

I have this day written a letter to Colonel Vance, complaining of my condition; but, as I concluded it, he called in to visit me, and I read him the contents, as follows:—

AT HOME, Feb. 15, 1862.

COLONEL ROBERT VANCE:

I am glad to learn that you are in command of this post, and I hope you may be continued while it is my lot to remain here under guard and in prison. As you are no doubt aware, I have not been able to write for several days; and this hasty letter I indite while propped up in bed. But I write to give you an account of my treatment by those associated with you and preceding you.

I think I may venture to say, by way of preliminary, that I am not prone to utter complaints, but usually exercise a good degree of patience. For the first five weeks of the last seven that a guard has been placed around and in my room, I have voluntarily given them three meals in each day, seating them at my table with my family, considering it no hardship, as I knew most of them to be Union men forced into the service. When even a different class of men were selected, who took possession of my library and office, where my two sons sleep,—when, I say, this was seized upon and turned into a guard-house, rocking-chairs broken to pieces, carpet ruined, and books damaged,—when my coal and wood were taken and consumed, though dear and difficult to procure,—and when I have furnished their guard-house candles all the time, though none are to be had in the market,—I have not complained. When your predecessor, *Colonel Leadbetter*, has refused my son John the privilege of collecting debts due me from the clerks and sheriffs of surrounding counties, which they are ready and anxious to pay me, and which, in my broken-down condition, I really need to live on, I have uttered no words of complaint. When, for several days past, out of a family of thirteen in number only my wife, my son John, and two negroes were off the sick-list,—when both the *mumps* and *measles* were introduced by armed sentinels standing day and night in my room and at my doors,—I have not uttered even a single word of complaint. When my house, and especially my passage and front portico, have been shamefully abused by these sentinels, disfigured with mud and tobacco, I have submitted in silence, though conscious of the bad treatment given me. When we have all been kept from sleep by the walking, talking, singing, and swearing, and by a change of these guards every two hours,—when they have rudely rushed into my bedchamber, as they said, to get warm,—I have submitted without one word of complaint. I have felt that there is a better day coming for me and my family, if I am not assassinated,—which is threatened me on every hand! I have had, and I still have, confidence in the final success of the principles for which I am made to suffer these cruel indignities; and hence I have been silent.

But last night, when my wife attempted to close and fasten a back door by which my bedroom is entered, and it the only fastening to my room in the rear of the building, she was insultingly notified by the sentinel, a drunken Secessionist, that *it must stand open all night*, and that such were his orders from *Captain Cook*, to whose company he was attached: she told him that it could not, and should not, stand open,—that there were three other sick persons in the room besides me, and one of them a little daughter with fever; and she accordingly closed it upon him, and locked it, expecting him to break it down.

Of this treatment, Colonel Vance, I do complain, and especially as threats are made that the door shall be kept open to-night. My appeal for relief is to you. To your predecessor, *Leadbetter*, I can make no appeal; for he never had a gentlemanly emotion of soul in his life; and, if he were capable of such feelings, he is the willing and malicious instrument of a villainous clique here, of most corrupt, vindictive, and despicable scoundrels, of whom *John H. Crozier*, *J. C. Ramsey*, and *W. G. Swan* are chief.

There is no call for this double guard around me. It is done to oppress me and my family. My wife and children are treated as prisoners; and all marketing is excluded from the house by a military order not to allow any persons to enter my door or yard. I hope, for the honor of the Southern character, that no other private family within the eleven Seceded States is subjected to such an ordeal. Certain I am that such tyranny and oppression, such outrages and insults, will never diminish my esteem for the old United States Government, or increase my respect for the Southern Confederacy.

Feeble as I am, I am ready and anxious to go beyond your lines, as it will relieve my family of this oppression. If I cannot be removed, in accordance with the pledge of your War Department, I am willing, nay, desirous, to go back to jail, if that will secure the repose of an afflicted, insulted, and outraged family.

I am, very truly, &c.,

W. G. Brownlow.

Sunday, Feb. 16.—Colonel Vance, as might have been expected of a gentleman of his known character, relieved my family of this great annoyance of a double guard, and stationed *two* sentinels there, to relieve each other during the day, with instructions to retire at night, so as to allow us to sleep in quiet. Cook's men left the same day for Cumberland Gap, where it is hoped the Secession portion of them will find employment.

Monday, Feb. 17.—A Georgia regiment arrived here to-day from Pensacola, under command of Colonel Mangum. A portion of them got drunk; took the town; called in front of the court-house to mob Colonel Baxter; Circuit Court in session; Baxter appeared, told them he was the man they were hunting, denounced the scoundrels who set them on him, and pointed out young Crozier as a goggle-eyed little scoundrel who had tried to set them on him.

Squads of the Georgia *patriots* have passed my house at different times, surveyed my premises, and inquired how strong the guard was. Colonel Vance to-night has put an additional guard of ten men at my house, to prevent their attacks.

Secessionists have received the news of the fall of Fort Donelson, but have kept it a profound secret, until the members of the Legislature have arrived and disclosed it. They are in great trouble.

Tuesday, Feb. 18.—The news of the fall of Fort Donelson no sooner reached here than several of our most *intense* Southern patriots packed up and left for other quarters. W. H. Sneed, John H. Crozier, W. G. McAdoo, C. W. Charlton, and poor *little Graves,* have fled to parts unknown, going mostly in the direction of the Cotton States. These men are all original Secessionists but McAdoo, and they were, less than a week ago, proposing to raise a regiment for home-defence, and proposing to die in the last ditch. It is said that most of these men were looking back, as they took to flight, to see if Lincoln's invaders were coming. Regiment after regiment of Georgia troops have been arriving; but this has only made it look more like a fight approaching. These men have not even taken time to sing their favorite hymn, commencing with these beautiful lines:—

> "How tedious and tasteless the day
> When the Federals no longer we see!
> Fair prospects, high fees, and good pay
> Have lost all their sweetness for *we.*"

The panic seems to have been general throughout

the State. A Secessionist writing from Chattanooga to the Knoxville *Register*—all Secession authority—thus describes the alarm of the Southern-Rights men :—

"Verily, these are days of trial to our young republic. In addition to disastrous reverses to our arms, we have some most humiliating examples of incapacity, if not worse, in the management of our military affairs. I am no 'croaker,' nor do I assume to dictate the war-policy of the Government; but certain moves have been recently made which astonish and confound the mere lookers-on, but ardent sympathizers with our cause. I refer to the evacuation of Nashville, and the incidents connected therewith.

"It seems that General Johnston informed the authorities of the city on Sunday last that he could not hold it, although no enemy was near or threatened it. Immediately all was consternation and alarm. The Governor and Legislature fled panic-stricken. With this example set them, nothing better could be expected of the citizens. Mr. V. K. Stevenson, Quartermaster-General, and President of the Nashville & Chattanooga Railroad, &c. &c., instead of standing sentry at his post and protecting the immense accumulation of military stores, and controlling the railroad so as to remove them, fled. Early on Monday morning he loaded several cars with his personal effects, his negroes, horses, carriages, and household furniture, including his own sacred person, and hastened to this city, where he has ever since remained. By his direction, all the rolling stock was hurried to this end of the road, and no effort —or next to none—was made to bring any of the Government property from the doomed city. Nearly a week has elapsed, and no enemy has approached. During this time every pound of bacon and ordnance and quartermaster's stores could easily have been removed to Murfreesborough, if no further. Instead of this being done, the doors of the storehouses were thrown open, the people invited to carry away all they wished, and the torch was applied to the rest! Was ever such wanton abandonment and destruction of property?"

Like the "Fishing Creek" warriors, these men will run on until they reach the other side of sundown. When they fled from Zollicoffer's battle-ground, they came into Knoxville bare-headed and bare-footed, on mules and stolen horses; and, although they were one hundred and fifty miles from where they got so terribly basted, they were still looking back to see if the "Lincolnites" were after them. A portion of these *racers* were the cowardly scoundrels who used to groan about my house and flourish their pistols and knives, swearing what they would do with my flag. They have at length come up with the Stars and Stripes in more hateful proportions than they found them at my house. Some of them have got their rights in this drive.

These rebels used to swear with emphasis, and with varied intonations, that they intended to "die in the last ditch." I think they are in search of this ditch, and in a fair way to find it. This heroic phrase is traceable to that country of dikes and ditches, Holland. It is said that William of Orange, when hard pressed by England and France, said that he would avoid beholding the ruin of his country by dying in the last ditch. His idea was to resist the invaders to the verge of the ocean, and there yield up his life. These Southern rebels are looking out for that huge ditch, the Mississippi River. If they cross that,—which I predict,—they will have no ditch left them to die in except the Gulf of Mexico, where I hope they will all drown, as did the swine in the Sea of Galilee when the devils entered into them.

Stronghold after stronghold of these rebels is being carried by the Federals, and they are refusing to die in the last ditch. They afford us other exhibitions, such as helter-skelter, pell-mell, harum-scarum, hurry-skurry, skadaddle-skadiddle, devil-take-the-hindmost-man in fleeing from the *first* ditch. But the *last* ditch of the whole concern has not been found. That is a desirable ditch, as there never was a drop of blood in it, and it is *the* place of all others where there is no dying. Thousands of legs stride over it at "Fishing Creek" and "Fort Donelson" rates, but they never stop to kick the bucket there. But if you want to see fighting, let a company of these *braves* be sent out to defend themselves against some Union Thermopylæ where the Spartans are unarmed, and you will see the Southern-Rights men "die in the last ditch."

Wednesday, Feb. 19.—Two additional regiments arrived from the South. Town overrun with troops, cutting up all sorts of shines, and taking possession of all vacant houses, and of the Methodist white and colored houses of worship in East Knoxville.

Captain Latrobe, a Baltimorean, of the artillery service, ordered to guard my house until otherwise instructed. The captain has acted the gentleman towards us, and his men are behaving very well.

Thursday, Feb. 20.—The remains of Captain Hugh L. McClung, Jr., who was killed at Fort Donelson, were interred to-day with military honors. I knew him well. He was very clever, and as a *merchant* and *man* I liked him. The insane madness of his relatives in favor of this rebellion had much to do with causing him to rush into this war. They would now reflect upon themselves, but that they have all learned the Southern slang of the righteousness of the Rebel cause and the sacredness of the Southern soil. Well, every man to his notion!

Captain Monserrat returned to-day from Nashville, and is again in command of this post, Colonel Vance having gone to Cumberland Gap with his regiment.

Friday, Feb. 21.—Two regiments from Georgia and Mississippi left for the Gap to-day. Their departure has given relief to the citizens. Whilst here, they have denounced, in unmeasured terms, Sneed, Crozier, McAdoo, Charlton, and Graves, and other Southern-Rights champions, for their inglorious flight. The

Cleveland (Tenn.) *Banner* is also down upon them for fleeing in such hot haste.

Saturday, Feb. 22.—Governor Harris, since his precipitate flight to Memphis, has issued a call for the entire militia of the State to be mustered into service. He even proposes to take the field himself, provided, in his alarm, he can halt long enough to organize.

Sunday, Feb. 23.—The two Methodist houses of worship in East Knoxville are to-day occupied with swearing and card-playing troops, and the congregations are driven out. The churches in the old part of the city are not disturbed, because their *pious* pastors are Secessionists, as well as their congregations, to some extent, while those in East Knoxville are for the Union, first, last, and all the time.

Monday, Feb. 24.—I have this day sent to Captain Monserrat, commanding this post, to consult him about letting me out of the Confederacy. He informs me that he has just received a dispatch from General Winder, commanding at Richmond, ordering him to deliver me to him in that city. I don't like this indication: it looks to me like another intended violation of faith, and as though I am to be badly treated.

Tuesday, Feb. 25.—The town and county are both

said to be in a perfect uproar, on account of the Governor's call for the militia. All hands are out, offering to raise companies, so as to avoid being drafted,—all wanting to be *captains*, none prepared to enter the service as *privates*.

Wednesday, Feb. 26.—A company of blackguards and vagabonds, called cavalry, rode by my house to-day, some of whom cursed and denounced my wife, who sat at the window sewing. These are some of the cowardly devils who ran from "Fishing Creek," and have been fitted out with new horses. A company of them can demolish any unarmed Union *woman* in the country!

Thursday, Feb. 27.—I addressed the following card to Secretary Benjamin to-day:—

KNOXVILLE, Feb. 27, 1862.

HON. J. P. BENJAMIN:—Satisfied, upon reliable information, that my personal safety forbids my going out of this Confederacy by way of Richmond, I ask the justice to allow Major Monserrat to send me through the lines, either over Cumberland Mountain or *via* Nashville. I prefer the latter, as I am not yet well enough to undergo the fatigues of travelling on horseback.

Very respectfully, &c.,

W. G. BROWNLOW.

Friday, Feb. 28.—This is Jeff Davis's day for fasting, humiliation, and prayer; and if ever a set of men needed to humble themselves before God and confess their sins, it is the men associated with him in this infernal rebellion. The hypocrites of the town, and many false pretenders to extraordinary piety, will, no doubt, turn out *in force.* The day is beautiful, the sky clear and serene, without a cloud; and the Rebels will, no doubt, flatter themselves that Providence is favoring them with good weather. This is a mistake: Providence is only drying up the roads that the Federal army can get at the retreating forces of the demoralized army of the South.

Saturday, March 1.—The elections came off to-day for sheriffs and other county officers, and, as far as returns have come in, the Union ticket prevails. Ay, and it always will prevail in East Tennessee, unless the present race of voters are extinguished.

Thirty Union men, well dressed, were arrested by the cavalry, who found them leaving for Kentucky, to avoid the draft ordered by Governor Harris. Seventeen of them agreed to join the Confederate army, to keep out of jail.

But a Sabbath past, they brought twenty Union men out of jail, arms tied behind them with strong ropes, and marched them with bayonets to the depot, cursing and insulting them, and sent them off to Tuscaloosa, to be held as prisoners during the war. To have seen them coming out of the jail-yard and entering the street, would have brought tears from the eyes of the unfeeling Sepoys of India.

Sunday, March 2.—The following dispatch has just been received by Major Monserrat, the officer in command of this post, and read to me by that officer:—

"RICHMOND, March 2, 1862.

"MAJOR MONSERRAT:—You are authorized to send Brownlow out of Tennessee by the Cumberland Mountains, or any other safe road.

"J. P. BENJAMIN, *Secretary of War.*"

As clouds of darkness are gathering around me, and dangers are multiplying in every direction, I have resolved, feeble as I am, to go, and I have notified the officer that I shall be ready to leave by morning, selecting as my route the railroad to Nashville. I will continue my journal on the road, if I can do so without detection.

Monday night, March 3.—I left home this morning at seven o'clock, with an escort of four citizens, under command of Adjutant-General Young and Lieutenant O'Brien, officers of my own selection; and upon reaching Loudon, thirty miles west of Knoxville, we were furnished with ten armed soldiers for an escort. These men were taken from Captain Dill's company of East Tennessee troops. Before starting, the captain made substantially this speech to his men:—"Soldiers! you are to escort Parson Brownlow to Nashville, under the command of these officers. He is sent out by the Confederate Government; and your duty is to protect him from insult and injury, at all hazards, come from what source they may. Treat him courteously and kindly, and discharge your duty as men, though you are engaged in a cause he opposes."

I feel grateful to Captain Dill for this manly advice to his men, and I have so far found his men of the right grit.

At Athens, some sixty miles west of Knoxville, we met a train filled with drunken vagabonds, on furlough, returning towards Yorktown. They learned that I was on board, and made a rush towards my car, but were repulsed by my guard, placed on the rear and front platforms by officer Young. This day has brought us to Bridgeport, on the Tennessee River, where we are all to lie over until to-morrow morning, when the Nashville train passes.

A gentleman who is well informed as to the condition of the Rebel army furnishes me with the following information as to the force they have in the field:—Alabama, 20,000; Arkansas, 10,500; Florida, 4500; Georgia, 32,500; Kentucky, 7200; Louisiana,

31,200; North Carolina, 25,000; Mississippi, 17,500; South Carolina, 20,800; Tennessee, 31,200; Texas, 7200; Virginia, 57,400; being in all 265,000 men, divided into 368 regiments.

Wartrace Depot, Friday, March 7.—We arrived here three days ago, and have all been detained for the want of authority from one of the Confederate generals to raise a flag of truce and proceed within the Federal lines. Moreover, the rolling stock on the road to Murfreesborough, leading to Nashville, has all been withdrawn. We have sent Mr. Rogers, a civilian, but one of our escort, to Shelbyville, on a branch road, only eight miles distant, to ask of General Hardee, in command of some ten or fifteen thousand troops at that post, to grant us a flag of truce. Rogers is back, and reports that Hardee refuses the flag. We have started Lieutenant O'Brien and Rogers to Huntsville, to head the Confederate generals Johnston, Crittenden, Carroll, Hindman, Breckinridge, Floyd, and Pillow, in their precipitate flight into North Alabama. Our messengers came up with General Albert Sidney Johnston at Huntsville, and obtained the following remarkable document:—

"HEAD-QUARTERS, CONFEDERATE DISTRICT,
"HUNTSVILLE, March 7, 1862.

"LIEUTENANT O'BRIEN, *Third Tennessee Regiment*:—

"SIR:—General A. S. Johnston, having just heard

that you have brought W. G. Brownlow to Wartrace, as a prisoner, instructs you to return him to his home, or release him where he now is, as he may elect.

"Respectfully,

"W. W. Mackall."

This order to return me to my home was in effect to send me back into the lions' den; and the one to turn me loose at Wartrace was to hand me over to Morgan's mob of cavalry, who were eager to get hold of me. Lieutenant O'Brien telegraphed us that Johnston had given this order, and we telegraphed back for him to follow on to Decatur and demand of General Crittenden a flag of truce, exhibiting to him our passports from the War Department. I hope before a great while that the Federal army may capture this man *A. Sidney Johnston,* and not release him until the war is over.

Lieutenant O'Brien came up with General Crittenden at Decatur, and obtained from him the following very different order:—

"Head-Quarters, Second Division,
"Central Army, March 8, 1861.

"In obedience to the orders of the Secretary of War of the Confederate States, the officers in charge of W. G. Brownlow will conduct him, under a flag of truce, to the most convenient and practicable point of the lines of the enemy, and deliver him over to the Federal authorities.

"By command of Major-General Crittenden.

"POLLOCK B. LEE,

"*Assist. Adjt.-General.*"

With this authority we came on to Shelbyville, and, to our astonishment, found this document, and the order of the War Department at Richmond, wholly insufficient to pass us through the Rebel lines, where Brigadier-General Hardee was in command, as the sequel will show. At the dirty hotel at Wartrace, where we could get nothing fit to eat, and had to lodge in a filthy room on still more filthy Secession beds, we paid, for six of us, for three days, SIXTY DOLLARS!

Shelbyville, March 14.—We have now been here seven days, being refused, by *General Hardee*, the privilege of proceeding to Nashville. Major Picket, a member of General Hardee's staff, called upon one of the officers having me in charge, and signified the general's intention to dispatch me to Montgomery, Alabama, and confine me in jail. He was told that, with the documents I held from the War Department and from General Crittenden, it would be a disgrace to the Confederate Government to re-arrest and imprison me.

There were some drunken scoundrels here from East Tennessee, connected with the army, who, upon our arrival, infused into the already corrupt and poisoned mind of this humbug of an officer, Hardee, all the hatred they could, and sought to prevent my safe conduct beyond the Rebel lines. A panic prevailed among these cowardly rascals, equal to that which backed them out from "Fishing Creek," Fort Donelson, and Bowling Green, and they were not inclined to respect the orders of their superior officers.

The truth is, this man Hardee is engaged in removing their Government stores to Georgia, Mississippi, and Alabama; and they are working in dread of General Buell's forces, who are only fifty miles distant. They feared—and so expressed themselves—that if I got through the lines safe I would inform the enemy of their condition and have them all bagged. I greatly prefer their being bagged down on the line of the Cotton States; and I am well enough posted to justify the prediction that this will be done before a great while. May God hasten the hour!

They had on hand, when I first arrived here, the bacon of *twenty-nine thousand hogs,* and the meat of *two thousand beeves.* They have seized upon the negroes and wagons of the citizens indiscriminately, and used them in brisk style to haul to the depot. In these hurried movements they have, nevertheless, discovered that the bacon of some *fourteen hundred hogs* is missing. They have instituted a search, and found the bacon of *two hundred* of their missing hogs in the basement story of a large brick house, one mile from town, occupied by the *father of the contractor with the Rebel Government!* This lot has just been captured by General Hardee and sent off on the trains; but no punishment is to be inflicted upon the thieves, as they are all Secessionists.

This man Hardee has demanded that "this Brownlow demonstration" shall cease; by which he means the visits of Union men to my room, and the visits of Union ladies, who all sympathize with me. This is Bedford county, and Shelbyville is the county town, and both are strongly Union; while the presence of a demoralized Southern army has only had the effect to increase the devotion of the people to the Union. Hardee is by no means adding strength to the Rebel cause. He is the well-known humbug whose book of "Tactics" is in use in the army. The translation is from the French: it was made in Philadelphia, by an officer of the army, and Hardee fathered the production, and claims the authorship of what he had not the ability to produce. This is known to the army-officers North, and has increased their contempt for this foolish and weak man. Hatred to General Scott, by Jeff Davis, while Secretary of War, instigated him to employ his willing tool, Hardee, to get up this new system of "Tactics," which was intended to displace

Scott's able work. The lake that burns "with fire and brimstone" will yearn for its promised aliment, until such men as these get there. The time is, however, rapidly approaching when the wailings of their damned ghosts will rise upon the flames, and, with one loud, deep, long wail, in bitter utterances of remorse, they will exclaim, "THIS REBELLION IS A FAILURE!"

I have never been more kindly treated than since I came here,—ladies and gentlemen visiting me every day, and expressing their kind regards for me. As a specimen, I give the following correspondence between the lady-like daughter of the mayor and myself.

"SHELBYVILLE, TENNESSEE, March 11, 1862.

"REV. W. G. BROWNLOW:—

"DEAR SIR:—Herewith I send you a collection of flowers, which I beg you will do me the favor to accept as a small token of the high esteem which I cherish for you on account of your great devotion to, and untiring efforts in behalf of, our once-glorious Union; and beg to express the hope that the Government established by our fathers will yet be sustained, and bound together by stronger ties than those by which we have heretofore been united.

"With sentiments of highest esteem,

"I beg to remain your friend,

"EDITH J. GALBRAITH."

SHELBYVILLE, TENN., March 13, 1862.

MISS EDITH J. GALBRAITH:—

During the six days I have been detained here I have been called upon by a number of the ladies of Shelbyville, both married and single, who have, in words of kindness, expressed their sympathies for me in my departure from my home and family. These evidences of regard have greatly comforted me, after my confinement in a crowded and uncomfortable *jail* for having reiterated to the people of East Tennessee what WASHINGTON taught us,—namely, that "THE CONSTITUTION IS SACREDLY OBLIGATORY UPON ALL;" and for having proclaimed, as JACKSON did, "THE UNION—IT MUST BE PRESERVED."

But your kind note of the 11th instant, and the accompanying "collection of flowers," have afforded me a pleasure for which I have no words suitably to express my thanks. I shall at least carry these flowers with me to the redeemed and disenthralled capital of our State, where I can see the glorious Stars and Stripes of our distracted country floating from the dome of the capitol.

I hope at no distant day to visit your noble Union town again, when, I feel perfectly confident, our loyal State—rushed out of the Union, at the point of the bayonet, under the lead of her worst men—will be back in the old Union, and her citizens, contented and happy, determined never again to embark in the hell-born and hell-bound cause of Secession.

I am, very respectfully, &c.

W. G. BROWNLOW.

I will record an incident that occurred on the train as I came to this point and to Wartrace, some ten days ago, and then close out my sojourn in Shelbyville. A tall, self-important Rebel officer, dressed in a full suit of uniform, learning at the depot that I was on board, came into the car, and inquired of one of our guards if I was on board, and, being told that I was, said, "Show me Brownlow." The guard pointed out Adjutant-General Young,—a very fine-looking man, dressed in citizen's clothes,—and said, "That is Brownlow, with the slouch-cap on." He gazed at him. He frowned with the scowl of a demon, wrinkled his brow, and, with a sour, sullen, frowning look, exclaimed, "I am satisfied. He is a mean-looking man. I believe all I have heard about him." Thus he retired, passing sentence against a clever gentleman and a man of really fine personal appearance. This shows what prejudice will do. Here was an officer in the Confederate ranks condemned as worthy of death for a *supposed bad countenance*, because he was erroneously reported to be a man against whom all Rebeldom entertains a strong prejudice.

Nashville, March 15.—To-day, at twelve o'clock, I was landed within the Federal lines, having come from Shelbyville, at a rapid rate, on the Knowlensville turnpike. We had up the white flag when we came upon the pickets. They halted us, and inquired by what authority we had that flag of truce up. I alighted from the buggy, and introduced myself to them as "Parson Brownlow,"—when, with one accord, they advanced and gave me a cordial shake of the hand. They said they had heard of me before, and were glad that I had come within their lines.

I was sent for by Colonel Jackson, an ex-Congressman, and a noble Kentucky gentleman, commanding a regiment of cavalry. I was treated with great kindness and with marked attention by the officers, while the privates crowded around to see me upon the mention of my name. I *felt* and *knew* that I was among friends. Nay, I felt like a bird out of a cage. Brigadier-General Wood, a noble son of Kentucky, within whose division we were, (five miles distant from Nashville,) came up to receive our flag of truce; and a more cordial welcome no man ever received. He at once commissioned Captain Leonard, of his staff, to turn me over to General Buell, the chief in command. Our only trouble was in regard to Lieutenant O'Brien, a Rebel officer, who, if admitted into Nashville, must be blindfolded. However, General Buell met me with the same cordiality with which I had been greeted before, and said that my friends—O'Brien, Rogers, Harrison, and others—should lodge with me at the hotel: accordingly, we were all landed at the St. Cloud Hotel.

General Buell, as I understand, is a native of Indiana, or hails from there. He is a man of liberal education and cultivated tastes,—a man of fine conversational powers, and a chivalrous, high-toned gentleman. Below six feet, he is heavily built, with an eagle eye. He was dressed in a handsome uniform, with a sort of foraging-cap. He has a fair complexion and blonde moustache, with suavity and politeness written in every line of his face. I take him to be about forty-five years of age,—certainly not so much as fifty. He has *ninety thousand men* here, and more arriving every day. He has the confidence of his command, and will move his forces in a few days into Alabama. He asked me many questions, in quick succession, touching East Tennessee. I answered him promptly, and, as I have reason to believe, quite to his satisfaction.

Nashville, March 20.—I have here found Governor Johnson, Horace Maynard, Emerson Etheridge, and Colonel Trigg,—all in good health, and glad to see me landed safe in the *United States.* Governor Johnson is here as Military Governor, with the rank of brigadier-general, and is now organizing a State Government. He will, as I suppose, declare all the offices in the State vacant held by men acting in pursuance of the Confederate Constitution and of the mobocratic oath they have taken. The Governor issued a proclamation yesterday, which is an able and well-timed document and meets the case as it exists here. After speaking of the heresy of Secession, the abdication of the Executive office, the dissolving of the Legislature, and the Judiciary being in abeyance, he concludes his proclamation in these words:—

"I shall, therefore, as early as practicable, designate for various positions under the State and county governments, from among my fellow-citizens, persons of probity and intelligence, and bearing true allegiance to the Constitution and Government of the United States, who will execute the functions of their respective offices until their places can be filled by the action of the people. Their authority, when their appointments shall have been made, will be accordingly respected and observed.

"To the people themselves the protection of the Government is extended. All their rights will be duly respected, and their wrongs redressed when made known. Those who, through the dark and weary night of the Rebellion, have maintained their allegiance to the Federal Government, will be honored. The erring and misguided will be welcomed on their return. And while it may become necessary, in vindicating the violated majesty of the law, and in reasserting its imperial sway, to punish *intelligent and conscious treason in high places*, no merely retaliatory or vindictive policy will be adopted. To those especially who in a private, unofficial capacity have assumed an attitude of hostility to the Government, a full and complete amnesty for all past acts and declarations is offered, upon the one condition of their again yielding themselves peaceful citizens to the just supremacy of the laws. This I advise them to do for their own good, and for the peace and welfare of our beloved State, endeared to me by the associations of long and active years and by the enjoyment of the highest honors.

"And, appealing to my fellow-citizens of Tennessee, I point them to my long public life, as a pledge for the sincerity of my motives, and an earnest for the performance of my present and future duties.

"ANDREW JOHNSON."

Accompanying this proclamation is the following ordinary oath of office, to support the Constitution of the United States and of the State of Tennessee:—

"STATE OF TENNESSEE, ——— county.

"On this the —— day of ——, 186—, personally appeared before me ———, of the ———, and took and subscribed the following oath, in pursuance of the first section of the tenth article of the Constitution of the State of Tennessee, which is as follows: 'Every person who shall be chosen or appointed to any office of trust or profit under this Constitution, or any law made in pursuance thereof, shall, before entering on the duties thereof, take an oath to support the Constitution of this State, and of the United States, and an oath of office,' (he having already taken an oath to support the Constitution of Tennessee,) to wit:

"'I, ———, do solemnly swear that I will support, protect, and defend the Constitution and Government of the United States against all enemies, whether domestic or foreign, and that I will bear true faith, allegiance, and loyalty to the same, any law, ordinance, resolution, or convention to the contrary notwithstanding; and, further, that I do this with a full determination, pledge, and purpose, without any mental reservation or evasion whatsoever; and, further, that I will well and faithfully perform all the duties which may be required of me by law. So HELP ME GOD.'

"Sworn and subscribed to before me,

"——— ———."

The Secessionists regard the appointment of Governor Johnson as a very unfortunate one; but the Union men, irrespective of old party associations, regard it as most fortunate, and say that we have the right man in the right place. I have no doubt his appointment to the office will give general satisfaction to Union men throughout the State. I am certain this will be the case in East Tennessee.

The feeling of opposition to the Federal Government and the occupation of this city by Federal troops is gradually giving way to a spirit of acquiescence, and to the "sober second thought" of sensible and patriotic men. The good order, strict discipline, and sober habits of *one hundred thousand troops* here are in striking contrast with the thieving, drinking, and other revolting habits of the so-called Confederate soldiers, who but recently committed all manner of outrages in these streets. Even the children and negroes see and speak of the difference.

The ladies of Nashville are more bitter and unyielding in their hostility to the Federal army than any other class of citizens. I can excuse them: most of them have sons, brothers, or husbands in the Rebel army, and they regard Federal officers and soldiers as their enemies, in search of their relatives.

Some amusing incidents occurred here upon the arrival of the Federal army, under command of General Mitchell, after the fall of Fort Donelson. The most *stirring* incident was the brass bands, on the gunboats and transports, playing that favorite Southern air, "In Dixie's land I take my stand," &c., while the loyal citizens cheered long and loud. A game lady, full of resentment, as they passed the Square, exclaimed, "Lack-a-day, what a great Lincoln circus!" "Yes," rejoined an Ohio soldier: "the last time we performed was at Fort Donelson." A second lady inquired, with an air of disdain, "How far do your lines extend?" The answer was, by an officer, "Our lines, madam, extend to the North Pole; and, when I left the other day, there were several regiments applying for transportation South!"

My room was entered last evening by some officers and civilians from Kentucky, and I was literally forced out into the crowd, in front of the St. Cloud Hotel, where a speech was demanded. I sought to be excused; but they would take no denial, and I proceeded to deliver this speech:—

Speech of W. G. Brownlow in Nashville.

GENTLEMEN:—I am in a sad plight to say much of interest,—too thoroughly incapacitated to do justice to you or myself. My throat has been disordered for the past three years, and I have been compelled to almost abandon public speaking. Last December I was thrust into an uncomfortable and disagreeable jail,—for what? *Treason!* Treason to the bogus Confederacy; and the proofs of that treason were articles which appeared in the *Knoxville Whig* in May last, when the State of Tennessee was a member of the imperishable Union. At the expiration of four weeks I became a victim of the typhoid fever, and was removed to a room in a decent dwelling, and a guard of seven men kept me company. I subsequently became so weak that I could not turn over in my bed, and the guard was increased to twelve men, for fear I should suddenly recover and run away to Kentucky. But I never had any intention to run, and, if I had, I was not able to escape. My purpose was to make them send me out of their infamous Government, according to contract, or to hang me, if they thought proper. I was promised passports by their Secretary of War, a little Jew, late of New Orleans; and upon the faith of that promise, and upon the invitation of General Crittenden, then in command at Knoxville, I reported myself and demanded my passports. They gave me passports, but they were from my house to the Knoxville jail, and the escort was a deputy marshal of Jeff Davis. But I served my time out, and have been landed here at last, through much tribulation. When I started on this perilous journey,

I was sore distressed both in mind and body, being weak from disease and confinement. I expected to meet with insults and indignities at every point from the blackguard portion of the Rebel soldiers and citizens, and in this I was not disappointed. It was fortunate, indeed, that I was not mobbed. This would have been done, but for the vigilance and fidelity of the officers having me in command. These were Adjutant-General Young and Lieutenant O'Brien, clever men, high-minded, and honorable; and they were of my own selection. They had so long been Union men that I felt assured they had not lost the instincts of gentlemen and patriots, afflicted as they were with the incurable disease of Secession!

But, gentlemen, some three or four days ago I landed in this city, as you are aware. Five miles distant I encountered the Federal pickets. Then it was that I felt like a new man. My depression ceased, and returning life and health seemed suddenly to invigorate my system and to arouse my physical constitution. I had been looking at soldiers in uniform for twelve months, and to me they appeared as hateful as their Confederacy and their infamous flag. But these Federal pickets, who received me kindly and shook me cordially by the hand, looked like angels of light, compared with the insulting blackguards who had been groaning and cursing around my house.

Why, my friends, these demagogues actually boast

that the Lord is upon their side, and declare that God Almighty is assisting them in the furtherance of their nefarious project. In Knoxville and surrounding localities, a short time since, daily prayer-meetings were held, wherein the Almighty was beseeched to raise Lincoln's blockade and to hurl destruction against the Burnside Expedition. Their prayers were partly answered: the blockade at Roanoke Island was most effectually raised!

Gentlemen, I am no Abolitionist; I applaud no sectional doctrines. I am a Southern man, and all my relatives and interests are thoroughly identified with the South and Southern institutions. I was born in the Old Dominion; my parents were born in Virginia, and they and their ancestors were all slave-holders. Let me assure you that the South has suffered no infringement upon her institutions; the Slavery question was actually *no* pretext for this unholy, unrighteous conflict. Twelve Senators from the Cotton States, who had sworn to preserve inviolate the Constitution framed by our forefathers, plotted treason at night,—a fit time for such a crime,—and telegraphed to their States dispatches advising them to pass ordinances of secession. Yes, gentlemen, twelve Senaters swore allegiance in the day-time, and unswore it at night.

Soldiers and citizens! Secession is well-nigh played out,—the dog is dead,—and their demoralized army are on their way to the Cotton States, where they can look back at you, as you approach their scattered lines. I have been detained among them for ten days, General Hardee refusing to let me pass. This was only fifty-five miles from here, in the sound Union town of Shelbyville. They were pushing off their bacon and flour and their demoralized men; and I hope you will follow them up. You will overtake them at the Tennessee River,—sooner, if they come up with new supplies of mean whiskey.

But, gentlemen, you see that I am growing hoarse in this fierce wind. I am otherwise feeble, not having attempted to make a speech in months. Excuse me, therefore, and join me in this sentiment, should this wicked and unholy war continue,—"Grape for the Rebel masses, and hemp for their leaders!"

Night before last I heard a speech from Etheridge, delivered before an attentive audience of twelve or fifteen hundred persons. He spoke over two hours. I never heard him in a regular stump-speech before. I saw at once the secret of his great success before the people. He is the *people's man*, and keeps up the interest all the time. He was severe on the leaders of this rebellion, but not more so than they deserved; and his blows met with a hearty response from the crowd.

This army is moving south, by divisions of twelve and fifteen thousand each day. Generals McCook, Mitchell, Nelson, Crittenden, and Thomas have all gone, taking the different pikes leading south. There will be a fearful conflict somewhere in North Alabama, or on the line of the Memphis & Charleston Railroad. I have apprized our friends of the strong force of the enemy, and assured them that they would have a bloody battle when they met.

Nashville, March 21.—No officer in this vast army has impressed me more favorably than Colonel Fry, the man who killed General Zollicoffer. He is a fine officer, a perfect gentleman, mild and unassuming, and a devout member of the Presbyterian Church. He enjoys the confidence and esteem of all who know him.

By the way, the Vandals under the lead of Floyd destroyed the wire suspension-bridge here, in which General Zollicoffer had some $25,000 of paying stock,—and about all he leaves behind to clothe and to educate his children—five little girls. This was a wicked act, wholly uncalled for, and one which, while it could do no sort of damage to the Federal army, brings ruin upon a number of orphan children. Floyd was remonstrated with by Secessionists, but all to no purpose.

The following correspondence will explain itself:—

"College Street, South Nashville, March 21, 1862.

"Mrs. Dr. Davis presents her compliments to W. G. Brownlow, and hopes that he will accept the accompanying bouquet."

NASHVILLE, March 21, 1862.

Mrs. Dr. Davis, of South Nashville, has my thanks for the beautiful bouquet sent to my room yesterday. It is gratifying to me to find that the ladies of Nashville are not all crazy upon the subject of this infamous rebellion. I took tea last evening with some Union ladies, whom I found in their right minds, as they have been since the commencement of hostilities. On yesterday I took my stand in front of R. H. McEwin's mansion, on Spruce Street, and, together with several Union ladies, waved our handkerchiefs as the large divisions of well-dressed officers and men passed, under the command of Generals Thomas and Schœpff. Each regiment as it moved south, upon the Franklin pike, halted, and played us a national air, cheering "Parson Brownlow and the ladies." The breeze carried the Star-Spangled Banner over us to its full proportions, and the sunshine illuminated its hues in all their beauty. The army of one hundred thousand men now leaving here and going south is a real army, magnificent in *matériel*, admirable in its discipline, sober in its habits, and elegantly equipped and armed. God and angels smile upon them, and victory must attend their march and struggles.

Our heretofore patriotic State is coming to her senses, and this sad and unnatural war must, in the very nature of things, soon close out. For myself I shall ask no higher honor than that of being booked as on the Union side of this struggle. Respectfully, &c.,

W. G. BROWNLOW.

I heard an able speech last evening from Hon. Horace Maynard. He spoke two and a half hours, to a large and interested audience. I have heard him on many occasions, but never have I heard him when he was so eloquent, forcible, and effective. His history of this infamous rebellion was pointed and convincing, and his language was chaste and beautiful. His arguments were unanswerable, and listened to in the most profound silence, only when interrupted by enthusiastic bursts of applause. The speech was, throughout, conciliatory, and could not fail to have a good effect.

Here, as in all parts of the South, the worst class of men are *preachers*. They have done more to bring about the deplorable state of things existing in the country than any other class of men. And foremost in this work of mischief are the Methodist preachers. Brave in anticipation of war, and prone to denunciation on all occasions, even in the pulpit, they have been among the first to take to their heels. Doctors McFERRIN, SUMMERS, and McTYEIR, of the Methodist Publishing House, have all fled in the direction of the Cotton States,—leaving their Book Concern vacant, and, I should say, not more than *solvent!* McFERRIN was escaping through Shelbyville as I approached the town, trying to exchange a refractory nag of Secession proclivities for one that would work and abide by *law and order*. I did not see him.

The notorious *J. R. Graves*, the Baptist editor, has also fled, and that most ingloriously. He went through the neighborhood of Shelbyville, John Gilpin-like, staying for the night with Major Goggin, a Union man, but a member of his church. He was following up his Methodist associates in the work of rebellion. Graves is a Northern man, and has been a strong anti-slavery man, as his past record shows; but to prove his loyalty to the South he has had to go to great Secession extremes. It is not difficult for him to fall in with Secession. He *seceded* from the Baptist Church a few years ago, and sought to destroy it. Failing in that *rebellion*, he is now about to take satisfaction out of the United States Government! He ought to get up a regiment of men and arm them with the *pikes* manufactured here to fight Yankees with.

A dreadful retribution awaits these men. Called of God, as they say, to preach the gospel of *peace*, they have been for twelve months preaching war, bloodshed, and plunder; but now they are ingloriously fleeing from the wrath of an approaching Federal army.

Bishop Soule.

It will be gratifying to the numerous friends of this venerable man of God, now upwards of eighty years old, to learn that he is still a staunch advocate of the Union and of the Constitution of his country. He is the senior bishop of the Methodist Church in the United States, and a man of learning, of great acquirements, and of a powerful mind. Chaplain Stephenson, of the Fifteenth Indiana Regiment,—a man whose acquaintance I have made,—had an interview with the bishop a few days since, at his residence near Nashville, which he thus describes in a letter to a friend:—

"General Wood's division encamped recently seven miles north of Nashville, in the vicinity of the quiet home of the venerable Bishop Soule. I called upon the bishop twice, and found in him the same social, courteous, Christian minister I have always regarded him. He remarked, emphatically and solemnly, 'I have never written a line nor uttered a sentence politically: I have been a man of one work.' Lifting his majestic form and reaching to the mantel-piece, he grasped affectionately a newly-bound old book, the Constitution of the United States. Resuming his chair, and opening the book, he said, with great deliberation, 'I have carefully read and closely studied the Constitution, and have never seen any clause in it authorizing or providing for division, or the secession of one or more States from the others.' 'We, the people, may change, alter, or amend.' This was the purport, and, as nearly as I can recollect, the precise language of the occasion: he authorized me so to represent him to his friends; and I take pleasure in disabusing a prejudice arising from a misapprehension of his views."

DR. JEPHTHA FOWLKER.—This is a distinguished

citizen of Memphis, and a large property-holder. He is a true man in every sense, brave, generous, and loyal, though forced by circumstances to bow to the storm of Secession which has raged with so much fury in West Tennessee. He is one of the owners and editors of the *Memphis Avalanche*, and in his issue for March 8 publishes the following:—

"PARSON BROWNLOW EN ROUTE FOR WASHINGTON.

"We learn that this distinguished individual left Knoxville on the 3d, under an escort or guard of ten men, for Nashville. He has doubtless reached his destination safely. We regret to part from an old and valued friend, one who stood by us in times past, when we needed his friendship. We are well assured he has left behind him at Knoxville a set of men far more detrimental to the Southern Government than he would ever have proven if he had been kindly treated. He is a true man to his principles and professions, while they are false to themselves, others, and the Government. He has our good wishes for himself and his family, whatever may betide him in life. His health, we learn, is much improved."

This article, as I understand, caused a split between the doctor and his partner and associate editor, and dissolution of partnership followed. Since then, through the machinations of an infamous clique at Knoxville, he has been arrested and confined in prison at Memphis. I hope the Federal army will relieve him soon. And should he appear in any one of the loyal States, sooner or later, I bespeak for him the treatment due to a TRUE MAN, a gentleman, and "a man of soul sin-

34

cere." I have known him long and intimately, and I would perform a pilgrimage to any quarter of the globe to serve him.

Fort Donelson, March 23.—I am now seventy-five miles west-by-north from Nashville, on the Cumberland River. This is Stewart county, and Dover is the county town. I came down on board that floating palace, the Jacob Strader. Dover is on the left bank of the river, elevated by a considerable rise in the hill. It will never be known hereafter by any other name than that of *Fort Donelson,* where the late terrible battle was fought. The marks of the fight are to be seen on every hand. The graves of the dead show arms and legs protruding out of the ground, and the odor is very offensive. Though our boat stays all night, I did not go out to see the evidences of the death and carnage that reigned here but a few days since.

The United States troops stationed here, and those on steamers just arriving from the Northwest, learning that I was on board, surrounded our boat, and called repeatedly, until I was forced out on deck, where I addressed them in substance as follows:—

SOLDIERS AND CITIZENS:—I suppose you think me a stubborn sort of man, as I have resisted so many calls, and calls so loud and enthusiastic, as have been made on me to-night. The truth is, I am not able to speak, and especially am I not able to face the wind blowing so fiercely on this river. I am fleeing from the wrath to come; and I stand before you to-night as a brand plucked from the scorching flames of a Southern Confederacy. I am just from the land of oppression, where there are no constitutional guards left for the protection of the rights of the citizens,—where they have abolished the *habeas corpus*, provided county dungeons for Union men, the sweets of which I have tasted; where they have instituted *lettres de cachet*, violated mails, disarmed communities and individuals, quartered drunken troops on private families, hung men for not being Secessionists, shot down others in their fields for adhering to the Stars and Stripes, muzzled the press, silenced free speech, debauched the pulpit, tortured women and children, and brought into service, at two and four dollars per day, a pensioned band of depraved spies and informers. You could not expect a man to speak in the open air, coming out of such a furnace as this. Still, I desire to bear testimony to the excellency of the most loving, forbearing, and beneficent of Governments, the Government of the United States. Compared with this miserable Southern Confederacy, it rises up on the highest pedestal of moral grandeur, and asserts a commanding claim on the magnanimity and chivalry of the loyal men of the whole country. You have lately done a noble work here, gentlemen, and the scenes of FORT DONELSON will long be remembered by the Rebels who fled from here under the lead of Floyd and Pillow. Nor will the ten or fifteen thousand prisoners you bagged at this point soon forget the drubbing you gave them on this memorable hill. With the deluded masses I sympathize, but with the corrupt and reckless leaders I cannot.

Gentlemen, I am but recently from Shelbyville, fifty-five miles from Nashville, where I was held over ten days by that miserable tyrant, *General Hardee.* He was engaged in removing meat and bread South, for the Rebel army to live on as they retire to the Cotton States in search of the last ditch, in which they have pledged themselves to die. They are congregating in force along the line of the Memphis & Charleston Railroad, and somewhere in North Alabama—probably below Florence and Tuscumbia—they will make a determined stand. A battle in that quarter is imminent, and I dread the consequences,—not but that I believe we shall whip them and drive them farther south, but because many of our brave men will be slain. Expelled from there, as they will be, they will fall back upon Grand Junction, and then upon Memphis, until finally they retire into Mississippi.

We are soon to have Memphis, New Orleans, and Mobile, and in their capture you may look for some of the finest military manœuvres of the war. A splendid field is presented for strategic and tactical skill on both sides; but we have the advantage of them in generals: our generals are capable of giving wings, legs, and motion to their armies. We also have the advantage in the powers of endurance on the part of our privates, and their clothing, arms, and means of transportation. When the war began, they could whip out five of you with *one* Southern man. Now they are not willing to fight you man to man.

But, gentlemen, I must close my remarks. You see I am not able to speak. I am retiring to the North for rest. Whenever you can get possession of my down-trodden country, I design to return to my family and home. I have no idea of leaving there. I want to go back and aid in driving out others who have expelled me. I therefore retire, and introduce to you my friend and townsman Colonel Trigg, who is a good speaker and good Union man, and a refugee from the persecutions of the Rebels in East Tennessee.

Arrival in Cincinnati.

At no point since I reached this Government have I been treated with more kindness and more real hospitality than in Cincinnati. Arriving there on Thursday night, I was met at the wharf by Messrs. Geffroy and Gibson, the proprietors of that well-kept, quiet hotel, the "Gibson House," on Walnut Street, and kindly tendered the hospitalities of their house as long as I chose to remain. Upon reaching the "Gibson

House," where I was most hospitably received, I was waited on by the Union Committee appointed by the Union Convention, and by them conducted to the Merchants' Exchange, where I found a vast assemblage of the best men in the Queen City, and was introduced to them by Joseph C. Butler, Esq., President of the Chamber of Commerce.

I delivered a very brief address, setting forth the state of things in East Tennessee,—excused myself for not speaking,—promised a speech at some length, at such future time and place as they might agree upon,—and made the acquaintance of quite a number of gentlemen. The committee furnished a suite of carriages, and with them I took a most agreeable drive through Clifton and Spring Grove, viewing at my leisure the surroundings of the most populous city of the West, alike remarkable for its extensive trade, rapid growth, genuine hospitality, and productive industry.

On the evening of the 4th of April I made my first regular speech in "Pike's Opera-House;" and I will let the Cincinnati *Gazette* relate the particulars of the introduction:—

"**Parson Brownlow's Public Welcome.**

"We very much doubt whether the Opera-House, since it was first opened to the public, ever contained a larger or more refined assemblage of our citizens than on last evening on the occasion of the welcome to our city of the illustrious Tennessee patriot, Parson Brownlow.

"Before the doors were opened, the crowd had commenced to gather on Fourth Street; and before half-past seven o'clock not a vacant seat was to be found in the house, and the aisles and every available spot were occupied. Many, we learn, were unable to obtain even standing-room, and left the house. The turn-out, considering that the admission-fee was fifty cents, must have been very gratifying to the Parson.

"The stage was decorated with a number of American flags, and across the front part of it were two rows of chairs, on which were seated the Vice-Presidents. Immediately in the rear was a raised platform, on which were seated three hundred and seventy-two boys and girls from the district, intermediate, and high schools of the city, who, under the direction of Mr. L. W. Mason, sang the following

"SONG OF WELCOME.

"All hail! all hail the hero unflinching!
The pure patriot we sing, unwavering and bold,
Who foul treason denounced, and with deeds was still clinching
His strong speech, when vile traitors, in numbers untold,
Howled hatred demoniac, and madly were clamoring
His life should be forfeit. Triumphantly sing,
And utter the welcome with the tongue's feeble stammering.
The welcome, the warm welcome, our hearts to him bring!
Safe, safe in our midst we shall hear the man's voice
That hath cowed all his foes, and made us rejoice;
Then hail him again, and forever and aye!
His country he loves, and for it he would die!

"Rejoice! rejoice! for Freedom is marching,
With her power resistless, to punish and crush,
And the iris of Union will soon be o'erarching
Again our loved country, when its brave children rush
To rescue its life from the demons now seeking
To blot out its name from the nations of earth;
But, rather than this, let their black blood be reeking
Unpitied from earth, so disgraced by their birth.
Thus speaks he, the hero! Then sing with one voice:
We love and revere him, in his presence rejoice!
Then hail him again, and forever and aye!
His country he loves, and for it he would die!

"Shortly after eight o'clock, Parson Brownlow came upon the stage, leaning upon the arm of Joseph C. Butler, Esq., the President of the Chamber of Commerce.

"Mr. Butler, in introducing Mr. Brownlow, said:—

"LADIES AND GENTLEMEN:—I have been honored with the pleasing duty of inaugurating the ceremonies of this occasion, in introducing a renowned and loyal citizen of our sister State of Tennessee,—a State forced, by usurpation, fraud, and violence, into rebellion against a Government that her sons in by-gone times have done so much to maintain and establish, and now suffers in being the field of conflict in a desolating civil war,—a State recently baptized again into the fold of the Union by the martyr patriots' blood shed upon her soil, and will be confirmed in that fold by continued deeds of heroic daring,—within whose limits has been exhibited by her loyal sons as unfaltering devotion and love of country as have ever been displayed in the history of any people. Surrounded by the armed bands of desperate and cruel military despots, given up to the mercy of ignorant and vicious mobs, cut off from all communication with and support from a Government they were sacrificing themselves to maintain, these patriots of Tennessee were driven from their homes, suffered in jails, and sealed, when called on, with their lives, on the scaffold, their devotion to the Union and Constitution established by their fathers. Through a long and weary summer, through the dreary fall and winter, with hearts sickened by many disappointed hopes, they suffered and faithfully endured. And now that the armies of the Union have entered their State, and the flag of freedom once more floats over its capital, may we not hope that the hour of their deliverance is at hand? God grant it may be speedy!

"One of this noble band of patriots is with us to-night. He will recount to you some of the scenes he has witnessed, and give you in brief the history of the rebellion in his once prosperous and noble State. He has sacrificed on the altar of his country all that man holds most dear, jeopardizing not only his own life, but the lives of his family and kindred, in vindicating the sacred cause of his country. If we honor the bravery displayed on the battle-field, how much more should we honor him who, almost alone, sick and in prison, tempted by seducing offers of power and place, and with an ignominious death daily threatened, maintains for weeks and months, with unfaltering trust, his faith and virtue! The instinctive homage of the human heart to genuine courage we pay to an endurance like this. The historian who will record for the perusal of our children the list of heroes that this wicked rebellion has brought forth, will name none whose matchless courage is surpassed, or the bold outline of whose character for outspoken patriotism so overshadows all cavil and criticism as the hero of the pulpit and the press I have now the honor of introducing,—Mr. W. G. Brownlow, of Knoxville, Tennessee."

I give a correct report of this Cincinnati speech, because it was substantially what I said at all other points, and, next, because it has been misrepresented in Tennessee and subjected to unjust criticism by the Rebel press. The speech occupied one hour and twenty minutes in its delivery.

Speech in the Opera-House.

LADIES AND GENTLEMEN:—

I appear before you to-night in accordance with the arrangement of a committee—a large and intelligent committee—of citizens of your own town. I am not before you for the purpose of making an effort at display, or of trying to play the orator. I have no wish to fascinate or to charm an audience with a fine style of speaking, or with elegant language. I therefore apprize you of what you will have discovered before I take my seat,—namely, that in my extemporaneous addresses, no matter what the theme may be, I do not present a subject with an eloquence that charms, with that critical and studied acumen that fascinates, nor yet with that richness of diction that captivates an audience. This I regret in the advocacy of a good cause like that of the preservation of the American Union; for there is no power like that of oratory. Cæsar controlled men by exciting their fears; Cicero, by captivating their affections and swaying their passions. The influence of the one perished with its author; that of the other continues to this day, and will continue with public speakers to the end of time.

I feel confident that I address an appreciative audience, who are here to learn facts in regard to the GREAT REBELLION,—the great event of the nineteenth century,—including the reign of terror in the South generally, and the murderous conduct of Secessionists in East Tennessee. I shall look more to *what* I say than to my *manner* of saying it,—more, if you please, to the *subject-matter* of my speech than to any exhibition of rare powers of analysis, wit, satire, or remarkable force and beauty of language. I will state what I know to be true, without drawing upon my imagination for any thing. I will give names, dates, and localities; and I challenge now, or hereafter, a contradiction of what I say touching the great Rebellion in the South, the persecution of my fellow-countrymen, and of their sufferings even unto death.

I have met, since my arrival in this city, with not a few intelligent and high-toned gentlemen,—men of years and of knowledge,—who have inquired of me, seriously, "Is it a fact that they hanged men, shot others down, and imprisoned not a few, for their sentiments?" You cannot, it seems to me, gentlemen, realize the horrible state of affairs existing beyond the mountains, and especially in East Tennessee.

I have been accustomed to public speaking for more than thirty years, and I have seen the day when I could make myself heard at any reasonable distance. Then I was a young man; and I admit, ladies, not now being a widower, that this was a long time ago. But those days with me have gone by, and are now numbered with the years beyond the Flood. For more than three years past I have been suffering from a stubborn case of *bronchitis*, and could not speak at times above a whisper. I was advised by Professor Horace Green, of New York, who performed an operation on my throat, to exercise my speaking-machinery frequently in short speeches. I have done so, sometimes preaching short sermons, and at other times delivering temperance-speeches,—both good causes. Strange to say, my voice has never returned in any good degree until since I landed in the United States and opened my batteries against this wicked rebellion and the infinitely infernal leaders who inaugurated it! Under the providence of God, and with my continued denunciations of the vile heresy of Secession, my voice is gaining all the while; and I should not be astonished, in the course of a few brief months, to find that "Richard is himself again."

Ladies and gentlemen, you will bear with me for a few moments whilst I make other remarks personal to myself. This I think I may venture to do, by way of preliminary, without incurring the charge of egotism. Circumstances, not now necessary to repeat, have connected my name with this rebellion in the South, and therefore I may be allowed to speak more freely of myself than would otherwise become a modest man, such as I am. Candidly, I deserve no credit for any thing that I have done, or for what I have endured. I have only done my duty; and the man who is not prepared to submit to insult, the confiscation of his property, the incarceration of his person, or even to death itself, in defence of this glorious Union, is not worthy of the name of an American citizen!

I am a native of Virginia; I was born and raised in the Old Dominion, as were my parents before me. They were, on both sides, slave-holders. I have lived for the last thirty years in East Tennessee, where I married, and where both my wife and children were born. I am perhaps the only man who ever did, or ever will, appear before a Cincinnati audience publicly confessing that he descended from one of the *second* families of Virginia. All others are descended from the F. F. V's., which, since their numerous retreats before Rosecrans and others, signifies *Fleet-Footed Virginians!* By the way, *Floyd* and I hail from the same county. I have endeavored to be honest all my life, and remained poor. *Floyd* was a good *financier*, whether you view him as Governor of Virginia or Secretary of War under James Buchanan, and he has money and to spare.

Since this rebellion commenced, I have been held up to the world in the corrupt and pensioned journals of the Southern Confederacy as a traitor to the South and the descendant of a Tory. I complain of this charge, when I reflect that my father was a private in the War of 1812 under General Jackson. One of his brothers—the one after whom I was named—was a naval officer, and his honored remains sleep in the navy-yard at Norfolk. Another brother was a lieutenant in the navy, and died in New Orleans while in the service. A third brother of his died at sea while in the service, and was given to the monsters of the deep. A fourth was among the first men who scaled the walls at the memorable battle of the *Horseshoe*. On my mother's side my relatives were in the battles of their country, and not a few lost their lives defending the flag of their country, fighting for the United States against the combined assaults of our British and savage foes. They did not fight for a *section*, either North or South, but for our common country,—for the American Union,—and died beneath the folds of the Star-Spangled Banner, the sacred shield of a common nationality.

I am not before you on this occasion to revive old party political prejudices, but I may as well make a remark or so upon the subject of party politics. In Tennessee we have done what you ought to do here, —merged all party questions into the great question of preserving the Union and crushing out this infamous rebellion. I claim to be an unconditional Union man; and before I would vote for a man who is not, I would see him, in the language of Milton, "where cold performs the effect of fire." Nay, in the still more nervous language of Pollok, I would see him "Where gravitation, shifting, turns the other way," and sends the parties in the direction that Ward's ducks went.

I have battled against Andrew Johnson, perseveringly, systematically, and terribly, for a quarter of a century. He has basted me on every stump in Tennessee. We have each given the other as good as he sent. Honors are easy with us now, and we are hand-in-hand fighting the same battle for the preservation of the Union. We will fight for each other against the common foe. He is now at the head of our new State Government; and I take pleasure in saying that he is the right man in the right place. If Mr. Lincoln had asked the Union men of Tennessee whom they wanted for a military

Governor, the answer would have been, Andrew Johnson!

It is no new thing with me that I am a Union man, for I have been that all my life long. I was living in the counties of Pickens and Anderson, South Carolina, —the latter the home of John C. Calhoun,—in 1832, during the Nullification Rebellion. I declared for the Union then,—wrote a pamphlet in which I denounced Disunion and defended the proclamation of General Jackson.

I commenced my political career in 1828, when I was one of a corporal's guard who got up an Electoral ticket for John Quincy Adams against Andrew Jackson. I name this fact to show that I have never been *sectional*, but always *national*, supporting men of integrity and talents, without looking to which side of the line they were born. I was for Adams because of his talents and pure moral character, and last, but not least, because of his Federal politics. I have always been a Federal Whig of the Alexander Hamilton and George Washington school,—believing in a strong central or concentrated Government, strong enough to sustain itself and to put down all such infamous rebellions as this is. Though I was opposed to Jackson, I would have resurrected him, if I could have done so, two years ago, and placed him in the chair disgraced by that mockery of a man, Buchanan, and had him to crush out this rebellion. Jackson was a true patriot, and a lover of his country, and a Union man; and if he had been living when this rebellion broke out, he would have hanged the leaders and prevented this unnatural war.

In 1832, I was for Clay for the Presidency; in 1836, I was for Hugh Lawson White, who was beaten by Mr. Van Buren; in 1840, I was a zealous supporter of General Harrison, of Ohio, a true man and a tried patriot; in 1844, I supported Clay and Frelinghuysen; in 1848, I supported Taylor and Fillmore; in 1852, I was for Daniel Webster, but he was not the candidate, and died before the election came off; in 1856, I was for Fillmore and Donelson; in 1860, I was for Bell and Everett, and I am for the hind-legs of this kangaroo ticket yet. A better or a more nobly disinterested man than Everett never lived. Bell has gone over to Secession; but he is at heart a Union man, and only yielded on account of the great pressure, which but few of our Union leaders found themselves able openly to resist.

And now let me call your attention to the subject of *Slavery*, the great topic of the day. I have no sentiments at the South that I do not hold here. I have no sentiments here that I do not entertain when I am in Tennessee. I should despise myself, and merit your scorn and contempt, if I held one set of opinions at the North and another set at the South. I have for years been publishing my sentiments upon the Slavery question, and I have only to say to-night that they have undergone no change.

The South, as I have repeatedly published there, is more to blame for this state of things than the North. The South brought on this war without any just cause. We had a Presidential election, and we had four different tickets in the field, the meanest and most unpatriotic of which was the *Breckinridge ticket*. In a fair and open-handed race, under the forms of law and of the Constitution, without violence, the *Lincoln ticket* was chosen; and it was the duty of every good citizen to submit to the will of the people, thus expressed. But the South lost the spoils, and her corrupt and designing men determined to overthrow the Government and to erect a new Confederacy, where they could get offices. We of the South have had the Presidency twice to your once since the formation of the Government. We have even re-elected five of our men to a second term, while no Northern man ever was re-elected. Besides this, we have used two or three of your Northern Presidents. We had a fugitive-slave law enacted to suit our wants; we annexed Texas that we might have more slave-territory; and we repealed the Missouri Compromise Line,—a thing that ought never to have been done, and a measure I opposed to the bitter end. All this ought to have satisfied us of the South; but no, we were for breaking up the Government. Pryor, one of the gang, telegraphed from Washington, "We can get the Crittenden Compromise, but we don't want it." Judge Douglas overheard and exposed Mason in the Senate for saying, "No matter what compromise the North offers, the South must find a way to defeat it."

If, then, the South, in her madness and folly, will make the issue of "No Union and Slavery, or no Slavery and a Union," I am for the Union, *though every institution in the country perish.* And if I had been authorized, some two or three years ago, to select about two or three hundred of your most abominable anti-Slavery agitators in the North, and an equal number of our God-forsaken and most hell-deserving Disunionists at the South, and had marched them to the District of Columbia, hanged them on a common gallows, dug for them a common grave, and embalmed their bodies with *jimson-weed* and *dog-fennel,* there would have been none of this trouble, nor should I have been here to-night!

Let the Federal Government now guarantee to all loyal men in seceded States the right and title to all their property, including negroes, and protect them in the enjoyment of the same; but let the title held by rebels seeking to destroy the Government be annihilated, both as to negroes and all other property. And I trust in God that it will be done, and that such confiscated property will go to make up the losses of loyal men.

When this war was commenced, we were all told at the South that the Federal soldiers were coming among us to run off our negroes. Some Southern cavalry came along one *Sabbath*, and pitched in and stole a valuable boy from me, worth about one thousand dollars, and they now have him in camp, in full uniform. I would have expected this from Lincoln's hordes, but would not have expected it from the chivalry of the South! the flower of the Southern youth! The truth is, they have regularly-trained bands of negro-stealers and negro-traders following the Southern army, and these have already stolen more negroes from the border States in one year than all the Northern Abolitionists have stolen in forty years!

About twelve months ago, a stream of Secession fire, red and angry, and almost as hot as hell, came along from the South through Knoxville. Then it was that the Rebel soldiers, made mad by bad whiskey, visited the houses of Union men in Knoxville, and insulted and abused the inmates; and my humble dwelling was honored—if honor it be—by these soldiers.

At the same time I was reading in my exchanges from Mobile and Charleston that they had been compelled to send the flower of the South to defend the border States. I said to my wife, "If these soldiers be the flower of the South, God deliver us from the rabble!" They became more and more insulting, until in May and June they commenced shooting down and hanging the Union men. One man named Douglas raised a pole and ran up the Stars and Stripes: for this he was shot down. The work of murder and slaughter went on, and they became so overbearing that a number of us had to flee to the mountains.

I cannot boast of my courage, but I believe I was never accused of personal cowardice. They seized my printing-office, and converted it into a shop in which to repair old muskets, which the thief Floyd stole from the Government. After taking possession of my office, I was out of employment. One regiment located in the town had decided to tear down my dwelling, and the plans were all ready. General Zollicoffer was informed of the facts, and issued orders forbidding any of his soldiers to go outside of their lines. He also sent a detachment of two hundred men to surround and protect my house. Many said he had done an act worthy of great credit, but I believe he did no more than his duty. I knew him for twenty-five years: he was a high-toned, honest, and brave man. He never stooped to any thing low; and the only mean thing that he ever did, that I am aware of, was to fight in such a cause as that in which the South is now engaged.

My family urged me, with tears and entreaties, to leave home, and to gratify my wife and children I did so. About that time there was an election for President and Vice-President. The ticket got only 25,000 votes in a State that has given 150,000 votes. In East Tennessee the Union sheriffs refused to open the polls. Judge Swan, the member of the Confederate Congress from the Knoxville district, had but 700 votes, while the same district has given Horace Maynard 12,000 votes. After Johnson and Maynard left, I was the only leader left in Knoxville,—only a second or third rate one at that. Mounting an old iron-gray horse one day, with a few friends, we—as the Secessionists say when beaten by the Union army—we retired. I retired, gentlemen. [Laughter.] We made up a company of twelve persons, and retired into the Smoky Mountains, which divide Tennessee from North Carolina, and in the month of November we lay out days and nights. We had taken some bread and meat; and when our provisions gave out we killed a black bear and some turkeys. We had friends who came to us every few days and informed us as to what was going on. We learned that the commanding officer had detailed four squads of cavalry, and their public instructions were not to take us, but to shoot us on sight.

In some mysterious way, one Saturday night about eleven o'clock, five bridges on the main line of railroad, some miles apart, were set fire to, and were in ashes by daylight the next morning. This put the very devil in the Secessionists, although he had been in their midst all the while.

This burning of bridges was all wrong, as it could serve no other purpose than that of setting the authorities upon Union men. The bridges ought to have been destroyed a year ago, but not when they were fired.

Meanwhile, the Rebels—largely reinforced from the

Cotton States—went to work and deprived the Union men of their guns, pistols, and knives, and cast many of them into the county prisons. Now the reign of terror set in. Houses were plundered, stock killed before the eyes of the owners, and horses taken. I could give the names and localities of men shot down in their fields for no other offence than that they were Union men.

Returning to the vicinity of Knoxville, I received a letter from General George B. Crittenden, stating that he had been ordered by the Confederate Secretary of War to give me a passport beyond the Confederate lines into the State of Kentucky, to a Union neighborhood. I accepted the general's proffer, but was immediately arrested on a charge of treason, for writing and publishing what had appeared in the Knoxville *Whig*. On the 6th of December I was thrust into the Knoxville jail. I found in the jail one hundred and fifty Union men,—the building crowded to overflowing. Every man confined was a personal friend. They crowded around me in astonishment, and asked what I was thrown into prison for. Some of them shed tears, others smiled, when they saw me enter the iron gates. I told them I was under arrest for treason on a warrant just issued.

PRISON-SCENES.

In that dirty prison we were so crowded that but two-thirds of our company could lie down, and there was neither bench, chair, block, nor other thing, to sit or lie upon. As a consequence, many took cold and were sick. A wooden bucket and a couple of tin cups, out of which we drank, were all the furniture we had. In five weeks I was myself prostrated, and had to be removed.

Among the inmates were three Baptist preachers. One of them,—Mr. Pope,—seventy-seven years of age, was charged with having prayed to the Lord to bless the President of the United States, to bless the General Government, and to put an end to this unholy war. Another old man,—Mr. Cate,—a minister, seventy-five years of age, was thrust into jail for having thrown up his hat and hurrahed for the Stars and Stripes when a company of Union Home-Guards marched by his house with the Union flag flying over them. The third—a young man—was confined for having volunteered as chaplain of a Union regiment.

WILLIAM HENRY HARRISON SELF.

The most affecting case, however, was that of an old man who, after a lengthy incarceration, was told, one morning, that he had been sentenced to be hung at four o'clock that afternoon. His name was William Henry Harrison Self. His daughter, an intelligent and well-educated lady, hearing this awful news during the day, hastened to the jail, and, with great difficulty, obtained permission to visit the condemned man. The meeting of the father and daughter was a scene which drew tears from the eyes of a hundred and fifty men long used to hardship and suffering. The father and daughter embraced and kissed each other, neither of them able to utter a word for some time. At about one o'clock the young lady asked me to write, in her name, a dispatch to Jeff Davis, at Richmond, asking him to grant a pardon to her father, which I did.

The young lady carried the dispatch to the telegraph-office, on Gay Street, in great haste, and had it sent to Richmond immediately. Shortly before three o'clock she received an answer from "President" Davis, commuting the old man's sentence to imprisonment for such length of time as the commanding general should see proper. The joy of his daughter was, of course, unbounded. When I left Knoxville, on the 3d of March, Self was still in jail.

Old Mr. Cate had three sons in jail. Madison Cate was on the verge of the grave with typhoid fever. He lay upon the floor of that damp prison, with an old overcoat under his head for a pillow, and a single thickness of old home-made carpeting between him and the cold, damp floor. In this condition his poor wife came twenty-five miles to see him, with an infant about six weeks old in her arms. She came into the yard of the prison and asked permission to see her husband. The officer said, "No! they did not allow anybody to have any thing to say to these infernal

Union-shriekers." I went to the window then, myself, and, by dint of perseverance, prevailed upon them at last to let her see her husband. They limited her to just twenty minutes. When she entered the door, her eyes fell upon her husband lying in the corner, so weak and emaciated that he could scarcely stir. He was nearly gone. She held her infant in her arms. The sight of her husband in that condition unnerved her completely. Seeing that she was upon the point of letting the child fall, I took it from her, and she sank down upon the floor beside her husband. Neither of them uttered a word, but, clasping each other's hands, they sobbed and cried together; and oh, my God! I hope that I shall never see such a sight as that again.

That, ladies and gentlemen, is the spirit, the hellish, inhuman, infernal spirit, of Secession. The devil himself is a saint, compared to the leaders in that scheme.

In Andrew Johnson's town they hung up two men to the same limb, and the bloody Colonel Leadbetter,—a man born and educated in the State of Maine, who went down to Mobile and married a lot of negroes, through one white woman,—the worst man, the greatest coward, and the blackest-hearted villain that ever made a track in East Tennessee,—this man tied the knots with his own hands, and directed that the bodies of the victims should be left hanging for four days and nights directly over the iron track of the railroad, and ordered the engineers to run their trains slowly by the spot, in order that the Secessionists on board might feast their eyes upon the ghastly spectacle. And it is a fact, as true as it is revolting, that men stood upon the platforms of every train that went by, kicked the dead bodies as they passed, and struck them with sticks and rattans,—with such remarks as "that they looked well hanging there," and that all "d——d Yankees and traitors should hang that way too." It is true that Colonel Leadbetter, as the weather was somewhat warm and the corpses were becoming somewhat offensive, ordered them to be cut down at the expiration of some thirty-six hours; but it was for the convenience of his Secession friends purely, and not from any other motive.

One day they came with two carts and took old Harmon—a Methodist class-leader—and his son. Old Mr. Harmon was seated in one cart upon his coffin, and his son in the other, and each cart was surrounded by a strong guard of Rebel bayonets and driven down the hill to a scaffold. The young man was hung first, and the father was compelled to look upon his death-struggles. Then he was told to mount the scaffold; but, being feeble and overpowered by his feelings, two of the ruffians took hold of him, one of them saying, "Get up there, you damned old traitor!" and the poor old man was launched into eternity after his son.

A few days after this, they came up to the jail with another cart. We never knew whose turn was to come next. I had "counted the cost." I intended, if my turn had come, to meet my fate with the best grace I could. I had prepared a speech for the occasion; and I can assure you that I should have pronounced a handsome eulogy, if I had been called upon; for, if I have any talent in the world, it is that talent which consists in piling up one epithet upon another. But it turned out that the cart was not intended for me. It was intended for a young man by the name of C. A. Haun, an excellent man, of fine morals and good common sense. He had a wife and two small children. Haun was informed one hour beforehand that he was to be hung. He immediately asked for a Methodist preacher, who lived in the town, to come and see him and to pray with him.

The reply was, "We don't permit any praying here for a damned Union-shrieker." Haun met his fate like a man.

My fellow-citizens, I congratulate you upon the fact—now sufficiently clear—that this rebellion is now pretty well "played out." We will wind the thing up this spring and summer. They are nearly "out of soap" down South. They lack guns, clothing, boots, and shoes. The boots I have on cost me fifteen dollars in Knoxville. They are out of hats, too. In Knoxville there is not a bolt of bleached domestic or calico to be had, nor a spool of Coates's thread; and, although "Cotton is King," we never made a spool of thread south of Mason & Dixon's line. Sewing-needles and pins are not to be had. The blockade is breaking up the whole South. It has been remarked on the streets of Knoxville that no such thing as a fine-toothed comb was to be had, and all the little Secession heads were full of squatter sovereigns hunting for their rights in the territories. [Laughter and applause.]

General S. F. Carey, of Ohio, and Lieutenant-Governor Fisk, of Kentucky, delivered brief, but eloquent and appropriate, speeches after me. The President offered the following preamble and resolutions, expressive of the sentiment of the meeting; and, on motion, they were unanimously adopted by a deafening AY:—

"*Whereas*, The foundations of this republic were established in wisdom, justice, and virtue, by men of courage, intelligence, and patriotism, against the Government of which a causeless and wicked rebellion has been instigated by unprincipled demagogues, to advance their political schemes at the expense of public liberty; and

"*Whereas*, We believe that no Government can be formed more conducive to the happiness and prosperity of the people, or which can give greater security to life, liberty, and property: therefore, be it

"*Resolved*, That we, a part of the free people of this nation, will never cease our efforts until the last vestige of treason shall have been effaced from the land, and the principles of Washington and his illustrious compeers immediately established.

"*Resolved*, That we will stand upon the Union as our platform, and claim that the unity of the Government is essential to its preservation and to the liberties of the people; that we are entitled to the whole area embraced by the thirty-four States and the territorial domain, not alienating one inch of its soil one moment of time, being in its political and commercial relations the common property of all the loyal citizens of the Union; that we claim the present Constitution as the sovereign and fundamental law of the land, subject to no change or abatement except by the will of the people through their constitutional representation; that we repudiate any terms with traitors; that we estimate neutrality, in its application to the present rebellion, as synonymous with treason.

"That no loyal citizen can remain neutral while foreign or domestic enemies of his country assail its Constitution and laws, and that we demand a vigorous and unceasing prosecution of the war, and a certain punishment of all the leading traitors, enforcing the doctrine of the immortal Clay,—'that we owe a paramount allegiance to the whole Union, a subordinate one to the several States.'

"*Resolved*, That the blood of the patriots of the Revolution, and of Ellsworth, Lyon, Winthrop, Baker, Lander, McCrea, Whitcom, and Budd, and of the host of heroes in the present war, both on sea and land, whose bravery has added fresh lustre to our country's history, together with the martyrs who have illustrated their devotion to the Constitution by the sacrifice of their lives on the altar of freedom, has indissolubly cemented the union of the States, and forever endeared it to the hearts of a gratified people, who can never forget the debt of justice they owe to the widows and orphans of the illustrious dead.

"*Resolved*, That the flag of the nation shall again float triumphantly from the walls of Sumter, and from every other fort belonging to the Union; that the mouths of the Mississippi shall never be closed against the commerce of the great Northwest, or be subjected to the laws of any foreign or rebellious power; and that no interference with the rights of the whole people to the free use of all the avenues of commerce, throughout the length and breadth of the land, will ever be tolerated.

"*And be it further resolved,* That we recognize in the Rev. W. G. Brownlow the true patriot, the intrepid and unflinching defender of the Federal Constitution, as the representative of that band of true men in the South who, in the midst of an atrocious rebellion, still assert their ancient loyalty and devotion to the Union.

"*Resolved,* That he has fixed the true standard of patriotism for all in the present crisis,—viz.: an unhesitating sacrifice of private interest, in the hope of an early peace, and, if necessary, of loved institutions, to the maintenance of the Constitution, without further compromises, and a vigorous prosecution of the war, until the authority of the Federal Government shall be fully established in every insurgent State, every armed rebel disarmed and every leader punished.

"*Resolved,* That our warmest sympathies are with our distinguished guest, as we reach across the border our hands to our loyal brethren of the South, especially to those of East Tennessee, greeting them as friends engaged in the same holy cause; and we call upon the Federal Government to afford them speedy relief, so as not only to exhibit the high appreciation of their constancy and patriotism in the midst of unparalleled suffering, peril, and persecution, which is entertained by the whole people of the loyal States, but also as a sacred duty due unto the Constitution and to all loyal men of the South."

The exercises were closed by the singing of "Hail Columbia."

Indianapolis, April 9.—General Carey and I addressed a large audience here last night, having come from Dayton, where we spoke the night before. We were the guests of Governor Morton, who is a true man, and has done great service for the country during this rebellion. The "Metropolitan Hall" in this city, it is said, was never better filled.

Governor Morton took us in his carriage to see the prisoners in Camp Morton,—some five thousand of them. I found the Tennesseeans glad to see me, and made them a brief speech; but the Kentucky and Alabama Rebels gave me no very graceful reception, crying, "Put him out!" "Don't want him here!" "Traitor to the South!" &c.

Chicago, April 11.—The citizens of Chicago having adopted the following complimentary preamble and resolution, I could do nothing less than visit their great and growing commercial emporium:—

"'*Whereas*, The citizens of Chicago, and of every loyal city and State, have watched with anxiety the independent, manly, and patriotic course during the past year of the Rev. William G. Brownlow, of Tennessee; and,

"'*Whereas*, His position upon the grand and momentous issue that has nearly broken to fragments and rent in twain our beloved country has commanded the admiration and gratitude of every loyal citizen, in supporting and maintaining the flag of our country, in an enemy's land, even at the peril of his life and the sacrifice of all its comforts; and,

"'*Whereas*, We have heard with great pleasure that he is to be in our city the present week, thus giving our citizens an opportunity of hearing the voice and words of the patriot, and of testifying their appreciation of the man who has suffered every thing but death in defending our Constitution: therefore,

"'*Resolved*, That a special committee of three be appointed by the Mayor, whose duty it shall be to make such arrangements as may be necessary in order that the hospitalities of the city be tendered to Rev. W. G. Brownlow upon his arrival and during his stay here.'

"On motion of Alderman Comisky, the resolution was adopted unanimously.

"The Mayor appointed Aldermen Hoyt, Hubbard, and Salomon, as a committee to carry into effect the resolution of Alderman Hoyt.

"On motion, the Mayor was added to the committee."

To this committee were added other gentlemen by the Commercial Exchange; and these met me at Michigan City, where I was welcomed by their chairman, Judge Drummond, of the Federal Court, in a complimentary speech.

My first day in Chicago was spent in visiting Camp Douglas, where I found five thousand more prisoners, many of them from Tennessee. They were glad to see me, and I made them a brief speech. When I announced to them that Tennessee would vote herself back into the Union again, they cried out, "We Tennessee prisoners would vote the State back now, if it were left to us!" Poor fellows! I felt sorry for them, because I knew they were mostly Union men, but had been deceived by the Secession leaders of the State.

At one o'clock I visited the Merchants' Exchange, where General Carey and I addressed the Board of

Trade. Mayor Ramsey introduced me to the immense throng, when J. C. Wright, Esq., on behalf of the Board, addressed me thus:—

"REV. W. G. BROWNLOW:—At the request of the officers of this Board of Trade, I have the honor, sir, of performing the most agreeable duty of welcoming you to our Exchange.

"It is not, sir, because of any official position you now hold, or have held, that this vast assembly has gathered here to receive you; but, sir, it is a mark of respect and admiration for your patriotic devotion to your country. When this horrid rebellion assumed its gigantic proportions, the loyal men of the North watched with anxiety the course of many men of the South whom we had delighted to honor with the highest positions of trust and power. With rare exceptions, we saw them retreating into the ranks of the traitors, using their influence, wealth, and position to strike down the mildest and most beneficent Government which God in his mercy had ever permitted man to establish. They beguiled and deceived the people who had been accustomed to look up to them and listen to their counsels. Many of the arch-traitors, not content to act with the popular voice of their States, joined the ranks of the Rebels, endeavoring to force their States to disregard their allegiance to that glorious Union which for nearly a century had thrown its genial influence and protection over a united, happy, and prosperous people. Amidst all this horrid exhibition of treason and malignant, hellish hate, when the heart grew sick at contemplating the dark and dismal scene before us, when your neighbors and friends around you, in vast numbers, had deserted that old flag, consecrated by our fathers' blood, and were trampling under foot that Constitution which had so long been our pride and our hope, you, sir, stood firm and unmoved in your devoted patriotism. Threatened with the halter, with the grave yawning before you, with scorn you spurned proffered freedom and such honors as traitors could confer. To you the grave had no terrors to be shunned by an act of disloyalty to your beloved and now grateful country.

"We are now rapidly making undying history for future generations to read. When the history of this wicked rebellion—for I cannot call it an honorable war—is written, it will be sadly deficient if its pages do not tell, in words that burn, the story of your wrongs, your fortitude, and your unswerving devotion to your country in the hour of her great trial. Our children will need no romance to stir their young hearts; but the truthful picture of your sufferings and heroism will fill the place of high-wrought fiction. We shall no longer point to the classic ages for noble examples of heroes who laughed at the halter and rack and scorned life at the price of dishonor.

"Sir, it is because you have so loved your country and suffered for your principles that we this day welcome you to our Exchange, to our hearth-stones, to our hearts.

"In behalf of the officers and of the more than nine hundred loyal members of this Board, again, sir, I bid you welcome. Amid the stirring, glorious news of the triumph of our arms, I bid you welcome."

At night General Carey and I spoke at length to an overwhelming audience, and were given the hospitalities of the "Sherman House" by the city authorities. The following night we addressed a large and enthusiastic audience at Lafayette, Indiana.

Columbus, Ohio, April 14.—I arrived here to-day from Cincinnati, having been previously invited by both branches of the Legislature and by the City Councils. I will let the Ohio *State Journal* give the particulars:—

"PARSON BROWNLOW'S RECEPTION.

"Pursuant to arrangements made by committee of the Legislature, the distinguished Parson Brownlow, the patriot of East Tennessee, was received here yesterday as the guest of the State. Upon the arrival of the train from Cincinnati the Parson was met at the depot by the 69th Regiment, Colonel Campbell, with their splendid band, and escorted to the Capitol.

"At a quarter-past three in the afternoon, the Senate was announced in the hall of the House, and was seated,—Hon. James Monroe, President *pro tem.* of the Senate, taking the Speaker's chair, with Speaker Hubbell and Colonel Campbell, as Grand Marshal, on his left. At precisely half-past three, Governor Tod entered the hall, arm-in-arm with Parson Brownlow. The hall was densely crowded by citizens, including a great number of ladies. Upon the appearance of the Governor, escorting Parson Brownlow, the audience greeted them with cheers.

"Upon reaching the Speaker's stand, Governor Tod said:—

"'Mr. President and gentlemen of the Legislature of Ohio, I have the honor to present to you, in the Capitol of Ohio, the distinguished visitor and guest of our State, Parson Brownlow, of Tennessee. And as such (turning to Parson Brownlow) I have the pleasure of taking you by the hand, in the name of our people, as the friend and the guest of our Commonwealth.'

"The President of the Senate then receiving him, he was seated on the right of the President with the Governor. Whereupon President Monroe spoke as follows:—

"'SENATORS AND REPRESENTATIVES:—

"'I rise not so much to occupy your time myself as to bid welcome to this Capitol, and to introduce to you, the honored guest whose presence graces the occasion. I am told that it is expected of me, in accordance with a time-honored custom which has obtained at receptions of this sort, to submit a few remarks in harmony with the spirit of the hour.

"'We are naturally reminded, under present circumstances, of that law established by a kind Providence, which ordains that the greatest evils shall bring with them great compensations. War is one of the direst calamities that can befall any nation, and yet important benefits and blessings are often incident to it. When waged in behalf of a just cause, it develops all the nobler and more heroic elements of human character. In time of peace, the commercial spirit—the spirit of traffic, of gain, of greed—rules society. Men live for themselves. They occupy a low plane of thought and action, and move round in narrow circles. They do not rise to the loftier heights of observation where the eye swoops a wider horizon and takes in a broader view of human relations. But when cherished institutions, country, home, are in peril, and the shock of war rouses the land, then the moral sensibilities of our nature are stirred to their depths. Men discover that they are brothers, and that what is for the interest of one is for the interest of all. Then, among the young and the old, in both sexes and all classes of the people, is revealed the spirit of self-denial, the disposition to suffer, to dare and to do, for the attainment of noble ends, and the heart which had been shrivelled by self-interest expands to the generous dimensions of great sacrifices and sublime endeavor.

"'Perhaps in no contest since the world began has a nobler heroism, or heroism in more varied forms, been manifested, than in that contest for constitutional liberty upon which we now daily invoke the blessing of God. It has indeed brought terrible desolations upon us, but it has also given us the most precious things that men or nations ever possess,—rare and costly human virtues.

"'When was a nobler heroism ever exhibited, by officers or men, upon the battle-field? When was ever seen in grander forms that courage which impels men to expose their persons, where bullets rain and shells burst, with no concern, except for the honor of the flag and the triumph of the cause? If this war has stained the page of our history with the treason of Davis, and Beauregard, and Buckner, and Pillow, and Floyd, it has also illuminated that page with the names of Halleck, and Shields, and Buell, and Grant, and Sigel, and Curtis, and the Christian hero, Foote; and it has forever embalmed in the hearts of the people the memories of Ellsworth, and Winthrop, and Baker, and Lyon, and Lander. It has also drawn forth from the mass of our soldiers displays of valor worthy of their Christian nurture, and of the high achievements of their ancestry on both sides of the Atlantic.

"'This war, too, has revealed to us the heroism of woman in those forms most precious to God and man,—a heroism which has shown itself both in giving up to the country those nearest and dearest, and also in toiling with patient meekness for the support of the family deprived of its natural protector, and in supplying, by an unremitting and laborious industry, comforts and necessaries for soldiers in the camp. Which of us has not been profoundly affected by seeing the wife or the mother weeping, agonized, broken-hearted at the thought of separation, and yet not permitting her sorrow to wring from her one dissuasive word to shake the resolution of one dearer than her own life to fight the battles of his country?

"Nor must I forget, though exhibited in other forms, the heroism of the artificer and the inventor. Who has not thought, as he retired to his own comfortable couch at night, of the faithful mechanics in our foundries, manufactories, and arsenals, who, ever since this war began, all day long and late into the night, have made our workshops resound with the music of their patriotic toil? who have employed willing mind and sturdy muscle in making powder and ball, shot and shell, sabre and bayonet, and rifled ordnance, to destroy treason? Who does not admire the inventor, who has brought all his powers of body and mind to the service of his country? Who does not honor the genius, patriotism, and courageous perseverance which, in the face of much criticism, with small means and no certain expectation of reward in the future, finally enabled Ericsson to give to the Federal Government, to give to the Rebels, and to give to France and England, a Monitor?

"'I must not delay you to speak of all the forms in which this war has developed the heroism of our people; but there is one of them which surely cannot be overlooked on the present occasion.

"'Among the noble men and women who, in these unhappy times, have enriched the history of the country with the exalted graces of their characters, certainly not the least honorable place will be assigned to those bold patriots in the border States who, when the whole mass of the people of those States seemed about to be swept away by the tide of Secession, dared to take their stand in the very face of the excited multitude, and rebuke the terrible madness,—who, with few and uninfluential sympathizers at the time, through persecution, imprisonment, and threatened death, maintained freedom of speech and freedom of the press. Cherished in the heart of the whole people are the names of such men as Andrew Johnson and W. G. Brownlow. Such valor is not noisy and ostentatious like that of the battle-field. It does not announce itself to the world by the blare of the trumpet or the roll of the drum. It is not plumed or epauletted; but God, in his own good time, will cover it all over with the stars and decorations of Heaven's nobility.

"'It is because the General Assembly of the State of Ohio appreciates and honors this manly endurance, that it heartily welcomes this our guest to this presence and these halls to-day.

"'And yet we cordially welcome our friend, not so much for the courage he has exhibited, as for the moral quality of that courage and the noble end to which it was devoted. We respect and honor his heroism, because it was made subservient to the establishment of a great principle, unspeakably dear, at this time, to all our hearts. This principle can be set forth in a single sentence. *If there is any one thing that the loyal people of America have irrevocably settled in their minds, it is this: that these United States do constitute, and, by the blessing of God, shall forever constitute, one permanent and indissoluble nation.* They have decreed that these States shall forever form one great united brotherhood,—that no such heresy as that of secession shall ever be tolerated in this land, and no such crime as that of secession shall ever be committed; and for the accomplishment of these great ends they have pledged all their financial, physical, intellectual, and moral resources. We have a Constitution, the best for the promotion of general happiness and prosperity that God ever gave to man. That Constitution may have defects; but, if such exist, provision has been made within the instrument itself for removing them in a just and lawful manner. The people will not tolerate, and—I say it with reverence—God will not tolerate, any attempt to subvert this Constitution by force of arms. Not only the principles of enlightened liberty and of all just government, but the precepts of religion and the dictates of philanthropy, require that this Constitution shall be respected and obeyed until lawfully amended. Whenever the ship of state, smitten by the tempest of rebellion, shall part her cable, and be driven out of this harbor of safety, nothing will be left for her but to become a hideous wreck upon some rocky and sterile shore. Some one will tell me of the rights of the States. I believe in those rights. But what rights, or what prosperity, would remain for the States or their people when once this great Federal bond shall be broken? I answer, the same prosperity that would be left to our earth if she, becoming impatient of the control of law, were to throw off the restraints of that gravitation which holds her in the neighborhood of central light and heat, and to rush from her orbit into some outer region of darkness and desolation. Every loyal heart will prefer the order which God pronounced good, to the dismal chaos which preceded it, and into which it will once more be dissolved when the authority of law no longer commands respect. Hence, the voice of the people—which, I would humbly trust, is also the voice of God—has declared that the Constitution which the fathers framed shall be reverenced and obeyed,—that the old Government, for whose establishment they toiled and prayed and shed their blood, shall still be our Government,—that the old flag shall still wave over the land and over the sea, with all its glories still bright upon it, with not a color faded nor a star obscured. This doctrine we love; to support this doctrine we will give all that we possess; and for it we are ready to die. And because we recognize in the patriot of Tennessee a gallant defender of this doctrine, a representative man of this principle of nationality, we welcome him here, with warm hearts and open hands, in the name of the General Assembly and the people of the State of Ohio.'

"President Monroe's eloquent remarks were received with frequent and hearty cheers. As he concluded, he presented the distinguished visitor to the Legislature and the citizens, by whom he was received with great applause. When the cheers that greeted him on rising had subsided, Parson Brownlow proceeded to address the Legislature and audience in the manner that is so peculiarly his own, and which stirs and fascinates by its tones of earnestness as well as by his words of power."

At night I spoke in the theatre, to a full house, for more than one hour. The orchestra gave us some stirring music, and Ex-Governor Dennison introduced me to the audience, in a brief and stirring speech. I was followed by General Carey and ex-Congressman Gallaway. The exercises continued until eleven o'clock at night.

Luther Donalson, Esq., President of the City Council, gave us a handsome entertainment at his residence on State Street. His elegant lady spread a magnificent table, and the Governor and many Senators and Representatives were present, also many handsome ladies.

Pittsburg, April 17.—Here I was met with carriages by the City Councils, Mayors, and Aldermen of Pittsburg and Alleghany City, tendered the hospitalities of both corporations, and conducted to one of their best hotels,—the "Monongahela House." At night I spoke one hour and a half to a crowded hall. Left on the morning train for Philadelphia, on the Pennsylvania Railroad. On leaving Pittsburg, I was invited by the conductor to ride on the locomotive, in order to enjoy the sublime scenery along the rivers and mountains. In this way I rode seventy miles. Poets and tourists may sing and write of "a life on the ocean wave," or "a home on the rolling deep;" but give me a seat in an open locomotive at the head of a long passenger-train, and let me cross the Alleghany Mountains from Pittsburg to the new mountain-city of Altoona, gazing on the dashing streams on the one hand, and the lofty and romantic mountains on the other. The sun was high in the hill of heaven, and rolling his chariot through a cloudless sky; all creation was calm, and sleeping on the bosom of serenity, until aroused by the heavy tread and clear whistle of the iron horse!

At Altoona, having descended the mountain, I was met by that prince of clever fellows, George W. Childs, the extensive and energetic Philadelphia publisher, and by other Philadelphians with him, among whom I name Mr. H. R. Edmonds, of the Philadelphia Bar, and Mr. G. A. Townsend, the able and clever correspondent of the Philadelphia *Press*.

Harrisburg, April 18.—At this ancient capital of the Keystone State the train was detained some fifteen minutes,—when an immense concourse gathered at the depot demanded my appearance on the platform of the rear car. Governor Curtin introduced me as "Parson Brownlow, of Tennessee." I responded, substantially in these words:—

MY FELLOW-COUNTRYMEN:—Governor Curtin introduces me as Parson Brownlow, of Tennessee. He should have stated that this is what is left of the late Parson Brownlow. Being a very modest sort of man, I have no wish to speak of my troubles and sufferings in the kingdom of Jeff Davis. I claim no consideration for any thing that I have said or done, having only done my duty as an American citizen. The Apostle Paul records the fact in his history that he had fought with beasts at Ephesus. Though not his rival, I can say more: I have fought the "devil and Tom Walker," and the infuriated legions of the so-called Southern Confederacy! True, they have wellnigh used me up; but I am now where I can breathe free and easy, and I hope soon to recover. In the towns where I have been, and at the depots along the road, my kind friends have *spoke me too often*, and I feel rather worsted by the operation.

My only ambition is to get up a new printing-establishment, and return to East Tennessee and resurrect my *Knoxville Whig*, the only Union journal in the Confederacy at the time the Rebels crushed it out. I want to go back and aid in restoring that glorious State to the old Union again. I want to go back and point out to the triumphant Federal army such men as deserve to hang, and suitable limbs upon which to hang them! Nay, I desire to tie the rope around some of their infernal necks.

We have suffered much. We have been hung, shot down on our own properties, tied to trees, and whipped to death; and all this because we would not desert the flag of our fathers, the Union, and the Constitution. These had protected us for years; and we won't give them up for the world or the devil! [Cheers.] I tell you, my friends,—and I do speak advisedly,—when Andy Johnson, our new Governor, orders an old-fashioned State election, and the withdrawal of the bayonets of Secession leaves us free to express our will, Tennessee will give the Union and the Government a majority of fifty thousand! [Cheers.]

A gentleman in the crowd calls out to know where his friend, Colonel Luttrell, of Knoxville, stands in this contest. Well, my friend, he is a Union man, good and true! [Cheers.] But a few weeks ago an election came off in Knoxville for Mayor and Aldermen. The Secession organ gave out that Colonel Luttrell and the candidates associated with him were Abolitionists and Lincolnites, and proclaimed *their* candidates, heading their ticket with the name of their postmaster, Parson Charlton, as the States-Rights and Jeff Davis ticket. They had the streets full of bayonets on the day of the election; but the result was that the Union ticket was carried two to one in every ward, carrying all that was heaped upon it,—Lincoln, the war, the blockade, and even the Chicago Platform. [Great cheering.]

The game of Secession is almost done. The ardent spirits in Secessia have almost got their rights, and will soon come in to renew their allegiance. Your blockade is ruining them at a greater rate than fire and sword. Although cotton is said to be king, there is not a spool of it in Knoxville, and they have no calico or domestic goods of any description.

Gentlemen, I cannot conclude without expressing my admiration for the great State of Pennsylvania, a State which has furnished so many gallant soldiers to battle for the Union,—more, I am authorized to say, in proportion to the population, than any other State. [Cheers.] Your Governor, too, has done his whole duty in this war. He is the right man in the right place, and, if he were not present, I should certainly speak of him in extravagant terms of praise. [Cheers and laughter.] As it is, I make you my best bow, and I join Governor Curtin, Ex-Governor Porter, and other members of the Executive Staff, in a cup of coffee in this Refreshment Saloon. [Prolonged cheers.]

Philadelphia, April 19.—After being immensely cheered at every station on the railroad, and loudly called for, I arrived here last night between the hours of eleven and twelve o'clock, and was met at the depot by a delegation from the Select and Common Councils, and was received by JOSEPH MEGARY, who spoke as follows:—

"MR. BROWNLOW:—SIR:—The Councils of Philadelphia have deputed us to tender to you the hospitalities of the city. In doing which, the city of Philadelphia has honored herself in paying honor to a patriot who has suffered so much in the cause of constitutional liberty. The people of Philadelphia, always loyal, will shout with joy at the reception of a patriot who has dared to tell those would-be destroyers of the greatest Government that God ever made, 'Thus didst thou.' Allow me again to tender to you the hospitalities of the city."

After briefly acknowledging the compliment paid me, I was escorted to the carriages, and our whole party was driven rapidly to the Continental Hotel,—perhaps the most elegant house in America. After making the acquaintance of a number of gentlemen, I was shown to my rooms, and retired, greatly fatigued, but much gratified at the kind treatment I had everywhere received.

At eleven o'clock this morning I spoke to the citizens in front of old INDEPENDENCE HALL, on Chestnut Street, for nearly one hour, to an immense audience. I there found a stand erected, draped with several flags, among which was the large flag raised on the 22d of February, 1861, by President Lincoln. It was a beautiful morning, and I was in front of the old Temple of Liberty, surrounded by a host of loyal men. I thought of the signers of the Declaration of Independence,—of the Congress that appointed Washington commander-in-chief of the Revolutionary army,—of Robert Morris, of Revolutionary fame,—of Rittenhouse, Penn, Logan, and the immortal Franklin. My speech, with some variations caused by the surrounding circumstances, was substantially the same as at Cincinnati and other towns where I had spoken at length. At the conclusion of my off-hand address I was greeted by three long and hearty cheers, when I retired.

Invitation to Baltimore.

The two brief documents which I annex to these remarks will show the feeling towards me in that city. A second letter from the Mayor, stating a similar action by the second branch of the City Government, I have mislaid. The reader may feel anxious to know why it is that I give so many of these documents complimentary to myself. It is because the corrupt and lying press of the Southern Confederacy are publishing that I have been treated with scorn and contempt at the North, and in some instances that I have been utterly repudiated by large public meetings! The Knoxville *Register* and Athens *Post*—two East Tennessee organs of Secession—have named *Baltimore* as having repudiated me officially. It is to brand these drunken, lying editors, and those who retail their slanders, with falsehood and infamy, that I intrude a portion of a vast number of similar documents I have received, upon the notice of the reader.

While in the South, I seldom took up one of the many pensioned and prostituted sheets printed there, that I did not read labored accounts of the sufferings of the North growing out of this war. We were all told there that the North was on the very "eve of starvation," and that all her principal cities were "threatened with bread-riots." I have seen much of the North in the last two months, and I have found a country prosperous and happy. Provisions are abundant and cheap. Goods of all kinds are to be had at former prices, almost; and money is abundant; while Government stocks are advancing. The only evidence to be seen of the existence of a war is in the newspapers, and the appearance in the cities and towns of a few officers and soldiers in uniform.

But to the documents from Baltimore. A third one I regret to have misplaced:—

"CHAMBER FIRST BRANCH CITY COUNCIL,
"April 8, 1862.

"JOHN LEE CHAPMAN, ESQ., *Mayor*:—

"SIR:—You are respectfully notified that the following is a true copy of a resolution adopted by this branch at its session of this date:—

"*Resolved*, by the First Branch of the City Council of Baltimore, That the Hon. John L. Chapman, the Mayor, be, and he is hereby, requested to invite that bold and uncompromising patriot, *Parson William G. Brownlow*, of Knoxville, Tennessee, to visit the city of Baltimore, and tender to him the hospitality of the city.

"By order. ANDREW J. BANDEL, *Clerk*."

"MAYOR'S OFFICE, CITY HALL,
"BALTIMORE, April 14, 1862.

"Rev. WILLIAM G. BROWNLOW:—

"DEAR SIR:—Enclosed please find copy of a resolution *unanimously* passed by the First Branch of our City Council.

"It affords me great pleasure to co-operate with the First Branch in this matter, and to assure you that every Union-loving heart in Baltimore will give you a most hearty welcome.

"We have watched your course and have sympathized with you in your sufferings, and rejoice to know that you are again permitted to breathe the pure air of freedom, untainted with Secession and treason.

"I will be pleased to hear from you at your earliest convenience.

"With great respect, &c.

"JOHN LEE CHAPMAN, *ex-officio Mayor.*"

Crosswicks, N. J., May 10.—I am now in a pleasant and quiet village in New Jersey, county of Burlington, —a county wanting but a few hundred inhabitants to equal in population the entire State of Florida. Here I have reposed in quiet and comfort, for three weeks, in the hospitable mansion of Robert E. Peterson, Esq., whose extensive library has been at my command whilst I have hurried through with this book. Mrs. Peterson is a lady of rare literary attainments, and is the authoress of a large work on Astronomy, alike extolled in Europe and America by the first scientific and literary men of the age. Their mansion is on the spot of ground occupied by General Howe in the Revolutionary struggle. The Indian name of *Crosswicks* signified *separation*. The creek separates into two branches close to the village. Here is a large and commodious brick meeting-house, belonging to the Quakers, which seats two thousand persons. During a Revolutionary battle, a cannon-ball struck the north side of the building. The hole made by the ball is yet visible. I have inspected it: it is situated between the sills of the two upper windows. The American troops, after the battle of Trenton, used the meeting-house for barracks; yet, unlike the Rebel soldiers in the South, who use churches for a similar purpose, they neither defaced this venerable building nor disturbed the Society in their public religious duties. A Quaker preacher and two prominent members waited on me and invited me to make them a speech, which I did, occupying one hour and a half, and speaking to a crowded house. This was considered a great compliment, as they never extend such favors to other churches, or to politicians. The cheering was considerable; and it was remarked that this venerable building had not received such a shock since the war of the Revolution.

At Bordentown, (situated four miles from Crosswicks,) from 1816 until 1842, Joseph Bonaparte, the ex-King of Spain, and brother of Napoleon, resided. His park and grounds comprised some fifteen hundred acres of land. His mansion was enriched by exquisite works of art, in painting and sculpture. Bordentown is also famed for once having been the residence of the celebrated infidel Tom Paine, who, let his religious opinions have been ever so odious, was a man of transcendent talents, and did much towards establishing this Union.

Expulsion of my Family from Tennessee.

Smarting under the lash I have applied to the rogues, liars, and traitors who have led off in this rebellion, since I came North, the vile miscreants have sought to damage me all they could. Ashamed of having retained my family there, and wanting to occupy my large and commodious dwelling as a hospital, they resolved upon driving my family out, and, with one sweeping act of usurpation and oppression, intending to give the lie to my charge that they were holding them as hostages for my good conduct while North. Churchwell, the provost-marshal, seeks to vent his spleen upon an innocent and helpless woman and children, and uses a contemptible scoundrel, clothed with the Rebel authority of a major-general, as a tool to enable him to carry out his malicious feelings of resentment for my exposures of his personal dishonesty, his false swearing in a bank-suit, and the subsequent selling of him out under the hammer.

My wife and children have arrived in New Jersey, after a long and fatiguing journey, *via* Fortress Monroe, under a flag of truce, and after the sacrifice of a large and well-furnished house and all I have succeeded in accumulating during twenty-five years of toil and industry. That the reader may fully understand the case, I submit for perusal the following documents:—

Proclamation.

"THE Major-General commanding this Department, charged with the enforcement of martial law, believing that many of its citizens have been *misled* into the commission of treasonable acts through ignorance of their duties and obligations to their State, and that many have actually fled across the mountains and joined our enemies under the persuasion and misguidance of supposed friends, but designing enemies, hereby proclaims:—

"1st. That no person so misled, who comes forward, declares his error, and takes the oath to support the Constitution of the State and of the Confederate States, shall be molested or punished on account of past acts or words.

"2d. That no person so persuaded and misguided as to leave his home and join the enemy, who shall return within thirty days of the date of this proclamation, acknowledge his error, and take an oath to support the Constitution of the State and of the Confederate States, shall be molested or punished on account of past acts or words.

"After thus announcing his disposition to treat with the utmost clemency those who have been led away from the true path of patriotic duty, the Major-General commanding furthermore declares his determination henceforth to employ all the elements at his disposal for the protection of the lives and property of the citizens of East Tennessee,—whether from the incursions of the enemy or the irregularities of his own troops,—and for the suppression of all treasonable practices.

"He assures all citizens engaged in cultivating their farms, that he will protect them in their rights, and that he will suspend the militia draft under the State laws, that they may raise crops for consumption in the coming year.

"He invokes the zealous co-operation of the authorities, and of all good people, to aid him in his endeavors.

"The courts of criminal jurisdiction will continue to exercise their functions, save the issuing of writs of *habeas corpus*. Their writs will be served and their decrees executed by the aid of the military, when necessary.

"When the courts fail to preserve the peace or punish offenders against the laws, those objects will be attained through the action of military tribunals and the exercise of the force of his command.

"E. KIRBY SMITH,

"*Major-Gen. Command'g Dept. of East Tenn.*

"HEAD-QUARTERS, KNOXVILLE, April 18, 1862."

"To the Disaffected People of East Tennessee.

"HEAD-QUARTERS, DEPARTMENT EAST TENNESSEE,
"OFFICE PROVOST-MARSHAL, April 23, 1862.

"The undersigned, in executing martial law in this Department, assures those interested, who have fled to the enemy's lines and who are actually in their army, that he will welcome their return to their homes and their families: they are offered amnesty and protection, if they come to lay down their arms and act as loyal citizens within the thirty days given them by Major-General E. Kirby Smith to do so.

"At the end of that time, those failing to return to their homes and accept the amnesty thus offered and provide for and protect their wives and children in East Tennessee, will have them sent to their care in Kentucky, or beyond the Confederate States lines, at their own expense.

"All that leave after this date, with a knowledge of the above acts, their families will be sent immediately after them.

"The women and children must be taken care of by husbands and fathers, either in East Tennessee or in the Lincoln Government.

"W. M. CHURCHWELL,
"*Colonel and Provost-Marshal.*

"KNOXVILLE, TENN., April 23, 1862."

"HEAD-QUARTERS, DEPARTMENT EAST TENNESSEE,
"OFFICE PROVOST-MARSHAL, April 21, 1862.

"MRS. W. G. BROWNLOW, Knoxville:—

"MADAM:—By Major-General E. Kirby Smith I am directed most respectfully to inform you that you and your children are not held as hostages for the good behavior of your husband, as represented by him in a speech at Cincinnati recently, and that yourself and family will be *required* to pass beyond the Confederate States line in thirty-six hours from this date.

"Passports will be granted you from this office.

"Very respectfully,
"W. M. CHURCHWELL,
"*Colonel and Provost-Marshal.*"

"KNOXVILLE, TENN., April 21, 1862.

"COLONEL W. M. CHURCHWELL, *Provost-Marshal*:—

"SIR:—Your official note as Provost-Marshal for East Tennessee, ordering myself and family to remove beyond the limits of the Confederate States within the next thirty-six hours, is just received; and I hasten to reply to it. My husband, as you are aware, is not here to afford me his protection and counsel; and, being well-nigh in the evening of life, with a family of dependent children, I have to request, as a matter of indulgence, that you extend the time for my exile a few days longer, as to leave within the time prescribed by your *mandate* would result in the total sacrifice of my private interests.

"I have to request the further information what guarantee of safety your passport will afford myself and family. Yours, &c.,

"ELIZA A. BROWNLOW."

"HEAD-QUARTERS, DEPARTMENT EAST TENNESSEE,
"OFFICE PROVOST-MARSHAL, April 22, 1862.

"MRS. W. G. BROWNLOW:—

"MADAM:—At your request, the time for your leaving to join your husband is extended until Thursday morning next. The route will be *via* Kingston and Sparta.

"Your safety will be the soldiers sent along for your protection to the enemy's line.

"Very respectfully,

"W. M. CHURCHWELL,

"*Colonel and Provost-Marshal.*"

"HEAD-QUARTERS, DEPARTMENT EAST TENNESSEE,
OFFICE PROVOST-MARSHAL, KNOXVILLE, April 25, 1862.

"The following-named persons are allowed (in charge of Lieutenant Joseph H. Speed) to pass out of the Confederate States Government by way of Norfolk, Va.:—

"Mrs. Eliza Brownlow and three children.

"Miss Mary Brownlow.

"Mrs. Sue C. Sawyers and child.

"John B. Brownlow.

"W. M. CHURCHWELL,
"*Colonel and Provost-Marshal.*"

EDITOR OF THE PHILADELPHIA PRESS:—

SIR:—I desire to publish in your widely-circulated journal a brief card, and I request your other city papers to copy. I consider that the Petersburg *Express*, in announcing the arrival in that city of my wife and children, and the wife and children of the Hon. Horace Maynard, has mendaciously assailed the reputation and patriotism of these ladies, in stating "that, though the husbands have evinced an unaccountable hostility to the South and its cause, *they* (the ladies) are firmly attached to the Confederacy."

There is not one word of truth in this statement, unless it be alleged that the homes and firesides of these ladies, in Knoxville, from which they have been unceremoniously expelled by an insolent order of the commanding general, constitute the Confederacy. The order was issued to these families by William M. Churchwell, provost-marshal at Knoxville, giving them thirty-six hours in which to leave the Confederacy, leaving their houses and furniture behind, and escaping with only a portion of their wearing-apparel. Churchwell, who issued this mendacious order, no doubt took great pleasure in doing so. His hatred of Mr. Maynard's family grows out of Maynard's having beaten him by two thousand votes in that district, in a contest for the United States Congress. His hatred for my wife and five helpless young girls arises from my having convicted him of *falsehood and dishonesty*, in a court of justice, in a certain bank-suit I brought against him. He ought now to drive out of the Confederacy five officers in his rebel regiment who preferred the grave charge against him, at Richmond, of trying to draw from the paymaster of the army, upon false papers, *forty thousand dollars* more than he was entitled to. A fit representative of the morality, virtue, and integrity of the bogus Confederacy!

My family are safe, in the vicinity of Bordentown, New Jersey, and feel that to have escaped with their lives and a part of their wearing-apparel from the savage beasts of the Confederacy is a great blessing, and that they can sing, in good faith,—

"God of my life, whose gracious power
Through *various deaths* my soul hath led,
Has shone upon the darkened hour,
Has lifted up my sinking head."

Every member of my family old enough to appreciate

the horrors of this infernal rebellion despises the so-called Confederacy and the unprincipled villains who inaugurated it. The only difference between us is, that I claim to be capable of despising the wicked concern, and all connected with originating it, with more *intense hatred* than they can. But, then, I have trained them up "in the nurture and admonition of the Lord," which implies obedience to law and order, and an undying hatred of Secession and its guilty authors.

The work of murder, arrests, and imprisonments goes bravely on in East Tennessee, as my family inform me, who left Knoxville six weeks after I did. They were shooting Union men down in the streets, arresting hundreds, and killed, in one instance, fifty or sixty after they had surrendered and were under an arrest. They marched between three and four hundred loyal citizens, some of them barefooted and their feet bleeding, to the depot, and shipped them to Atlanta, Georgia, to work upon their fortifications. These men were denied water: they would lift out of *mud-puddles* in the streets, with their hands, after a rain, what they could to quench their thirst.

In God's name, I call upon President Lincoln, and upon his Cabinet and army-officers, to say how long they will suffer a loyal people, true to the Union and to the Government of their fathers, to suffer in this way. The Union men of East Tennessee are largely in the majority,—say three to one,—but they have no arms;

they are in the jails of the country; they are working on Rebel fortifications, like slaves under the lash, and no Federal force has ever yet been marched into that oppressed and down-trodden country. Let the Government, if it have any regard for its obligations, redeem that country at once, and liberate these people, no matter at what cost of blood and treasure. They have suffered these outrages for the last twelve months, and are now desponding,—nay, despairing of any relief.

Let an army—"a terrible army, with banners"—go at once into East Tennessee, and back up the loyal citizens, while the latter shoot and hang their persecutors wherever they can find them. I want the army to serve for me as a forerunner,—a sort of John the Baptist in the wilderness,—so that I may go back with a new press, type, and paper, and resurrect my Union journal, and tell one hundred thousand subscribers, weekly, what is going on upon the borders of civilization.

In conclusion, I return my most sincere thanks, and the thanks and gratitude of my persecuted family, to Lieutenant Speed, the Rebel officer who had them in charge, for the kind, courteous, and gentlemanlike treatment they received at his hands, in protecting them against the insults of Secession blackguards, seeing after their baggage, and turning them over to General Wool, at Fortress Monroe. The gentlemanly instincts of a Whig and a Methodist have not been crushed out in this true-hearted Virginian by the incurable disease of Secession; and, whatever may betide him in the ups and downs of this unholy war, he will have my good wishes, and the good wishes of my family.

I am, &c., W. G. Brownlow.

Crosswicks, New Jersey, May 3, 1862.

This man *Churchwell* hopes, by sending my family over the lines and destroying all I have in Tennessee, and thus reducing me to poverty, to prevent my return to that country, and to rid the country of me altogether. Vain delusion! *There* I am bound to live, and *there* I am resolved to publish a Union paper, and to expose to the gaze of an inquiring and active world the deep depravity and damning offences of all such as this man *Churchwell!* Unrenewed by grace, steeped to the chin in personal and political corruption, and deeply imbued with the malice, hatred, and meanness of a land-pirate, with a nature inclining him to take a willing part in all villainies, he has never figured in an honorable enterprise in his life. While in Congress, he *sold* his votes to those who gave him most money, not caring whether the measure he voted for would defraud the Government or meet with the approval or disapproval of his constituents. A base man, whose grovelling passions assume full sway on all occasions, and whose innumerable moral delinquencies are to be seen wherever his footprints go,—lost to all sense of honor and shame, degraded in his nature, corrupt in his principles, sold to the great enemy of God and man,—he is a true representative of the morality and integrity of the Southern Confederacy, and displays its criminal intentions in all their hideous deformity. And yet how little, how sordid, how mean, and how contemptible must be that man *E. Kirby Smith* to be used as a tool by *such a* man!

Can any cause employing *such men* and inflicting *such wrongs* be expected to prosper? Are not the frowns of God upon them? No wonder they retreat from Yorktown, Williamsburg, Corinth, Bowling Green, Manassas, Nashville, Huntsville, and other points, and surrender New Orleans! The time is not far distant, to use their own favorite expression, when they will "retire" from the United States. Their leaders, who have the capital, will go to France, and their *plunderers*, such as this man Churchwell, will go to Mexico!

To illustrate the corruptions of this *bogus* Confederacy, and the utter want of principle on the part of its leading men, I conclude this book with an extract from a letter from East Tennessee:—

"You are aware that a number of our Union friends were sent from the Knoxville jail to Tuscaloosa, to be held as prisoners during the war, some of whom died. As no trial was allowed to any of them, and as nothing like justice could be had, it was resolved in Bradley county to try what virtue there was in *money*. So a purse of TWENTY-FIVE HUNDRED DOLLARS was made up, and given to a leading Secessionist, who is, or has been, a member of a certain brigadier-general's staff, on the condition that he would go to Richmond and have twenty-five East Tennesseeans, whose names were given him, released. He accepted the bribe, went to Richmond, and got twenty-four released, mostly Bradley-county men. The one not released had been set free by death. This is a beautiful commentary upon the morality of the officials of the new Government!

"One other case, and I shall close. John Anderson, a brother of the late Congressman Josiah M. Anderson, was on his death-bed in Mobile, with a number of the East Tennessee prisoners around him from Tuscaloosa. He said that he desired to make a statement of facts, and was not willing to die without doing so. He called around him quite a number of our Union prisoners,—among whom were Dr. Brown, Stephen Beard, Samuel Hunt, Dr. Hunt, and John Kinchelo,—and stated to them that, while he lay sick in Cleveland, in Bradley county, *W. H. Tibbs*, the member elect to the Richmond Congress from the Third Tennessee District, had approached him and offered him a bribe of five hundred dollars if he would go to the Knoxville court and swear that Dr. Hunt and Levi Trewhitt, Esq., were concerned in burning the Hiawassee bridge. He declined the bribe, and said that he did not know or believe them to be concerned!"

I have now finished this sketch of Secession by an eye-witness. It has been a sad record. I have no particle of sympathy for the leaders in this criminal rebellion; but I commiserate the multitudes who have been swept into its vortex by a current of overwhelming fanaticism and terrorism which they were powerless to resist. I have spoken plainly, vehemently,—perhaps bitterly: I could not do otherwise in so dear a concernment as my country's good. I feel that I may appropriate the prophet's language: the "word was in mine heart as a burning fire shut up in my bones; I was weary with forbearing, and could not stay." I can spare no denunciation when I see demagogues and traitors deliberately plunging us into a fratricidal war fit only for the leadership of Cain. But I lay down my pen with the conviction that the bold, bad men who have appealed to the arbitrament of arms will be discomfited in that issue. The thronging victories of the Constitution are the presages of returning peace and prosperity. God grant that the people may now raise their eyes and lift their hands to the eternal and propitious Throne, in fervent supplication that the Father of Mercies will compose the distractions of our suffering land, and eclipse the splendor of our annals in the past by the future renown, for ages to come, of the Re-United States!

THE END.

RECENT PUBLICATIONS

OF

GEORGE W. CHILDS,

628 & 630 CHESTNUT ST., PHILADELPHIA.

Sparks's Life and Writings of Dr. Franklin, containing several Political and Historical Facts not included in any former edition, and many Letters, Official and Private, not hitherto published. With Notes, etc., by Jared Sparks, LL.D. A new edition, with 23 steel plates, beautifully printed on fine paper. 10 vols. octavo, superior cloth binding......$15 00

Same, sheep, library style, marble edges...... 18 00

This is the only complete edition of Franklin's Works, and contains about six hundred and fifty letters and miscellaneous pieces (more than one-third of the whole bulk of the new edition) not to be found in any other collection. Of these, upwards of four hundred and sixty had never been printed. The Familiar Letters of Franklin, published in 1833 by Dr. Sparks, are included in this edition; and magazines, pamphlets, and newspapers have been industriously examined, and no printed paper omitted which is known to have been written by Dr. Franklin. The number of books, papers, etc.—excluding letters—is no less than 304!

Sparks's Illustrated Life of Franklin. 1 vol. octavo, cloth......$1 50

The Great Iron Wheel Examined, or its False Spokes Extracted, and an Exhibition of Elder Groves, its builder. By William G. Brownlow. New edition, revised and improved. 12mo....$1 00

*** 100,000 copies of this work have been sold.

Brazil and the Brazilians. 5th thousand. By Rev. D. P. Kidder, of the Methodist Episcopal Church, and J. C. Fletcher, of the Presbyterian Church. One large vol. 8vo, beautifully illustrated......$3 00

Copies sent by mail, free, on receipt of price.

PROSPECTUS

OF THE

KNOXVILLE WHIG.

THE undersigned proposes, during the summer of 1862, to resume the publication of the "KNOXVILLE WHIG," and hopes to start with a list of 50,000 subscribers, which he expects to increase to 100,000 at no distant day. It will be a large WEEKLY JOURNAL, issued every Saturday, upon good paper, handsomely printed. The price per annum will be TWO DOLLARS, invariably in advance; and when the subscription expires the paper will be discontinued unless renewed in due time.

The 'Whig' will be INDEPENDENT in all things and NEUTRAL in nothing,—taking a hand in all the controversies of the day. It will be an *unconditional* Union Journal, holding up all participants in the *late* Rebellion—now almost played out—as a choice collection of men for a Rogues' Gallery! At the same time, it will make war upon all the gamblers, the thieves, North and South,—those whose trade it is to rob the public, as well as private pilferers, the whiskey-bloats, the bullies in elections, oppressors who grind the face of the poor, extortioners in trade, who swindle by wholesale and retail, and all foul-mouthed Secession sympathizers and other disturbers of the peace in the various sink-holes of society!

RATES OF ADVERTISING.

One square, of twelve lines of nonpareil, one insertion........	$ 2.00
Each continuance of same advertisement..........................	1.00
Half-square of six lines, per year..................................	10.00
One square of twelve lines, per year................................	15.00

Advertisements will be considered due when inserted, except those around and about home, with whom we shall keep regular accounts. Liberal discounts will be made to those who advertise liberally. Finally, if you want any thing,—if you have any thing to sell,—if you want to buy any thing,—if you want customers,—TELL IT TO ONE HUNDRED THOUSAND PEOPLE BY ADVERTISING IT IN A JOURNAL THAT FRIENDS AND FOES ALIKE READ!

☞ All orders and remittances from Northern States will be addressed to the undersigned, until the paper is received, by mail, at PHILADELPHIA or CINCINNATI, from which points they will be conveyed to me by Express. Journals friendly to me will confer a great favor by inserting once and calling attention.

W. G. BROWNLOW, *Editor and Publisher.*

PHILADELPHIA, May, 1862.